Collins

BTEC

NATIONAL

Children's Play, Learning and Development

Janet Stearns, Clare Schmieder
and Kate Young

Published by Collins Education
An imprint of HarperCollins*Publishers*
77–85 Fulham Palace Road
Hammersmith
London
W6 8JB

Browse the complete Collins Education catalogue at
www.collinseducation.com

©HarperCollins*Publishers* Limited 2013

10 9 8 7 6 5 4 3 2 1

ISBN 978-0-00-747981-8

British Library Cataloguing in Publication Data

A Catalogue record for this publication is available from the British Library.

Project managed by Caroline Low
Edited by Melanie Birdsall
Proofread by Lucy Hyde and Elizabeth Evans
Index by Annie Dilworth
Picture research by Grace Glendinning
Design and typesetting by Jouve India Private Ltd.
Illustrations by Ann Paganuzzi
Cover design by Angela English
Printed and bound in Lego, Italy

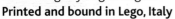

Contents

Introduction

Welcome to the Edexcel BTEC Level 3 National Diploma in Children's Play, Learning and Development (CPLD).

Working with young children is an extremely rewarding career, but it is also challenging and demanding. It takes a very special person to meet the different needs of children and their families. The role of an early years practitioner can be as diverse as working with babies, encouraging young children's development through play, assisting children's learning in school, and supporting parents and families – in addition to working with a wide variety of other professionals.

It is increasingly being recognised that high-quality early years education can make a real difference in the lives of children and their families. Early years practitioners need to have a sound understanding of child development and play, as well as being able to communicate effectively with a wide range of people, process information and make decisions. They also need to understand the importance of valuing individual differences such as working with families from different cultures or children with special educational needs.

Whether it is your intention to use this qualification to pursue employment in the early years sector or to go on to higher education, this book will help you to appreciate the breadth of learning and skills involved in becoming an early years practitioner, and the varied scope of career opportunities available in the sector.

How is the book organised?

The material in this book covers all of the core and mandatory specialist units required for the Level 3 National Diploma in Children's Play, Learning and Development. You will also need to undertake some optional units to achieve the full qualification and your tutor or assessor will help you choose the most relevant units to do this. Each unit of the book covers a specific Level 3 unit. You will see that the units are divided into different sections, which are exactly matched to the specifications for the Level 3 Diploma.

How is assessment covered?

In order to achieve your Level 3 Diploma, you will need to provide evidence of your knowledge and understanding of children's play, learning and development.

- Each unit clearly outlines the assessment criteria required to achieve a Pass, Merit or Distinction grade.

- The activities and case studies in each unit will help you to prepare for both the internal assessment and the external examination.

- The practical exercises will support you in making links with your experience in placement and will help you to complete your Skills for Practice Log.

- The assessment tables at the end of each unit will help you to keep track of your progress.

We hope that the material in this book is accessible, interesting and inspires you to pursue a rewarding career with young children. Good luck with your course!

Janet Stearns, Clare Schmieder and Kate Young

Qualification information

This book has been written to cover the core and mandatory specialist units of the Edexcel BTEC Level 3 National Diploma in Children's Play, Learning and Development. Learners aiming to achieve the Level 3 Diploma must complete and pass the eleven core units and three mandatory specialist units listed below.

Edexcel BTEC Level 3 National Diploma in Children's Play, Learning and Development

Unit	Core units	Assessment method	GLH
1	Child development	External	120
2	Play in early years settings	Internal	60
3	Meeting children's physical development, physical care and health needs	Internal	60
4	Health and safety practice in early years settings	Internal	60
5	Collaboration with parents, colleagues and other professionals in early years	Internal	60
6	Supporting children's communication and language	Internal	60
7	Supporting children's personal, social and emotional development	Internal	90
8	Child protection	Internal	30
9	Observation, assessment and planning for play and development	Internal	60
10	Diversity, equality and inclusion in the early years	Internal	60
11	Reflecting on own early years practice	Edexcel-set assignment	60
Unit	**Mandatory specialist units**	**Assessment method**	**GLH**
12	Research skills	Edexcel-set assignment	60
13	Health, education and social services for children and their families	Internal	30
14	Food and mealtimes in the early years	Internal	30
Total Guided Learning Hours (GLH)			**840**

In order to complete the full qualification, learners also need to undertake a minimum of 800 hours' work experience and some optional specialist units to make up a total of 1080 GLH.

In order to gain full and relevant occupational competence, learners will also need to achieve the Level 3 Diploma for the Children and Young People's Workforce (CYPW).

Alternative routes for study

Many parts of this book also provide a supportive study guide for learners who want to achieve any of the four smaller qualifications within the Edexcel BTEC Children's Play, Learning and Development Nationals suite. For example, these may be learners who wish to take CPLD alongside A-levels or progress onto the National Diploma at a later date. (It should be noted that learners enrolled on these courses of study are not required to undertake mandatory placement experience and therefore some of the placement-related activities included in this book may not be suitable.) Details of these smaller qualifications are outlined below:

Edexcel BTEC Level 3 National Subsidiary Award in Children's Play, Learning and Development

Unit	Core units	Assessment method	GLH
1	Child development	External	120
2	Play in early years settings	Internal	60

Edexcel BTEC Level 3 National Award in Children's Play, Learning and Development

Unit	Core units	Assessment method	GLH
1	Child development	External	120
2	Play in early years settings	Internal	60
3	Meeting children's physical development, physical care and health needs	Internal	60
4	Health and safety practice in early years settings	Internal	60
5	Collaboration with parents, colleagues and other professionals in early years	Internal	60

Edexcel BTEC Level 3 National Subsidiary Certificate in Children's Play, Learning and Development

Unit	Core units	Assessment method	GLH
1	Child development	External	120
2	Play in early years settings	Internal	60
3	Meeting children's physical development, physical care and health needs	Internal	60
4	Health and safety practice in early years settings	Internal	60
5	Collaboration with parents, colleagues and other professionals in early years	Internal	60
6	Supporting children's communication and language	Internal	60
7	Supporting children's personal, social and emotional development	Internal	90
8	Child protection	Internal	30

Edexcel BTEC Level 3 National Certificate in Children's Play, Learning and Development

Unit	Core units	Assessment method	GLH
1	Child development	External	120
2	Play in early years settings	Internal	60
3	Meeting children's physical development, physical care and health needs	Internal	60
4	Health and safety practice in early years settings	Internal	60
5	Collaboration with parents, colleagues and other professionals in early years	Internal	60
6	Supporting children's communication and language	Internal	60
7	Supporting children's personal, social and emotional development	Internal	90
8	Child protection	Internal	30
9	Observation, assessment and planning for play and development	Internal	60
10	Diversity, equality and inclusion in the early years	Internal	60
11	Reflecting on own early years practice	Edexcel-set assignment	60
Plus 800 hours of work experience			

Preparation for your assessment

In order to successfully complete your Edexcel BTEC Level 3 National Diploma in Children's Play, Learning and Development you will need to pass three different types of assessment as follows:

1. Externally set assignments

2. Internally set assignments

3. Practical skills in placement (Skills for Practice Log)

Externally set assignments

Units 1, 11 and 12 are all externally set, although Units 11 and 12 are internally marked. A summary of the externally set assignments is shown below:

Unit	Assignment set by	Assignment marked by	Description	Time allowed	No. marks/ grades available
1 Child development	External examination	Externally marked	A paper-based test with two sections. Section 1 has short- and extended-answer questions based on a sector-based scenario (case study) Section 2 has short- and extended-answer questions	1 hour 45 mins	80 marks
11 Reflecting on own early years practice	Edexcel	Internally marked by your tutors	Reflective practice with a focus on communication and language	n/a	Pass, Merit, Distinction, Unclassified
12 Research skills	Edexcel	Internally marked by your tutors	A research project that must relate to work with young children	n/a	Pass, Merit, Distinction, Unclassified

Unit 1: Child development is the only unit that is assessed by means of an external examination. Preparation for an examination requires a considerable amount of hard work and revision. Time spent in learning and revising child development will help you to strengthen your knowledge and understanding and boost your confidence. In order to be successful in this examination, you need to be able to identify children's stages of development and demonstrate your skills of analysis and evaluation. Test yourself using some of the exercises in this book and practise applying your understanding of children's development to unfamiliar scenarios using the case studies provided in Unit 1 of this book. Use your experiences from placement and the practical activities in Unit 1 to help you analyse how different theories and models of development relate to your observations of children and to understand the importance of recognising atypical development.

The grading of the external assessment for Unit 1 is based on the following criteria:

To achieve a Pass at Level 3 you need to:

• recall and apply knowledge in familiar and unfamiliar situations

• use relevant material from identified sources

- show a sound understanding of theory through appropriate use of concepts

- show some awareness of different perspectives/approaches relating to child development

- present and explain your judgements

- select and explain solutions for specific problems

- communicate your knowledge and understanding using appropriate language.

To achieve a Distinction at Level 3 you need to:

- independently synthesise your knowledge of the subject

- bring together your understanding of concepts and strategies and apply it to sometimes unfamiliar situations or problems

- integrate material from a variety of independently identified sources

- show a thorough and deep understanding of the subject, with a justification of arguments and analysis in different situations

- show and apply significant awareness of different perspectives and approaches relating to child development

- make reasoned and confident judgements and recommendations based on independent analysis and interpretation of knowledge.

You can resit the external assessment up to **two times** after the first sitting.

Unit 11: Reflecting on own early years practice is also assessed by means of an external assignment, although your tutors will mark this work. The assignment will focus on reflective practice, using the topic of communication and language, as all practitioners need to be able to support children in this area. Reflective practice has become a central part of working in early years and it is very important for you to understand how reflective practice contributes to work with children in early years settings.

Practise your skills using some of the exercises in Unit 11 of this book, and use your experiences in placement to help you select evidence from your own practice.

Unit 12: Research skills is also assessed by means of an external assignment, although again, your tutors will mark this work. You will need to carry out your own research project using different methods to gather information and you will need to consider the purpose and role of research that is relevant to work with children. Use some of the exercises in Unit 12 of this book to help you to create a realistic research proposal, discuss and present your findings and explain the implications of your research for current early years practice. Your tutor and placement supervisor will help you to plan your project and develop your work.

Internally set assignments

Internally set assignments are the main form of assessment for Units 2–10 and 13–33. The tutors at your centre will create the assignments and mark your work based on the unit learning outcomes and assessment criteria. Edexcel will also verify your work through a process of postal sampling.

The internal assignments will take a variety of formats (for example, reports, projects or case studies), to be decided by your tutor, and will allow you to demonstrate a range of skills and ways of presenting information.

The assessment criteria are hierarchical and you must achieve all the assessment criteria for the grade awarded. In other words, you can only achieve a Merit grade if you provide sufficient evidence for both the Pass and Merit criteria. Similarly, you can only achieve a Distinction grade if your work contains sufficient evidence for the Pass, Merit and Distinction criteria.

In order to be successful in the internal assessment, you need to:

- apply your knowledge and understanding with reference to relevant concepts
- apply practical and technical skills
- demonstrate the development of critical thinking skills
- manage your time efficiently in order to plan your work and meet the required deadlines
- be motivated to work consistently and independently and take responsibility for your own learning
- understand that any work you submit must be your own
- reference all your source materials and understand what would constitute plagiarism.

Use the practical activities and case studies in this book to help you practise your skills and prepare for the internal assignments.

You may be allowed to retake a completed assessment after a summative grade has been given.

Practical skills

In order to successfully complete your Edexcel BTEC Level 3 National Diploma in Children's Play, Learning and Development you are required to undertake 800 hours of placement experience in three different settings and complete a Skills for Practice Log. The log consists of 100 practical skills that you will need in order to work in early years settings with children of different ages and completion of this log will show employers that you have the skills required to be part of the early years workforce.

The log also includes reports that will be completed at the end of each placement. In these reports, your supervisors will summarise your professionalism and review your strengths and areas for improvement. There will also be an opportunity for you to reflect on your own progress.

Calculation of your final grade

Your final grade will be calculated using a points system based on the Guided Learning Hours (GLH) for each unit.

The table below shows the number of points awarded per 10 guided learning hours at each grade.

Grade	Points awarded per 10 GLH
Unclassified	0
Pass	4
Merit	6
Distinction	8

For example: if you achieve a Pass grade for Unit 6 (Supporting Children's Communication and Language), the unit size is 60 guided learning hours (GLH), therefore you would gain 24 points for that unit, i.e. 4 points for each 10 GLH.

Your tutor will help you to monitor your progress and you can use the assessment tables at the end of each unit in this book to help you keep track of your evidence for assessment.

1 | Child development

Learning aim A:
Understand how the principles of growth and development apply to children's developmental progress from birth up to 8 years

- ▶ The principles of growth and development
- ▶ The sequence of development from birth to two years
- ▶ The sequence of development from two to four years
- ▶ The sequence of development from four to eight years

Learning aim B:
Understand theories and models of development and how they relate to aspects of children's development

- ▶ Theories of behaviour and moral development
- ▶ The development of cognition and language
- ▶ Personality, self-esteem and attachment theory
- ▶ Strengths and weaknesses of theories and models of child development

Learning aim C:
Be able to apply theories and models of child development to support children's development

▶ Applying theories to professional early years practice

Learning aim D:
Understand how a range of factors influence children's development

▶ Factors affecting development

Learning aim E:
Understand the importance of recognising atypical development

▶ Recognising and responding to atypical development

11

The principles of growth and development

The unique child

Every child is an individual, with unique characteristics and qualities. The way each child grows and develops will vary and is dependent on a wide range of different factors.

Principles of growth

Growth means an increase in physical size and a child's rate of growth will generally increase as their development progresses. However, this will vary according to their genetic predisposition, medical history, nutrition and lifestyle. Different parts of the body grow at different rates and most children experience 'growth spurts' at certain periods. Children's growth is usually monitored by measuring height and weight (and the head circumference of babies).

Principles of development

Development is a continuous process, which begins at conception and continues throughout life into old age. It involves the development of skills and abilities, such as learning to walk and talk, and the maturing of body systems, such as bowel and bladder control.

Development occurs in an orderly sequence, which is always the same. For example, children will always learn to walk before they can run, climb, jump or hop. However, the rate (or pace) of development varies a great deal between children. For example, some children begin to walk at a very early age but learn to talk much later than others.

Physical development begins with the control of head movements and continues down the body. Physical movements progress from being large and uncontrolled (for example, random kicking) to being more precise and refined (for example, using a pencil).

All children develop in different individual ways

Key terms

Cortisol: a stress-related hormone

Neural pathway: an interconnected set of neurons that form a network in the brain and transmit information

Neural pruning: the process of removing neurons that are no longer used in the brain

Neurons: the core cells of the brain and nervous system

All areas of development are interrelated and can be affected by a wide range of different factors. You should never compare children with each other. Remember that there is a very wide range of what is normal and every child will progress in his or her own individual way. (See also Unit 3: Meeting children's physical development, physical care and health needs, pages 84–113.)

Brain growth

The maturation process of the brain plays an extremely important role in child development. At birth, the human brain consists of around 10 billion **neurons**. These neurons connect with each other to form **neural pathways**, which are responsible for processing and transmitting information.

Research shows that the development of neural pathways is actively encouraged by sensory stimulation and positive interactions. If children are not exposed to this kind of stimulation, the neural pathways will be lost through the process of **neural pruning**. This will result in the child's brain not developing to its full potential.

Research has also shown that leaving babies to cry for long periods results in higher levels of the hormone **cortisol**, which is toxic and damaging to the developing brain.

Understanding child development

Child development is the key to really understanding children. As a practitioner, having a thorough understanding of child development will help you to:

- 'tune in' to children's individual needs

- monitor children's developmental progress

- plan appropriate experiences and activities to encourage and support development

- recognise difficulties or delays in development

- implement early intervention if necessary.

Practitioners usually monitor children's development by examining milestones or developmental norms. Milestones provide an average guide to what is typically expected at specific ages and stages and can be used for assessing children's progress. However, it is important to remember that there is a very wide range of 'normal' and every child's progress will be unique and individual. You also need to understand children's development in the context of their cultural environment, as well as the many other factors that can influence developmental progress.

Research

In your placement or work setting, observe the physical sizes and abilities of different children. What differences do you notice? Keep a record of your findings.

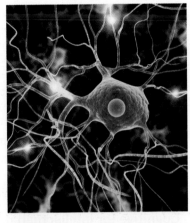

A neuron

Your assessment criteria:

Learning aim A: Understand how the principles of growth and development apply to children's developmental progress from birth up to 8 years

> Understand how the principles of growth and development apply to children's developmental progress from birth up to 8 years.

> Use relevant information to recognise children's developmental stages.

 ### Discuss

Can you remember (or have you been told) at what age you learned to walk, said your first word (do you know what it was?) and learned to read?

Reflect on some of the influences on your early development, for example having older/younger brothers or sisters, influences from your family, community or culture. Compare and contrast your ideas with others in the group. What differences do you notice?

The sequence of development from birth to two years

Areas of development

The study of child development is often broken down into five specific areas, as described below.

Physical development

This involves the development of **gross motor skills**, such as running, climbing and pedaling a tricycle, as well as the development of **fine motor skills**, such as fastening buttons and using scissors or a computer keyboard. Children are developing physical skills such as balance, hand–eye and body coordination, the ability to manipulate objects and dexterity.

Cognitive (or intellectual) development

This involves the development of thinking skills, including problem solving, imagination and creativity, memory and concentration, and understanding concepts such as colour, size, shape and time. Children are learning about the world around them and starting to make sense of their experiences, for example by piecing together a jigsaw.

Communication development

This involves the development of speech, language and all types of non-verbal communication, including gestures and body language. Children are learning to use language to express themselves, communicate their needs, ask questions and develop conversation and listening skills.

Emotional development

This involves the development of a positive sense of self, **resilience** and wellbeing. Children are developing confidence, self-esteem and learning how to express and manage their feelings.

Social development

This involves the development of social behaviour and learning how to get along with others. Children are learning about sharing, turn taking, cooperation, social rules and the difference between right and wrong (moral development).

Your assessment criteria:

Learning aim A: Understand how the principles of growth and development apply to children's developmental progress from birth up to 8 years

> Use relevant information to recognise children's developmental stages.

> Anticipate the next stage(s) of development.

> Analyse how development in one area may affect development in other areas.

Key terms

Fine motor skills: *body movements that use small muscles, such as those in the hands*

Gross motor skills: *the larger movements of the body*

Holistic: *emphasising the importance of the whole child*

Primitive reflex behaviours: *basic automatic responses present in the baby at birth*

Resilience: *the capacity to recover from difficulties*

Spatial awareness: *an understanding of our own position in space and the positions of the objects around us*

Holistic development

All areas of development are linked and influence each other. For example, in learning to walk, children need the physical skills to move their body, but also confidence in their own abilities and an understanding of spatial awareness in order to move around safely. It is important to view child development in a holistic way, which views the child as a whole person and emphasises that all areas of development are interrelated.

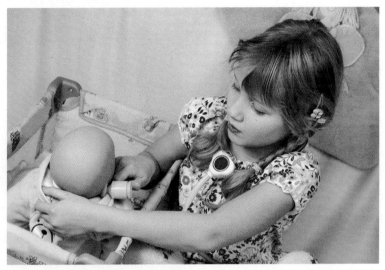

Children's play involves many different areas of development

Early development

Babies are born with a range of primitive reflex behaviours, which are actions they perform without thinking. These reflexes are linked to basic survival and most disappear within the first three months of life, as they are replaced by more coordinated movements. Some examples of these reflexes are described in Figure 1.1.

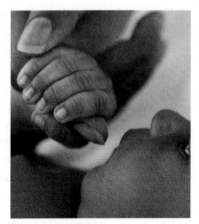

The grasp reflex

Figure 1.1 A baby's primitive reflex behaviours

Primitive reflex behaviour	Action shown by the baby
Swallowing and sucking reflexes	Babies will instinctively suck on anything placed in their mouth. This enables them to feed and swallow milk from birth.
Grasp reflex	Babies will grasp tightly onto an object (e.g. a finger) placed in the palm of their hand.
Rooting reflex	If the baby's cheek is stroked gently, the baby will turn its head to search for the nipple or teat. This helps the baby to find milk.
Startle reflex	When babies hear a sudden, loud noise or see a bright light, they will react by moving their arms outward and clenching their fists.

Development from birth up to two years

Children's development progresses extremely rapidly in the first two years of life as follows:

- Physically, their bodies become stronger and they learn to coordinate their movements.

- Cognitively, children's thinking skills are developing as they learn to figure things out for themselves and become problem solvers.

- Communication also progresses at an amazing rate as babbling babies develop into talking toddlers.

- Emotionally and socially, children are starting to become independent, confident individuals.

Physical development: gross motor skills

In the first year of life, most babies will gain control of their neck and back muscles, which helps them to support their own head and eventually to sit up.

Most six-month-old babies can sit up with some support. As they develop more strength and coordination, babies gradually become mobile, often by rolling over and over at first, but also by crawling (although it is important to remember that not all babies will crawl). Many nine-month-olds will start to pull themselves up on the furniture. As they gain confidence, this will progress to walking while holding on to furniture (often called 'cruising') and eventually to taking their first hesitant steps alone. With encouragement, most children will start to take their first steps between the ages of one year and 18 months. With practice, they will progress to walking with the help of an adult or a push-along toy and most 18-month-olds can walk by themselves, although they will often be quite unsteady. By the age of two years, children can usually run and kick a football.

Physical development: fine motor skills

From birth, most babies will start to explore their own hands (called 'hand regard') and at around four months of age, they will start to reach out and grasp toys. They start by using their whole hand (palmar grasp), but this soon progresses to a pincer grasp (using the thumb and index finger) at around 10 months old. Toddlers become more skilled in using their hands as their manipulative ability and hand–eye coordination develop. By the age of one year, most children will use an accurate pincer grasp to pick up very tiny objects and most two-year-olds can scribble with a chunky crayon.

Most children will take their first steps between the ages of one year and 18 months

Cognitive development

Babies rely on their senses to provide them with information about their world. For example, they will learn to recognise their parents by sight, the sound of their parents' voices and their smell. Gradually, babies learn to make sense of this information and start to piece it together as their thinking skills develop. Parents can encourage cognitive development through sensory play experiences, for example with musical toys, treasure basket play and at bath time.

Around the age of 10 months, most babies start to develop an understanding of object permanence. This means understanding that objects exist even though they are out of sight. Most toddlers will use simple problem solving skills such as cause and effect as they learn how things work. For example, they learn that 'if I push this knob, then the jack-in-the-box will pop up'. Most two-year-olds can complete a simple inset puzzle and enjoy putting things into containers and taking them out again. See also Unit 2: Play in early years settings, page 63, for more information about treasure basket play.

Treasure basket play

✎ Key terms

Cause and effect: *the relationship between an event and the reason why it occurred*

Object permanence: *the understanding that objects continue to exist even though they cannot be seen*

Palmar grasp: *immature hand movement in which the palm, rather than the fingertips, makes contact with an object*

Pincer grasp: *refined, mature hand movement in which the thumb and first finger are used to pick up a small object*

Treasure basket play: *an approach to early learning that involves providing a range of sensory experiences for babies to explore (developed by Elinor Goldschmied)*

🔍 Research

Investigate treasure basket play and make a list of items you could include in a treasure basket for an eight-month-old baby.

🔍 Research

Investigate the Foundation Years website at: www.foundationyears. org.uk. Explore the Parents Area on 'Helping your baby develop'. Watch the video and write a brief review that analyses how effective the information is for parents in supporting their baby's development.

Communication development

Babies communicate by crying, as they attempt to make their needs known. Most parents will soon learn to recognise the difference between a cry that means 'I'm hungry!' and a cry that clearly indicates 'I'm in pain!' The first year of life is often referred to as the **pre-linguistic** phase, as babies communicate without the use of words. By the age of four months, most babies will vocalise tunefully, using a range of different sounds and soon learn to babble using repetitive, single syllables, like 'ba ba ba'. Research has shown that babies are particularly responsive to a high-pitched, sing-song tone of voice, which is often referred to as '**parentese**'.

With encouragement, most one-year-olds will start to experiment with their first recognisable words.

Receptive language refers to the language that a child understands and **expressive language** is the words they actually speak. Most toddlers can understand far more than they can actually say. At this stage, children often make themselves understood by using lots of gestures such as pointing and, as they gain more experience, their language skills develop rapidly. Most two-year-olds will have a vocabulary in excess of 100 words and will use two words together, for example 'all gone'.

Key terms

Expressive language: *the ability to use verbal and non-verbal communication*

Parentese: *the sing-song, exaggerated speech pattern that adults use when talking to infants*

Pre-linguistic: *the stage before a baby starts to develop language and speech*

Receptive language: *the ability to understand verbal and non-verbal communication*

Most toddlers can understand far more than they can actually say

Emotional development

Babies are totally dependent on the attention of a responsive carer. The development of a strong attachment relationship (see Unit 7, pages 184–185) is extremely important for building trust and security. It creates the foundation for the baby's emotional development. In the first year of life, most babies will become distressed when separated from their main carer and will usually be very wary of strangers. Very young children do not have the level of understanding or the language skills to express their feelings and this can lead to a lot of frustration, often demonstrated through 'temper tantrums'. By the age of two years, most children are gaining confidence and developing a strong sense of who they are.

Social development

Babies are very social and, from an early age, most babies will smile as a social response to a familiar carer. This will soon progress to copying simple actions, such as sticking out their tongue and responding to social interaction and communication.

Learning to get along with others can be quite challenging for young children. In the first two years of life, children are very egocentric, which means that their viewpoint is centred on themselves. Social skills such as sharing, turn taking and cooperating have to be learned and don't always come easily!

Learning to play with others takes time and, in the first year of life, babies will usually engage in solitary play. Most two-year olds will play alongside other children (parallel or onlooker play), although they still do not play together. At this age, children are also starting to learn about acceptable and unacceptable behaviour. They can usually follow simple rules, but need consistent guidance from caring adults to help them with this process.

Parallel (or onlooker) play

Developmental milestones: birth up to two years

Figure 1.2 Summary of major developmental milestones: birth up to 2 years

Age	Physical	Cognitive	Communication	Emotional	Social
Birth	Primitive reflex behaviours Hand regard	Explores using the senses Recognises main carer	Expresses needs through crying	Developing attachments through close physical contact with main carers	Smiles as a social response to familiar carers
6 months	Sits with support Rolls over; reaches out and grasps toys (palmar grasp)	Explores toys and objects in their mouth Enjoys simple play activities (e.g. peek-a-boo)	Makes babbling sounds (e.g. 'ba ba ba') Uses gestures to express needs (e.g. arms up)	Expresses feelings by laughing, squealing or crying Shy with strangers	Plays alone Enjoys the company of familiar adults
1 year	Stands alone May walk with help Fine pincer grasp	Anticipates familiar routines (e.g. bath time) Imitates simple actions (e.g. waving 'bye-bye')	First recognisable words Follows simple instructions Points at objects to express needs	Seeks reassurance from and shows affection for familiar adults Fearful of unfamiliar situations	Joins in social activities (e.g. birthday celebrations) Shows an interest in the play of others
18 months	Walks alone Walks upstairs using two feet to each step Squats without falling Feeds self with a spoon Builds a tower of three blocks	Recognises own reflection Understands simple instructions Does basic problem solving using cause and effect	Produces several recognisable words Receptive language skills are more developed than expressive language Responds to more complex instructions	Shows frustration through temper tantrums Shows greater independence	Much more sociable More comfortable with strangers
2 years	Runs Kicks a ball Turns the pages of a book Screws and unscrews	More inquisitive Completes a simple jigsaw puzzle Points to four body parts on request	Names familiar objects Puts two words together (e.g. 'all gone')	Still expresses frustration through temper tantrums, but increased language helps to express feelings	Refers to self by name Engages in parallel (onlooker) play

Case study

Mia is a healthy one-year-old girl who lives with her mum, dad and three-year-old brother. Mia attends a local parent and toddler group with her mum three times a week and she enjoys playing with the wide range of toys at the group, both indoors and outdoors.

1. Describe two aspects of Mia's physical, cognitive, communication, emotional and social development that you would expect at this stage.

2. Summarise the developmental progress, in all areas, that you would expect Mia to make over the next year.

Your assessment criteria:

Learning aim A: Understand how the principles of growth and development apply to children's developmental progress from birth up to 8 years

Use relevant information to recognise children's developmental stages.

Anticipate the next stage(s) of development.

Recognise delays, difficulties or advanced progress in relation to growth and developmental norms.

Recall, apply and synthesise knowledge of child development and apply it to unfamiliar scenarios.

 Design

Think about the children in your placement, work setting or other children that you know, aged from birth to two years old. Make a list of the skills and abilities you have observed in their holistic development. Remember to include:

- *physical skills (both gross and fine motor)*
- *cognitive skills*
- *communication skills*
- *emotional and social skills.*

Push-along toys can help children develop confidence in walking

The sequence of development from two to four years

Development from two years up to four years

Children's development continues to progress at an amazing rate between the ages of two and four years. Physically, their bodies become much stronger and they develop more coordinated mobility and balance. Cognitively, children start to understand much more about themselves and the world around them, developing more creative thinking skills and learning through their play. Communication develops very rapidly as children become confident talkers and their vocabulary expands. Emotionally and socially, children are becoming more independent and learning the rules of social behaviour.

Physical development: gross motor skills

From the age of two years, muscle strength, balance and body coordination develop rapidly. Outdoor play provides opportunities for children to develop their physical skills and to practise risk taking.

Most three-year-olds can jump, climb and run around obstacles and, by the age of four years, children can usually pedal a tricycle skilfully.

Physical development: fine motor skills

Children are becoming more skilled in using their hands as their manipulative skill and dexterity develop. Most three-year-olds can hold a pencil using a tripod grasp and, by the age of four years, most children can thread small beads and build a tower of 10 blocks.

Cognitive development

Between the ages of two and four years, children's cognitive development progresses rapidly as they are learning more about the world around them. Play provides a wide range of rich opportunities for children to develop creative, critical thinking and problem solving skills. Heuristic play, imaginative play, construction play and messy play with natural materials all offer experiences for children to explore and investigate. Memory and concentration are also developing and repetition plays a very important role in children's learning at this stage. Most three-year-olds will have an understanding of basic concepts such as colour and size and, by the age of four years, children can usually compare different concepts such as shape and weight.

Your assessment criteria:

Learning aim A: Understand how the principles of growth and development apply to children's developmental progress from birth up to 8 years

> Use relevant information to recognise children's developmental stages.

> Anticipate the next stage(s) of development.

> Analyse how development in one area may affect development in other areas.

Key terms

Dexterity: skill in performing tasks with the hands

Tripod grasp: holding an object using the thumb, index finger and middle finger (the optimal position for holding a pencil)

The tripod grasp

Communication development

Communication progresses at an amazing rate during this time. Children's vocabulary expands as they learn to communicate in different situations and constantly ask questions. Most three-year-olds can communicate using simple sentences, although infantile substitutions are still common at this stage, for example 'par cark'. By the age of four years, children's language is becoming more fluent and their sentences will be more complex, although grammatical errors are still common, for example 'I goed outside and I played'. Children who live in a bilingual family will be learning more than one language.

Emotional development

Between the ages of two and four years, children become more confident and independent. Being in different situations helps children to learn about managing their feelings, although most three-year-olds will still be anxious about separating from their parent or main carer.

Play provides a very effective way for children to express their feelings, especially through role play and imaginative play. However, even four-year-olds are still very egocentric and find it difficult to understand the feelings of others.

Social development

For many children, this will be the stage at which they start nursery or pre-school. Friendships develop and children are learning how to share, cooperate and get along together in social play. Children are also developing more understanding about the rules of acceptable behaviour and will respond to positive reinforcement. Most four-year-olds are becoming more proficient in self-help skills such as washing and dressing themselves. It is also common at this age for some children to have an 'imaginary friend', and this is quite normal.

Research

Find out more about heuristic play. Make a list of objects that you might use for a heuristic play session with a group of two-year-olds.

Key terms

Bilingual: speaking two languages fluently

Concepts: ideas that form the building blocks of our knowledge and understanding

Heuristic play: an approach to support early exploration and problem solving by providing a wide range of natural objects for toddlers to investigate spontaneously

Infantile substitutions: the confusion of similar speech sounds in early language development

Research

Investigate the main areas of Communication and Language in the Statutory Framework for the Early Years Foundation Stage. Make a list of how you encourage children's:

a) listening and attention

b) understanding

c) speaking

in your placement or work setting.

Friendships develop through social play

Developmental milestones: two to four years

Figure 1.3 Summary of major developmental milestones from 2 to 4 years

Age	Physical	Cognitive	Communication	Emotional	Social
2 years	Runs Kicks a ball Turns the pages of a book Screws and unscrews	More inquisitive Completes a simple jigsaw puzzle Points to four body parts on request	Names familiar objects Puts two words together (e.g. 'all gone')	Still expresses frustration through temper tantrums, but increased language helps to express feelings	Refers to self by name Engages in parallel (onlooker) play
3 years	Walks upstairs, one foot to each step Jumps with both feet together Runs around obstacles Holds a pencil in a tripod grasp Feeds self using a fork and spoon	Matches primary colours Understands 'same/different' Copies simple shapes Knows own name	Asks 'what?', 'where?' and who?' questions Speaks in simple sentences Has a vocabulary of more than 200 words Follows simple instructions	More able to express feelings, especially through play Still experiences anxiety in new or unfamiliar situations Irrational fears are common (e.g. monsters under the bed)	Enjoys helping with household tasks Engages in social play with other children Understands acceptable and unacceptable behaviour
4 years	Pedals a tricycle skilfully Hops Threads small beads Uses scissors Builds a tower of 10 blocks	Recognises and names primary colours Draws a person with head and legs Understands 'bigger/smaller' and 'less/more than' Counts to 20 by rote	Can describe events accurately Tells jokes Uses complex sentences Makes some grammatical errors	Expresses more feelings verbally Has a sense of humour Shows pride in achievements Seeks frequent adult approval	Friendships are more important Beginning to have a 'best friend' Participates in group activities and cooperative play

Case study

Julie and Alena are newly qualified early years workers who are both employed at a small, private nursery. Their manager is planning an information evening for parents and has asked Julie and Alena to give a short presentation on the sequence of expected all-round child development between the ages of three and four years.

1. Outline the main points that Julie and Alena should include in their presentation for the parents.

2. Explain how Julie and Alena could support parents to anticipate some of the major milestones of expected development for children aged three to four years.

Three- and four-year-old children enjoy playing together

Case study

Calum is a healthy, active four-year-old, whose development has followed the expected pattern since birth.

1. Describe Calum's emotional and social development at this stage, with examples.

2. Explain how Calum's emotional and social development is interrelated with his cognition and language at this stage.

Your assessment criteria:

Learning aim A: Understand how the principles of growth and development apply to children's developmental progress from birth up to 8 years

- Use relevant information to recognise children's developmental stages.

- Anticipate the next stage(s) of development.

- Recognise delays, difficulties or advanced progress in relation to growth and developmental norms.

- Recall, apply and synthesise knowledge of child development and apply it to unfamiliar scenarios.

 Key term

Rote: *a method of memorising by repetition*

The sequence of development from four to eight years

Development from four years up to eight years

Between the ages of four and eight years old, children make great strides in their development. They are physically bigger, with more developed muscle strength and coordinated body movements. Cognitively, children's thinking is becoming more critical as their experiences widen and they ask endless questions and engage in conversation. Emotionally and socially, children are becoming much more confident and capable individuals, learning how to manage their own feelings and behaviour in different situations.

Physical development: gross motor skills

Physically, children will have more stamina and improved body coordination as they learn to control their movements more skilfully. Children will enjoy practising their physical skills through exercise and outdoor play. For example, they may take part in running races, playing football, climbing trees, gymnastics and dancing. By the age of five, many children can hop and skip, dance with rhythm and kick and control a football. Most eight-year-olds can swim and ride a bicycle without stabilisers.

Physical development: fine motor skills

Children are learning how to use their manipulative skills to complete more complex tasks. Some activities require more practice, such as tying shoelaces, but most five-year-olds can fasten and unfasten buttons and use a dominant hand (either right-handed or left-handed). Most eight-year-olds have legible handwriting and can create quite detailed drawings.

Cognitive development

From the age of five years, children will start to attend primary school, where learning becomes more formalised and children begin to understand more difficult concepts. Children will develop their skills in literacy (reading, writing, speaking and listening) and their understanding of problem solving and mathematical skills such as counting, calculating and estimating. By the age of five, most children are learning to read and write and, at eight years old, most children can do quite complex calculations. Around the age of seven, most children are developing the ability to think logically and use reasoning to explain why things happen.

Most five-year-olds can fasten and unfasten buttons

They will understand Piagetian principles of conservation (see pages 32–33), for example with mass or volume.

Communication development

Adults who talk with children and listen to them carefully will help them learn to communicate more confidently. Communication skills also develop a great deal as children learn about descriptive language and the rules of grammar. Bilingual children may be learning two systems of communication: one that they use for their learning at school and a different one for communicating at home. Most five-year-olds have a wide vocabulary and can communicate using long sentences that are mostly grammatically correct. Most eight-year-olds can engage in complex conversations and enjoy telling jokes.

Emotional development

With their improved language skills, children are much more capable of expressing their feelings and managing their behaviour. By the age of five, children are generally more in control of their emotions and will be more caring and thoughtful towards others. Most eight-year-olds are becoming confident individuals with a well-developed sense of self.

Most eight-year-olds are becoming confident individuals

Social development

Friendships are very important at this stage and most children will have a 'best friend', usually of the same gender. Children at this age are very concerned about rules and the difference between 'fair' and 'unfair'. They will often remind others about the rules and tell others when rules have been broken. Most five-year-olds are able to do things for themselves, such as going to the toilet independently. By the age of eight years, most children will have stable friendships and enjoy being part of a group.

Research

Investigate the Early Years Foundation Stage Profile and make a list of the Early Learning Goals for Mathematics, including:

a) Numbers

b) Shape, Space and Measures.

Design

Make a list of all the children's games you can think of that have rules, for example about taking turns, deciding who goes first or who the winner is.

Share your list with others in the group and see how many more you can think of.

Developmental milestones: four to eight years

Figure 1.4 Summary of major developmental milestones from 4 to 8 years

Age	Physical	Cognitive	Communication	Emotional	Social
4 years	Pedals a tricycle skilfully Hops Threads small beads Uses scissors Builds a tower of 10 blocks	Recognises and names primary colours Draws a person with head and legs Understands 'bigger/smaller' and 'less/more than' Counts to 20 by rote	Can describe events accurately Tells jokes Uses complex sentences Makes some grammatical errors	Expresses more feelings verbally Has a sense of humour Shows pride in achievements Seeks frequent adult approval	Friendships are more important Beginning to have a 'best friend' Participates in group activities and cooperative play
5–6 years	Hops, skips and dances with rhythm Kicks and controls a football Fastens and unfastens buttons Uses a knife and fork	Draws detailed pictures Is beginning to read and write Counts (with understanding of number value) Can do simple calculations	Has a wide vocabulary Communicates using long sentences that are mostly grammatically correct	More in control of their emotions More caring and thoughtful towards others	Enjoys games with rules Has a clear understanding of right and wrong Responds well to adult praise
7–8 years	Swims Rides a bicycle without stabilisers Has legible handwriting Uses scissors skilfully	Reads silently Thinking is more logical Can do quite complex calculations (using fractions or decimals)	Engages in complex conversations Enjoys telling jokes and chatting	Confident and independent More aware of the feelings of others (empathetic)	Has stable friendships Clear differences between the play activities of boys and girls

Q Research

Investigate a range of party games that would be suitable for a group of five-year-olds. Make a list and keep it for future reference. You may even want to try out some of the games with your class colleagues!

Case study

Alice is a healthy seven-year-old pupil in a Year 2 class at a local primary school. Her teacher, Mrs Knight, is preparing some worksheets with mathematical exercises for the children to complete. The National Curriculum guidance states that pupils should be taught to:

- use subtraction in 'take away' and 'find the difference' problems
- compare and order numbers from 0 up to 100
- recognise, name and write fractions ¼, ⅓, ½, ⅔ and ¾ of a whole.

1. Create five questions for a worksheet that would test Alice's mathematical understanding of these concepts.

2. Give examples of three other mathematical concepts that you would expect Alice to understand at this age/stage.

The Primary National Curriculum outlines the key areas of learning for children in Key Stage 1

Case study

Jaafar is five years old. He attends the local primary school and is picked up every day by Madhu his childminder. Madhu likes to provide a range of stimulating activities for Jaafar after school, which helps to support his learning and development. Madhu has a large, indoor playroom and an enclosed garden with some outdoor toys and a sandpit.

1. Describe two aspects of Jaafar's physical, cognitive, communication, emotional and social development that you would expect at this stage.

2. Give examples of some of the toys and play materials that Madhu should provide, both indoors and outside, in order to support Jaafar's learning and development.

Your assessment criteria:

Learning aim A: Understand how the principles of growth and development apply to children's developmental progress from birth up to 8 years

> Use relevant information to recognise children's developmental stages.

> Anticipate the next stage(s) of development.

> Recognise delays, difficulties or advanced progress in relation to growth and developmental norms.

> Recall, apply and synthesise knowledge of child development and apply it to unfamiliar scenarios.

Q | Research

Investigate the Primary National Curriculum for English at Key Stage 1. Summarise some of the key areas of learning for pupils in both reading and writing.

Q | Research

Investigate a range of suitable books for six-year-old children (both fiction and non-fiction). Select one of the books and explain to a colleague how the book would support the learning and development of an average six-year-old. Keep a list of titles for future reference.

Theories of behaviour and moral development

Theories about children's behaviour

Current early years practice is based on years of knowledge and experience, which helps us to understand children's learning, development and behaviour. Even though some of these theories were developed many years ago, they form the foundation on which many of the principles of our current early years' frameworks are based. As an early years practitioner, it is important for you to understand theoretical models of child development and to use these ideas to inform your professional practice.

Albert Bandura (born 1925)

Albert Bandura is a Canadian psychologist who developed social learning theory. He studied children's behaviour in different situations, most significantly with his 'Bobo doll' experiments. Through these experiments, Bandura found that if children observed aggressive behaviour, they were more likely to act in physically aggressive ways themselves. Bandura's work suggests that children learn by observing and imitating others and he emphasised the importance of adults being good role models for children.

Ivan Pavlov (1849–1936)

Ivan Pavlov was a Russian behaviourist, who developed the theory of classical conditioning. He observed the responses of dogs when they were being fed, and noticed that the dogs always salivated just before the arrival of their food. He theorised that the dogs were making an association between the arrival of food and other factors (such as the sound of footsteps) and this was causing them to salivate. He explored his theory by ringing a bell every time the dogs were fed, and eventually, the dogs salivated at the sound of a bell, even when no food was produced. Pavlov called this a conditioned response and suggested that it forms an important part of the learning process.

B. F. Skinner (1904–1990)

Burrhus Frederic Skinner was an American psychologist and behaviourist. He developed the theory of operant conditioning. His work was based on the study of rats in a specially constructed box, which was designed to 'train' the rats to behave in a particular way. If the rats travelled the right way through the box, they were rewarded with food (positive

Research

Investigate Bandura's Bobo doll experiments. Reflect on some of the different ways in which young children can be exposed to aggressive behaviour (including the internet and video gaming).

reinforcers), but if they travelled the wrong way, they received a mild electric shock. Skinner discovered that the rats learned to travel the correct way because they were encouraged by positive reinforcement (food). He also found that by maintaining the positive reinforcement, the rats continued to repeat the 'correct' behaviour.

This theory has a direct influence on the way we understand children's behaviour today. Examples include the use of praise and encouragement, stickers and other rewards to encourage appropriate behaviour.

Theories about children's moral development

Moral development is the process of children learning the difference between right and wrong. It is a gradual stage in child development and can help to explain many aspects of children's behaviour.

Lawrence Kohlberg (1927–1987)

Lawrence Kohlberg was an American psychologist who was well-known for his theory of moral development.

His theory proposed three levels of moral development:

- **Pre-conventional:** children are born with no sense of right and wrong, but quickly learn that some behaviours are rewarded while others are punished.
- **Conventional:** from approximately nine years of age, children learn to behave according to what others want or need. They have now learned the conventional ways of behaving according to what is right and what is wrong.
- **Post-conventional:** from approximately 16 years of age, people mature morally and have a genuine interest in the needs of others.

Piaget's theory of moral development

Jean Piaget (see page 32) believed that children's moral development is related directly to their stage of cognition and their social relationships with adults. He described the state of moral realism as a way of explaining why very young children are more concerned about the outcome of their actions than the intention. For example, a young child will be more concerned about spilling a large amount of milk accidentally than by spilling a small amount of milk on purpose.

(see page 32)

Key terms

Classical conditioning: learning that results from a reflex response to a specific stimulus

Conditioned response: a reaction that has been learned in response to a specific stimulus

Operant conditioning: the process by which an individual's behaviour is shaped by reinforcement or punishment

Social learning theory: the theory that learning occurs through observation and imitating the behaviour of others

Reflect

Reflect on the different forms of positive reinforcement for children's behaviour that you have observed in your placement or work setting.

How effective do you think this is?

Key term

Moral realism: a belief that there is an absolute truth regarding what is moral; children's understanding that the rules of adults are firm and unquestionable

Very young children are more concerned about the outcome of their actions than the intention

The development of cognition and language

Theories about children's cognitive development

Theories about the development of children's thinking skills have direct relevance for early years practitioners. Many of the main principles of the Early Years Foundation Stage are based on this research.

Jean Piaget (1896–1980)

Jean Piaget was a Swiss theorist who developed a constructivist approach to child development. He claimed that children learn actively through their play and suggested that children build up (or construct) their knowledge and understanding based on their experiences of the world around them. Piaget suggested that children's learning progresses in four distinct stages, as outlined in Figure 1.5.

Figure 1.5 Piaget's four stages of cognitive development

Stage and approximate age	Characteristics
Sensori-motor (birth–2 years)	Learning about self and the environment through senses and movements, e.g. recognising main carer through sight and smell; learning that moving a rattle causes a sound
Pre-operational (2–7 years)	Children learn to use language to represent thoughts and objects, and express themselves Thinking is very concrete and egocentric
Concrete operational (7–11 years)	Ability to think logically and use reasoning to solve problems and work things out based on the ability to conserve
Formal operational (11–15 years)	Ability to think in the abstract (without using concrete representations) and understand concepts like feelings, and to organise ideas and perform mental calculations

Conservation

Piaget conducted a number of studies to explore the development of children's reasoning and logical thinking. He did this by giving children a variety of conservation tasks, involving the properties of objects, such as volume and mass. For example, if you have a ball of clay, the amount of clay in the ball does not change if you squash it down into a flat shape,

Key terms

Abstract thought: the ability to think about concepts and ideas and to make generalisations

Concrete thought: thinking in terms of real physical objects and events

Conserve: to maintain at a constant overall total (for example, a quantity such as mass or volume)

Constructivist: describes the theory that knowledge is generated through interaction and experiences

Schema: an organised pattern of thought or behaviour

even though the appearance changes. Piaget discovered that children in the pre-operational stage would say that the flattened shape had more clay than the ball, because it looks bigger. Children in the concrete operational stage would understand that the amount is the same.

Children in the pre-operational stage are not able to understand the conservation of properties such as mass and volume

Egocentrism

Young children are egocentric, which means they tend to see the world only from their own point of view. To demonstrate this, Piaget used a three-dimensional model of three mountains, with a different object on each peak. A child is given several pictures showing different views of the mountains. A doll is then placed at various points around the model and the child is asked to choose the picture that shows what the doll sees. Piaget discovered that children in the pre-operational stage would choose the picture showing what they could see (not what the doll could see). Children in the concrete operational stage would choose the correct picture.

Chris Athey (1924–2011)

Chris Athey was also a constructivist who developed Piaget's ideas about schemas in relation to children's learning. A schema is a pattern of linked behaviours, which children explore at different levels and in a variety of situations to support their cognitive development. For example, a baby will try out a wide range of schemas on one object, such as sucking, shaking and throwing a rattle. (See also Unit 2: Play in early years settings, page 72.) Figure 1.6 gives some examples of schemas.

In your placement or work setting, ask your supervisor if you can try some of Piaget's tasks with children of different ages.

Q | Research

In your placement or work setting, ask your supervisor if you can try some of Piaget's tasks with children of different ages.

Reflect on your findings and think about how this influences our understanding of children's thoughts and actions.

Children exploring the rotation schema may be fascinated by a spinning top

Figure 1.6 Examples of children's schemas

Schema	For example, a child may...
Transporting	carry all the bricks from one place to another in a bag move toys around in pushchairs, wheelbarrows, etc.
Enveloping	cover themselves with a flannel when washing wrap a doll in a blanket cover their whole painting with one colour
Rotation	be fascinated by the spinning washing machine or anything with wheels, rolling down a hill or spinning around and around

Lev Vygotsky (1896–1934)

Lev Vygotsky was a Russian theorist who claimed that children learn predominantly through their interactions with adults and the environment. He emphasised the role that adults play in extending children's learning and helping them to achieve their full potential. Vygotsky defined the zone of proximal development as the difference between what children can do by themselves and what they could achieve with adult help and encouragement. (See also Unit 2, page 72.)

Jerome Bruner (born 1915)

Jerome Bruner is an American psychologist who developed ideas about children's thinking and problem solving skills. He emphasised the role of adults in 'scaffolding' children's learning, by providing a framework to support children's thinking. (See also Unit 2, page 72.)

Information processing

The information processing theory of cognitive development focuses on how children acquire, store and use knowledge. Children deposit information into their working memory through the process of 'encoding', which relies on active participation and constant repetition. It is also important to present material to children in a variety of different ways, for example visual, auditory and kinaesthetic. In order for children to store information in their memory, they need lots of opportunities to rehearse and recall the information and to link it to their own experience.

In order for children to remember information over time, it needs to transfer from the working memory into the long-term memory. The ability to do this is linked to brain development and it steadily improves as children get older. You can encourage children's ability to recall information by using games and activities such as picture pairs or Kim's game.

You can encourage children's ability to recall information with games like picture pairs

Research

In your placement or work setting, listen to children talking. What do you notice about how they construct sentences and use grammar?

Make a list of some of the unusual expressions that you hear children use.

Key terms

Innate: *inborn and occurring naturally*

Telegraphic speech: *speech that sounds like a telegram, using only the main words of a sentence*

Theories about children's language development

There are many different theories about children's language and communication development. The development of language and communication is discussed in detail in Unit 6, pages 163–181.

Noam Chomsky (born 1928)

Noam Chomsky is an American linguist and philosopher whose ideas have had a major influence on our understanding of children's language development. He claims that children are born with an innate ability to learn languages, which he calls the 'language acquisition device' (LAD). He argues that the LAD explains why all children follow the same pattern of language development and acquire complex language so rapidly. Chomsky's theories also explain why children often make mistakes such as 'I drawed', showing that they are applying rules rather than learning language through imitation alone.

Roger Brown (1925–1997)

Roger Brown was an American researcher who developed explanations of language acquisition by focusing on the uses of language. His findings have stimulated further research into telegraphic speech, children's use of negatives and tenses, and the structure of early sentences.

Brown described five stages of language acquisition:

- Stage 1: simple two- or three-word sentences
- Stage 2: naming objects and events
- Stage 3: questions such as 'what?', 'why?', 'where?'
- Stage 4: joining short sentences
- Stage 5: complex sentences.

Children gradually learn to apply the rules of grammar in their speech

Personality, self-esteem and attachment theory

Theories about children's personality and the development of self-esteem

Theories about children's personality and self-esteem help us to understand how children develop a sense of who they are, how they develop confidence and self-assurance and the role of adults in this process. This is explored in more detail in Unit 7: Supporting children's personal, social and emotional development, pages 182–205.

Erik Erikson (1902–1994)

Erik Erikson was a German-American psychologist who is best known for his theories about the stages of psychosocial development. He described a series of life stages and challenges that all children and young people must go through and overcome on their journey to adult maturity. He argued that each stage must be understood and accepted as an integral part of personality development. The first four of these life stages are described in Figure 1.7.

Figure 1.7 Erikson's first four stages of psychosocial development

Life stage	Challenge	Emphasis
Infancy: birth to 18 months	The development of trust versus mistrust	Through the mother's positive and loving care, particularly through visual contact and touch, the child learns to trust and have basic confidence in the future. Failure to experience trust can result in the child having feelings of worthlessness and a mistrust of the world in general.
Early childhood: 18 months to 3 years	The development of autonomy versus shame	Children learn to master skills for themselves. They have opportunities to build self-esteem and autonomy as they gain more control over their bodies and acquire new skills. Children can be very vulnerable if they are shamed when learning important skills (e.g. toilet training) and may suffer low self-esteem as a result. The most significant relationships are with the parents.
Play age: 3 to 5 years	The development of initiative versus guilt	Children experience a desire to copy adults and take the initiative in creating play situations. They make up stories and play out roles, experimenting with what it means to be an adult. Children's identification with gender roles becomes more important. The most significant relationship is with the basic family.
School age: 6 to 12 years	The development of industry versus inferiority	Children are capable of learning and accomplishing numerous new skills and developing a work ethic. If children experience unresolved feelings of inadequacy among their peers, they can doubt their own competence and have serious problems with self-esteem. As their world expands, children's most significant relationship is now with the school and neighbourhood. Parents are no longer the complete authorities they once were, although they are still important.

The most significant relationships for very young children are with their parents

Charles Cooley (1864–1929)

Charles Horton Cooley was an American sociologist who developed the concept of the 'looking glass self'. This theory states that an individual's sense of self is largely created by what other people think about them. This can help us to understand different levels of self-confidence in children, which develop as a direct result of their experiences with other people.

Charles Cooley argued that children's sense of self is largely created by what other people think about them

Cooley's work influenced Susan Harter's theory of self-esteem. She recognised that in order to develop self-esteem, children require not only the approval of others, but also need to experience competence and success. This helps us to understand the significance of helping children to achieve mastery and feel good about their accomplishments in order to build their self-esteem.

? | Reflect

Reflect on how much you are influenced by what other people think about you.

How does that affect your own confidence or behaviour in different situations?

Using Charles Cooley's concept of the 'looking glass self', write a brief report that analyses some of the ways your own behaviour is influenced by other people's opinions about you.

Attachment theory

Attachment theory is also discussed in Unit 7, pages 186–187, and you might want to review that unit alongside this section.

John Bowlby

John Bowlby was a British psychologist who developed attachment theory. His work emphasised the importance of young children developing a strong attachment relationship (emotional connection) with their main carer and the significance of this attachment for children's security, self-esteem and emotional development. This attachment relationship is particularly important in the first year of life. Building on this firm foundation, most young children are able to develop confidence, become more independent and learn to get along with others.

Mary Ainsworth (1913–1999)

Mary Ainsworth was a Canadian psychologist who studied the quality of attachment relationships between young children and their main carers through her 'strange situation' studies. She studied infants (aged 10 to 24 months) and observed their reactions when their parent left the room and then returned a short while later. She used the results of these studies to define different categories of attachment, which are described in Figure 1.8.

Your assessment criteria:

Learning aim B: Understand theories and models of development and how they relate to aspects of children's development

- Understand aspects of theories of development.
- Identify the strengths and weaknesses of theories.
- Apply different theoretical approaches to unfamiliar scenarios.
- Compare theoretical approaches to specific areas of child development.
- Analyse how theories and models of development relate to observations of children.
- Identify which theories or models of development link to what has been observed and explain why associations have been made.
- Use theories or models of development to make a judgement about what is being observed.

Figure 1.8 The four categories of attachment relationships

Category of attachment	Characteristics
Secure attachment	The infant was distressed when the parent left the room, but immediately sought out comfort from the parent on their return. This child has a basic sense of trust and seeks comfort naturally.
Ambivalent insecure attachment	The infant was distressed when the parent left the room and exhibited ambivalent or angry behaviour on the parent's return. This child has a basic sense of mistrust and is often aggressive.
Avoidant insecure attachment	The infant was detached and ignored the parent's return to the room. This child has a basic sense of mistrust and avoids involvement.
Disorganised attachment (added later by Ainsworth's colleague Mary Main)	The infant was dissociative and confused. This child has a basic sense of chaos and often has behavioural difficulties. The mothers had frequently experienced trauma during the birth or post-natal depression.

Attachment theory underpins the development of the key person approach in many settings and helps us to understand children's reactions to being separated from their main carers.

Ecological systems theory

Ecological systems theory is one of many different theories related to human development. It was developed by Urie Bronfenbrenner (1917–2005), a Russian-American psychologist. This theory emphasises the importance of environmental factors in influencing child development, although this does vary between cultures. Bronfenbrenner described how children's development does not happen in isolation, but is closely interrelated with their family, school and local community, as well as the wider society. Bronfenbrenner's theory is often represented as a series of concentric circles, as shown in Figure 1.9.

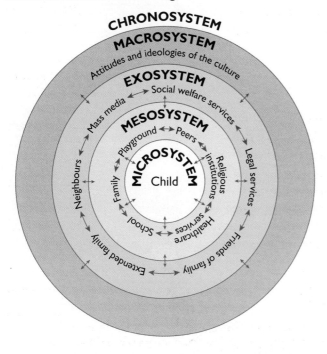

Figure 1.9 Bronfenbrenner's ecological theory

Research

In your placement or work setting, ask your supervisor if you can observe children when they are separating from their parents or main carers, for example when they first arrive at the setting.

Make notes on your observations of the children's reactions. What differences do you observe?

Research

Investigate more about Bronfenbrenner's Bio-ecological systems theory in the Early Childhood Education Journal at: www.usd.edu/~mremund/bronffamily.pdf

Case study

Tanya is six years old and lives with her large, extended traveller family in a caravan. The family move around a lot and Tanya's attendance at school is very erratic. She has attended three different primary schools so far and the family are about to move on again. They usually stay on established caravan sites but sometimes park on waste ground or the roadside. Tanya has two brothers and one sister and they all share the same sleeping space in the caravan.

1. Using Bronfenbrenner's ecological systems theory, describe some of the factors that will influence Tanya's development.

2. Explain why it is important for Tanya's teachers to understand these influences in order to maximise Tanya's potential achievement in school.

Strengths and weaknesses of theories and models of child development

Identify the strengths and weaknesses of theories

Early years practitioners need to be able to use child development theories appropriately. That means not only having an understanding of relevant theories, but also being able to analyse how theories and models of development relate to professional practice. Understanding the strengths and weaknesses of different theories helps practitioners to compare theoretical approaches and identify which theories are the most suitable in supporting observations and assessments of children's development.

Behaviourism

A key strength of behaviourist theories is that positive reinforcement clearly does lead to learning. However, one of the main weaknesses is that this approach does not support children's innate motivation to explore their world and construct their own knowledge.

Albert Bandura's social learning theory moves behaviourism closer toward the constructivist theories of Piaget, in that children are viewed as actively influencing their own development through mental processes as they interpret and select which behaviours to imitate. This is just one of the reasons why Bandura's theory has more recently been referred to as social cognitive theory.

Constructivism

A key strength of Piaget's constructivist theory is that it helps to explain children's development of logical thought. However, Piaget's four stages of cognitive development are not widely accepted among researchers today as children have been observed to develop different cognitive skills at a wide range of different ages and stages. One of the main weaknesses of Piaget's theories is that they focus on age trends in cognitive development with very little emphasis on the process of learning, or how children move from one stage to the next. Piaget believed that mental maturation is a prerequisite for learning, not a result of learning.

In contrast, Vygotsky believed that learning causes mental maturation and that good instruction actively encourages cognitive development. One of the strengths of social constructivism is that children clearly do learn through social interaction and dialogue with adults. However, this approach does not support children's self-directed learning through hands-on exploration.

Key terms

Prerequisite: a thing required as a prior condition for something else to happen

Social cognitive theory: the idea that children's learning can be directly related to observing others within the context of social interactions, experiences, and outside media influences

Social constructivism: a theory about children's learning that emphasises learning as an active social process in which children develop meaning through their interactions with others and with the environment they live in

 Design

Compare and contrast Skinner's, Piaget's and Vygotsky's theories about children's cognitive development. Write a report to summarise the key differences in these three approaches.

Children learn through social interaction as well as self-directed hands-on exploration

Language and communication theories

A key strength of Chomsky's theory about the innate nature of language, or the 'language acquisition device' (LAD) is that it supports the fact that children do not merely imitate what they hear but can generate an infinite number of sentences that they have never heard before. Chomsky's theories also support children's mistakes in the application of grammar rules, for example when they say 'foots' instead of 'feet', even though they have never heard adults say 'foots'. This approach also explains why all children follow the same pattern of language development and acquire complex language so rapidly.

However, Chomsky's theories do not emphasise the child's active role in learning language using their information processing abilities. Recent research has shown that infants can identify words in adult speech and can then begin to link words with meanings. Therefore there is more emphasis on the process of learning language rather than it being biologically determined.

Personality and self-esteem

John Bowlby's attachment theory is probably one of the most important and widely recognised theories about children's emotional development. The key strengths of this approach are that it explains the function of children's behaviour in two very important ways:

- it supports children's vital need to feel secure and to instinctively seek out the protection of a significant adult when they feel anxious or afraid

- it supports the idea of a 'secure base' from which children can move outward to explore the world.

However, one of the main weaknesses of this theory is that Bowlby emphasised the importance of the first years of life as a critical period for children to develop secure attachments. Subsequent research has shown that although a strong attachment relationship in infancy is extremely important for children's emotional development, changes in attachment security are possible in later life. Sensitive intervention through therapy programmes can enable attachment-disordered children to restore damaged attachment relationships and to develop healthy new ones.

While Bowlby emphasised the importance of attachments during the early years, subsequent research has shown that changes in attachment security are possible in later life

One of the major criticisms of attachment theory comes from Judith Rich Harris, who argues that the influence of nurturing and parental upbringing is not solely responsible for how a child develops; she calls this the 'nurture assumption'. Harris's view (*The Nurture Assumption*, 2009) is that parents do not shape their child's personality or character, but a child's peers have more influence on them than their parents.

Key terms

Attachment-disordered: *a behavioural disorder caused by the lack of an emotionally secure attachment to a caregiver in the first two years of life*

Critical period: *a period during a child's development in which a particular skill or characteristic is believed to be most readily acquired*

One of the main strengths of Erikson's theory of psychosocial development is that it emphasises the important role of the parents in the child's life. However, a key weakness is that in focusing on the specific stages, it does not explain the variable influence of external factors, including culture and different life experiences, on identity and personality development.

Ecological theory

A key strength of Bronfenbrenner's theory is that it primarily focuses on the social contexts in which children live and the people who influence their development. It emphasises the importance of what happens in children's families, neighbourhoods, and peer groups. However, it does not focus on the biological and cognitive factors in children's development or address the step-by-step developmental changes that are the focus of theories such as Piaget's and Erikson's.

Using theories in practice

Early years practitioners need to be able to use a combination of different theories and models in their professional practice. It is important not only to identify which theories are most appropriate in supporting practice, but also to be able to analyse how theories help to support observations, assessment and planning for children's learning in early years settings. This is explored further on pages 44–45.

🔍 Research

Research Bowlby's attachment theory and analyse how his theory might relate to your observations of children in the following situations:

- a distressed two-year-old arriving at the setting and separating from their main carer at the beginning of the day

- a key person changing the nappy of one of their key children, aged 10 months

- a one-year-old whose key person is absent from the setting due to illness.

🔍 Research

Research some of the key theories and models of children's development. Make a chart that identifies the strengths and weaknesses of each approach.

Ecological theory emphasises the importance of the family

Factors affecting development

Influences on children's development

There are many different factors that can affect children's development, both positively and negatively. Every child develops in his or her own unique way; even twins who are genetically identical will experience life differently. A variety of factors can combine to influence children's all-round development. Some of these influences can be the result of biological factors, such as health or disability, and some are due to external factors, such as poverty and stress. Research has shown that high-quality, early education is one of the most significant factors in improving outcomes for young children.

Figure 1.10 summarises the factors that influence children's development, which are detailed on pages 47 to 49.

Your assessment criteria:

Learning aim D: Understand how a range of factors influence children's development

Analyse a range of factors that support or hinder a child's development.

Make a judgement about the extent to which factors may affect the child's development in the short- or long-term.

Analyse the likely strength of each factor's effect compared with other factors.

Figure 1.10 Factors that influence children's development

Factors	Examples	Possible influences on children's development
Prenatal	Down's syndrome	Developmental delay, learning difficulties and health problems
	Smoking during pregnancy	Low birth weight
	Rubella virus (German measles)	Vision and hearing impairment Brain damage
	Prematurity	Developmental delay Hearing impairment
Biological	Chronic conditions (e.g. asthma)	Repeated periods of absence from school Restricted opportunities to play and learn
	Infections (e.g. meningitis)	Vision and hearing impairment Brain damage
	Cerebral palsy	Problems with speech, muscle tone and movement
Social, cultural and political	Family values Culture	Impact on children's opportunities to socialise or access early education
	Parenting style Provision of childcare services	Lack of stimulation and encouragement resulting in lower achievement and negative outcomes
Emotional	Quality of attachment relationship	Negative impact on children's wellbeing, sense of security and self-esteem
	Family trauma	Childhood depression, self-harming behaviour
	Bullying	School refusal
	Abuse	

Prenatal factors

The pre natal period is extremely important in child development, and maternal health in pregnancy can have significant consequences for children's growth and later development. Smoking cigarettes during pregnancy can significantly reduce the oxygen supply to the growing foetus, which can result in a low birth weight. This can cause respiratory problems for the newborn in addition to delayed development.

The Rubella (German measles) virus can be very damaging to the developing foetus, particularly if the mother contracts this infection in the first 12 weeks of pregnancy when the majority of the vital organs are being formed. This can result in vision or hearing impairments with a subsequent impact on a child's overall development.

Down's syndrome (also known as trisomy 21) is a chromosomal condition caused by the presence of an extra chromosome number 21. Children who are born with Down's syndrome frequently experience different degrees of all-round developmental delay and learning difficulties. This can affect children's speech and language development, body coordination and cognitive abilities. In addition, many children will also be affected by congenital heart disease, visual and hearing impairments.

Babies born before the 37th week of pregnancy are referred to as premature (or preterm), and this can impact on development in a number of ways. Premature babies often have respiratory problems at birth and many also have some degree of hearing impairment. Being born too early means that babies have some catching up to do, and it frequently takes extra time for premature babies to reach developmental milestones such as sitting up or learning to walk.

Biological factors

Disability, long-term medical conditions and short-term illnesses can all impact on a child's development in a variety of different ways.

- Cerebral palsy is a group of disorders that can involve brain and nervous system functions, such as movement, learning, hearing and vision. It is caused by injuries to or abnormalities of the brain, often while the baby's brain is still developing and sometimes as a result of low levels of oxygen (hypoxia). Children with cerebral palsy will often be affected by muscle weakness or loss of movement and poor body co-ordination, which affects their mobility. In addition, some children may also have speech problems and visual or hearing impairments.

- Meningitis is a serious infection that can be life threatening. Children who contract bacterial meningitis can sustain permanent neurological

Children born with Down's syndrome frequently experience different degrees of all-round developmental delay and learning difficulties

Research

Investigate more about premature babies at www.nhs.uk or www.bliss.org.uk and analyse the impact of prematurity on a baby's all-round development.

Key terms

Cerebral palsy: a group of conditions caused by brain damage before or during birth, which can result in problems with speech, muscle tone and movement

Down's syndrome: a chromosomal disorder, which can result in developmental delay and learning difficulties

Meningitis: inflammation of the meninges (the tissues that surround the brain or spinal cord) caused by a viral or bacterial infection

Prematurity: born before the 37th week of pregnancy

The impact of atypical development

Atypical development in a specific area can result in problems for children in many other areas. For example, if a child's social development is delayed, this will have an impact on their ability to interact with others, join in play, make friends, learn to share and cooperate. This will result in subsequent effects on the child's:

- physical development (through not joining in physical play or activities)

- cognitive development (through reduced participation in learning and play activities)

- language development (through reduced interaction with others)

- emotional development (through reduced opportunities for developing confidence, self-esteem and independence).

Further examples are given in Figure 1.11.

Research

Examine Figure 1.11, which shows some examples of how atypical development in one or more areas can affect other areas of development. Analyse, using examples, the extent to which the following would impact on other areas of a child's development:

- *delayed cognitive development of a four-year-old*

- *delayed physical development of an eighteen-month-old.*

Figure 1.11 Examples of the impact of atypical development on children

Area of delay	Can have an impact on children's...
Delayed social and emotional development	• physical development (through not joining in physical play) • behaviour and language development (through reduced interaction with peers) • play capacity (due to being shy, withdrawn or aggressive) • confidence and self-esteem (through social or behavioural difficulties and the possibility of bullying)
Delayed cognitive and language development	• learning (literacy, mathematics, problem solving) • speech, language and ability to express themselves • social interaction, behaviour and friendships • ability to express ideas, feelings and needs • ability to play cooperatively • confidence, self-esteem and independence
Delayed physical development	• opportunities to explore their environment • ability to play with others and join in • approach to risk taking (with subsequent effects on their emotional, social and behavioural development) • confidence, self-esteem and independence

Delayed social development can have an impact on children's confidence and self-esteem

Case study

Hannah is two years and three months old. She can walk sturdily by herself, run without falling and kick a football. She enjoys playing with building blocks and shape sorters and digging outside in the garden. Hannah is not talking yet and she generally makes her needs known by pointing or using other gestures. Hannah has just started to attend a local playgroup and her mum is concerned that her lack of speech will affect her ability to play with the other children.

1. Explain, using examples, how Hannah's atypical speech and language development might affect all other areas of her development.

2. Discuss why it is important for Hannah's atypical development to be recognised at this stage.

Q Research

Investigate the National Association for Gifted Children at http://www.nagcbritain.org.uk.

Make a list of some of the resources available to help gifted and talented children in early years and school settings.

Write a brief report for early years staff that highlights the advantages of early recognition of the atypical development of gifted children.

Gifted and talented children

Children whose development exceeds the expected pattern can also experience difficulties in a range of areas, for example:

- frustration or boredom due to under stimulation

- difficulties in making friendships or interacting with peers.

It is important for early years practitioners to recognise when children's development exceeds the expected pattern in order to provide appropriate stimulation and prevent further problems from occurring.

The development of gifted and talented children often exceeds the expected pattern

Case study

Kurt is four and a half years old and has just started in the reception class of the local primary school. From the age of three, Kurt has attended a small, private nursery school and his mother has informed the reception class teacher that Kurt is 'gifted and talented', with his development exceeding the expected pattern in all areas. He has an extensive vocabulary and can read fluently, he knows the names of a wide range of colours and shapes, and can count to one hundred.

In the reception class, his teacher has observed that Kurt frequently behaves in a silly way, he does not follow instructions and he is often rude and irritating with the other children.

1. Discuss using examples, how Kurt's atypical development may be affecting his behaviour at school.

2. Describe some of the difficulties that gifted and talented children may face if their atypical development is not recognised.

Assessment checklist

This unit is externally assessed under examination conditions. The external paper will test your understanding of the knowledge base of this unit, including your ability to synthesise and apply the information. You will be required to analyse issues presented in scenarios, including evaluating evidence, making judgements, drawing conclusions and justifying your responses.

Use the checklist below to decide which areas of the learning aims you understand and which you need to study further.

Learning aim A: Understand how the principles of growth and development apply to children's developmental progress from birth up to 8 years ✓

- Understand the principles of growth and development. ☐

- Use relevant information to recognise children's developmental stages. ☐

- Anticipate the next stage(s) of development. ☐

- Recognise delays, difficulties or advanced progress in relation to growth and developmental norms. ☐

- Analyse how development in one area may affect development in other areas. ☐

- Explain a child's development in the context of their cultural environment. ☐

- Recall, apply and synthesise knowledge of child development and apply it to unfamiliar scenarios. ☐

Learning aim B: Understand theories and models of development and how they relate to aspects of children's development ✓

- Understand aspects of theories of development. ☐

- Identify the strengths and weaknesses of theories. ☐

- Analyse how theories and models of development relate to observations of children. ☐

- Apply different theoretical approaches to unfamiliar scenarios. ☐

- Compare theoretical approaches to specific areas of child development. ☐

- Identify which theories or models of development link to what has been observed and explain why associations have been made. ☐

- Use theories or models of development to make a judgement about what is being observed. ☐

Learning aim C: Be able to apply theories and models of child development to support children's development ✓

- Use a range of theories in relation to different aspects of development. ☐

- Understand that theories of learning and development are not necessarily mutually exclusive. ☐

- Be aware that in practice a combination of theoretical approaches will need to be used. ☐

Learning aim D: Understand how a range of factors influence children's development ✓

- Analyse a range of factors that support or hinder a child's development. ☐

- Make a judgement about the extent to which factors may affect the child's development in the short- or long-term. ☐

- Analyse the likely strength of each factor's effect compared with other factors. ☐

Learning aim E: Understand the importance of recognising atypical development ✓

- Analyse the ways in which atypical development in one or more areas may affect other areas of development. ☐

- Understand atypical development in relation to norms and any other factors that may be affecting children's development. ☐

- Analyse the advantages of early recognition of atypical development. ☐

2 | Play in early years settings

Learning aim A:
Understand the links between play and children's development

- ▶ How play supports the development of young children

Learning aim B:
Understand how a range of play opportunities and types can support children's development

- ▶ How different types of play support development
- ▶ Providing play opportunities to support development
- ▶ Differentiating play opportunities to support development
- ▶ Selecting play resources to support development

Learning aim C:
Understand how a range of perspectives influence current approaches to play

- ▶ The development of theories about play
- ▶ Approaches to play in current practice

Learning aim D: Understand adults' involvement in children's play

▶ The benefits of adult involvement in children's play

▶ Effective adult involvement in children's play

How play supports the development of young children

Introduction to this unit

In this unit you will find out about the ways in which children's play and development are linked and about the types of play opportunities that support different aspects of child development. You will find out about the range of theories and approaches to play that influence current thinking and practice, as well as the benefits of effective adult involvement in children's play.

Your assessment criteria:

Learning aim A: Understand the links between play and children's development

P1 Explain how play supports the physical, cognitive, language, social and emotional development of young children.

M1 Discuss the role of play in supporting the physical, cognitive, language, social and emotional development of a child at different stages.

Linking play and children's development

The Statutory Framework for the Early Years Foundation Stage (2012) in England says: 'Play is essential for children's development, building their confidence as they learn to explore, to think about problems and relate to others.'

Play is important because it provides opportunities for children to develop, practise and refine a wide range of skills across all the areas of human development, as shown in Figure 2.1.

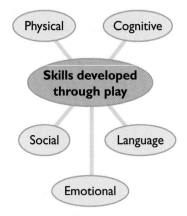

Figure 2.1 Skills developed through play

The range of skills that can be acquired and supported through play are:

- *Physical development*: increasing coordination, stamina, balance, fine and gross movements

- *Cognitive development*: learning new concepts, problem solving, higher level thinking skills (perhaps with adult support)

 Design

Imagine you are building a den with a small group of five-year-old children.

Draw a table using the headings shown in Figure 2.1.

Under each heading, write an example of how den building can support each area of development for these five-year-olds.

Can you think of examples for all of them?

- *Language development*: increasing vocabulary, creating opportunities to use language, using talk to organise action

- *Emotional development*: making sense of the world, freedom to make mistakes, supporting transition, providing a safe outlet for children who have experienced trauma

- *Social development*: sharing, cooperating, building relationships.

Child-initiated play

Children are very skilled at initiating their own play because play is intrinsically motivated. Children do not play because they are asked to or rewarded by others. They are naturally driven to play as a way of finding out about and interacting with their world.

Child-initiated play is characterised as play activities which are wholly:

- decided by the child

- motivated by the child (intrinsic motivation)

- controlled by the child.

However, the activities happen within a context that is influenced by adults, in terms of the available space, time and resources for play.

Play is particularly beneficial for children's development, as it supports a number of positive dispositions and attitudes to learning, including:

- developing independence
- creativity
- confidence
- concentration
- imagination
- exploration

- involvement
- collaboration
- flexibility
- engagement
- decision making.

Social stages of play

Through play, children learn and practise many basic social skills. They develop a sense of self and they learn to interact with other children and how to make friends.

In 1932, Mildred Parten observed children between the ages of two and five. She defined six different stages of play, as outlined in Figure 2.2 on page 60. These categories are still useful today to help us understand how children's developing social skills are reflected in their play.

Children are naturally driven to play as a way of finding out about and interacting with their world

 Key terms

Disposition: tendency, inclination or attitude towards something

Initiating: getting going, taking the first step

Intrinsically motivated: the motivation comes from within and is not influenced by external factors such as reward

Your assessment criteria:

Learning aim A: Understand the links between play and children's development

P2 Explain how children play at different stages of development.

Figure 2.2 The six stages of play

Stage of play	Characteristics
Unoccupied	The child spends periods of time observing the play of others. They may make small involuntary movements as if to join in.
Solitary/ independent play	This is more common in younger children. The child may appear unaware of or uninterested in the play of others and totally absorbed in their own activity.
Onlooker play	This is more common in younger children. The child will show interest in the play of others by looking on or commenting but will not join in.
Parallel/ adjacent play	The child's play behaviours mimic those of others close by. This is often seen as supporting the transition to more sociable types of play.
Associative play	The child has a greater interest in the social interactions of the play than in the play activity itself, which may appear random or unfocused.
Cooperative play	Both the activity and the people involved are important. This type of play requires high levels of social skills such as cooperating and negotiating. Often the play activity is highly organised, with individuals carrying out specified roles.

Although you are more likely to see the earlier stages of play among younger children, a young child who knows their play partners extremely well (for example, siblings) may well demonstrate more associative/ cooperative play. Similarly, an older child may appear quite solitary if deeply engrossed in a task.

Children can appear to be at more than one stage of play, depending on the context in which they are playing

Case study

Sam is the deputy manager of a small community pre-school that takes children aged two to four. As part of their quality improvement cycle, the staff team have decided to look at 'partnerships with parents' and have agreed that Sam will put together a display to support parents in their understanding of play.

Outline the key messages that Sam and the staff team need to include in their display for parents regarding:

1. how play and child development are linked

2. why child-initiated play is important

3. how play can reflect the different stages of social development.

How different types of play support development

Types of play

Play activities are often grouped by type, according to the particular area of development they best support. (See also Unit 9: Observation, assessment and planning for play and development, page 222.) The types of play most often available to young children are shown in Figure 2.3. The characteristics of each type of play and the skills children develop are described in Figure 2.4 on page 62.

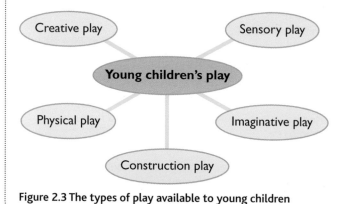

Figure 2.3 The types of play available to young children

Construction play helps to develop spatial awareness and hand–eye coordination

Your assessment criteria:

Learning aim B: Understand how a range of play opportunities and types can support children's development

P3 Explain how types of play support the development of young children to include:
- physical play
- imaginative play
- sensory play
- creative play
- construction play.

M2 Analyse how selected types of play meet the needs of a child and support the child's all-round development.

D1 Evaluate the extent to which different examples of play and selected resources support the all-round development of children from birth to two years and children from two up to eight years.

Research

While you are on placement with children aged two to five years, observe them playing. Note down the different activities they choose (the ones that are child-initiated, not the ones they are directed to by the practitioner).

Reflect on the types of play you see. Compare and contrast the play activities chosen by boys and girls or by younger and older children. Analyse your observations to see if any patterns emerge.

Figure 2.4 How different types of play support children's all-round development

Type of play	Characteristics	Supports the development of:
Physical play	Physical play is characterised by activities that use large and small physical movements that allow children to use their energy. It may also involve equipment or apparatus.	• physical skills • confidence • social skills
Creative play	Creative play is characterised by self-expression. It enables children to create unique works of art, sculptures and drawings.	• fine motor skills • hand–eye coordination • emotional expression/release
Sensory play	Sensory play is characterised by the exploration of materials using one or more of the five senses. Children can be provided with a few tools and containers and given the freedom to explore and manipulate.	• fine motor skills and hand–eye coordination • early mathematical concepts such as volume and shape • learning about the properties of materials such as texture
Imaginative play	Imaginative play is characterised by 'pretend'. Children might pretend to be another person or pretend that one object represents another. Imaginative play is often (though not always) supported by 'props' such as dressing up clothes or pretend food.	• communication and language • social skills • identity of self (through taking on different roles)
Construction play	Construction play is characterised by the building of three-dimensional objects using construction sets or collections of recycled objects.	• spatial awareness • hand–eye coordination • interest in structures and how things work

Case study

The staff team at Honeysuckle Day Nursery have decided to audit the provision they offer to children during the holiday play scheme. They want to be sure that the range of play activities and resources they provide are supporting children's all-round development across all the age ranges. (During the school holidays, children's ages can range from birth to eight years old.) The staff plan to carry out structured observations of children from different age groups engaging with the full range of activities and resources provided.

Design a tick sheet for the staff to use that will be quick and easy to use and will show:

1. the type of play that is being observed

2. the age of the child that is being observed

3. the aspects of development the practitioner will expect to see

4. the resources that are being used.

Research

On placement, discuss with your supervisor about how the setting provides for these different types of play.

Analyse how well the planning supports different types of play.

Compare and contrast how well resourced each type of play is – what might this tell you about practitioner attitudes to the different types of play?

While the children are engaged in the activities, try to identify the different aspects of their development.

Key term

Audit: to inspect, confirm, correct

Providing play opportunities to support development

Play opportunities (birth to two years)

Rich play opportunities, enabling environments and caring attentive adults will support the youngest children as they interact, explore and develop their physical skills.

The Statutory Framework for the Early Years Foundation Stage (2012) in England identifies 'Playing and Exploring' as one of the characteristics of effective learning. It also recognises as prime areas of learning:

- communication and language

- personal, social and emotional development

- physical development.

Some simple play opportunities for children aged from birth to two years are identified in Figure 2.5, together with some examples of how they support children to interact, explore and develop their physical skills.

Your assessment criteria:

Learning aim B: Understand how a range of play opportunities and types can support children's development

M2 Analyse how selected types of play meet the needs of a child and support the child's all-round development.

D1 Evaluate the extent to which different examples of play and selected resources support the all-round development of children from birth up to 2 years and children from 2 up to 8 years.

Figure 2.5 Play opportunities from birth to two years

Treasure basket play	What is it?	
	A treasure basket is a collection of natural objects and objects made from natural materials gathered together in a sturdy, low-sided basket. Treasure baskets are particularly beneficial when babies can sit unaided but are not yet mobile.	
How it supports interaction	**How it supports exploration**	**How it supports physical skills**
Unusually, this play activity is **not** intended to support interaction. Adults are observant and alert, but should sit back to allow babies to take the lead, following their own lines of interest.	• No right or wrong way of playing with the objects • Engaging all the senses as babies seek to find out 'what is this like?' • Making connections between things • Experiencing cause and effect • Concentrating for long periods of time	• Refining fine motor skills – picking up objects, passing them from hand to hand • High levels of sensory input (As an extension of their sense of touch, young babies will explore objects in their mouth. This is normal and is not dangerous when sensible health and safety precautions are followed.)

Figure 2.5 Play opportunities from birth to two years (*continued*)

Heuristic play	What is it?
	This is a natural follow on from 'treasure basket play' when sitting babies become mobile toddlers. Collections of objects, together with a variety of containers, provide opportunities for multiple combinations of collecting, transporting, dropping and pouring.

How it supports interaction	How it supports exploration	How it supports physical skills
As with treasure basket play, this activity is **not** intended to support interaction. Adults are observant and alert, but should sit back to allow toddlers to take the lead, following their own lines of interest.	• Properties of materials such as texture • Concepts of shape and weight • How sounds are made • Concentration and perseverance	Developing hand–eye coordination

 Design

Research the work of Elinor Goldschmied.

Put together a treasure basket of safe objects to use in your placement or work setting with babies who are able to sit unaided but are not yet mobile.

Take the basket into your placement and talk to your supervisor about the benefits of treasure basket play for young children.

Do a risk assessment so that you know how to ensure children's safety while they play.

 Key terms

Characteristics of effective learning: *how children learn, rather than what they learn*

Prime areas of learning: *the three areas of learning that are 'particularly crucial for igniting children's curiosity and enthusiasm for learning...form relationships and thrive.' (EYFS 2012)*

Proprioception: *the sensation that tells us where our body is in space and how it is moving*

Reciprocal: *describes an action that involves both give and take, which feels equally satisfying for both people*

Peek-a-boo	**What is it?**
	This is a game played with babies. In the game, the older player hides his/her face, pops back into the baby's view and says 'Peek-a-boo!' sometimes followed by 'I see you!' The baby quickly learns this game and then enthusiastically re-enacts it.
How it supports interaction	**How it supports physical skills**
This is a reciprocal activity, which encourages babies and young children to respond to and mimic the play partner. The turn taking elements of 'you lead' then 'I lead' mirror the pattern of all interactions.	Being able to cover your eyes with your hands is dependent on a good sense of proprioception.

Roll-the-ball	**What is it?**
	This is a game played with older babies and young children. The adult sits on the floor opposite the child with legs spread wide apart. They roll a ball slowly towards the child, intending it to stop at the child's feet. The child is then encouraged (verbally and/or non-verbally) to roll it back.

How it supports interaction	**How it supports exploration**	**How it supports physical skills**
A similarly reciprocal activity, which encourages babies and young children to respond to and engage with the play partner.	• Cause and effect – what happens when I push an object? • What if I push harder? • Round things roll – do all objects roll? • How far does it need to go? • How do I make it go in the right direction?	• Hand–eye coordination • Large and small movements

Differentiating play opportunities to support development

Play opportunities (two to eight years)

Children will often play in different ways as they get older (see the section 'Social stages of play' on pages 59–60), but they may well be engaged by the same activities throughout this period. Figure 2.6 indicates how the use of familiar play activities develops alongside the child.

Key terms

Malleable: *easy to work or handle into shape*

Outcome: *something that follows from an action or situation*

Process based: *with a focus on how something is done rather than the final result*

Product based: *with a focus on the end product*

Figure 2.6 The development of play activities from two to eight years

Play activity	At 2 years	At 5 years	At 8 years
Role play	Dressing up, 'pretend' play, and taking on real or imaginary roles Based on real life experiences May involve representational objects, e.g. a box as a boat	Often influenced by media characters May be supported by a costume or outfit	Can have highly imaginative storylines Often has rules
Small world play	Enacting real or imaginary scenarios with small toys, and with objects and characters that are familiar, e.g. animals	Often influenced by media characters More imaginative/fantasy based	Enacting detailed stories using small world items as props
Painting	Experimental Discovering the properties of paint Process based	Has an intention – product based Experimenting with effects and techniques	Understands what paint can do and how to use it to different effects Paints with purpose and intention
Mark making	Experimental Enjoys the effect of making marks	Will have an intention – product based May enjoy writing stories	Enjoys producing detailed and illustrated stories, posters, etc.

Play activity	At 2 years	At 5 years	At 8 years
Jigsaw puzzles	Small number of pieces Randomly successful No logical strategy for completion	Understands how jigsaws work Employs logical strategies Tackles more difficult pictures or with more pieces	Enjoys the challenge of more difficult jigsaws Uses a range of strategies to complete them successfully
Water	Enjoys the physical sensation of water Finding out what water does	Using water to find out about the world – solids and fluids, floating and sinking Plays with a purpose	Likely to use water for scientific purposes, experimenting with what it can/can't do or its impact on other materials
Sand	Exploring the texture of sand Finding out what sand does Exploring the difference between wet and dry sand	Uses sand as a tool, e.g. building a wall around animals Knows what wet and dry sand can do and uses this knowledge in their play	Enjoys creating elaborate structures and sculptures on both a small and large scale
Malleable materials	Exploring the properties of malleable materials such as dough, clay, modelling clay, etc. How soft is it? How hard is it? How malleable is it?	Enjoys experimenting with different types of materials Uses tools to shape materials More likely to make a model, e.g. an animal or food item	Uses malleable materials to create models or 'purposeful objects', e.g. a clay bowl May want objects to be more permanent – to make a collection or to give to someone

Differentiating play

Differentiation is the process of adapting an activity so that it can meet the differing developmental needs of a group of children. This may mean reducing the difficulty for some and making it more challenging for others. (See also Unit 9: Observation, assessment and planning for play and development, page 222.)

- **Differentiation by input** means altering the amount of resources or practitioner support given to an activity.

- **Differentiation by** outcome means having different expectations of how children will play with resources, how long they will be engaged by the activity or how likely they are to produce an end product.

The need to differentiate activities may arise because of the children's ages, developmental level, skill level or previous experience of the activity.

? Reflect

When children are given new resources, regardless of their age, they will need a period of time to explore and experiment. Think about how to plan for this.

Your assessment criteria:

Learning aim B: Understand how a range of play opportunities and types can support children's development

P4 Explain how to differentiate play to meet the development needs of individual children.

Selecting play resources to support development

Selecting resources to support children's development

The most useful resource in any play activity is usually the practitioner. However, certain pieces of equipment can also enhance the play experience. As a general rule of thumb, all play activities (and associated resources) that take place indoors can and should be replicated outdoors. You can sometimes use the outdoors so that children can play and learn in a larger space or in a more physical way. A few examples are given in Figure 2.7 opposite.

Playing safe

As with any activity, keeping children safe will be a priority. However, knowing how to face challenge and risk is a valuable life skill for children to learn. As an attentive practitioner, you can ensure that safety precautions do not detract from a high-quality learning experience. (See Unit 4, page 114.) In order to ensure children's safety at play, you should:

- know the capabilities of individual children (this will help you to recognise when a child is ready to go higher on the climbing frame or jump from the balance beam)

- conduct frequent maintenance checks of both large and small equipment to ensure that nothing is damaged or broken

- carry out daily risk assessments to ensure that the play area is free from hazards

- stay close during treasure basket or heuristic play to minimise potential accidents

- recognise the age and developmental stage of children in order to determine the most suitable resources, for example small babies could choke on smaller items of play equipment because of their tendency to put things in their mouths.

✍ Design

Using the information in Figure 2.4 on page 62 and Figure 2.7 opposite, create a chart to show how different play opportunities and selected resources support the all-round development of children from birth up to two years and from two up to eight years.

Your assessment criteria:

Learning aim B: Understand how a range of play opportunities and types can support children's development

P5 Explain how resources can best support different types of play in early years settings.

M3 Discuss the suitability of selected types of resources to support play and play opportunities in early years settings to meet the needs of children at different stages of development.

D1 Evaluate the extent to which different examples of play and selected resources support the all-round development of children from birth up to 2 years and children from 2 up to 8 years.

🔍 Research

Research the types of risk assessments that are carried out by your placement to keep children safe while they are playing. Talk to your supervisor about how often risk assessments are carried out and evaluate how effective they are in impacting on practice.

Attentive practitioners can help children find out about risk and challenge while ensuring they stay safe

Figure 2.7 Resources for indoor and outdoor play

Indoors		Outdoors
Fine motor: Threading, cutting and sticking, painting and drawing, clay and dough, dressing dolls, pegs and boards **Gross motor:** Depending on the space available, any of the outdoor resources	**Physical play** (indoors → outdoors)	As indoors, plus: **Fine motor:** Weaving, gardening, pegging out washing **Gross motor:** Climbing frames, wheeled toys, hoops, bats and balls, spinning tops, obstacle courses, stepping stones, planks and crates
Bags, scarves, shoes, hats, jewellery, dressing up clothes Blankets, lengths of fabric, safety blankets, netting Large cardboard boxes 'Real' objects such as old telephones Theme-led resources such as garage, shop, hospital, café	**Imaginative play** (indoors → outdoors)	As indoors, plus: Den-building materials, tents/camping gear, clothes horse (as a frame), tarpaulins
Sand, water, clay, dough, gloop, cornflour, shaving foam, lentils, pasta, wood shavings, pea gravel Containers and tools for spooning, moulding, pouring, etc.	**Sensory play** (indoors → outdoors)	As indoors, plus: Compost, bark chippings, pebbles, sticks, mud, hay/straw/grass
Paint, drawing materials, modelling materials, brushes, modelling tools, resources for printing Musical instruments, a variety of types of music to listen to Space (perhaps with scarves and ribbons) for dancing A variety of types of music to dance to	**Creative play** (indoors → outdoors)	As indoors, plus: Large areas of floor, wall and paper for large-scale painting Weaving frames Large frames for creating natural collage Large sound/music making resources such as pans, lids, metal pipes
Construction sets Small wooden blocks 'Junk' modelling materials such as cardboard boxes and tubes with tape, glue and paper clips for joining	**Construction play** (indoors → outdoors)	As indoors, plus Large-scale construction sets Large wooden blocks/replica bricks and breeze blocks Large-scale 'junk' for large constructions

Treasure basket play (both indoors and outdoors)

A sturdy, low, straight-sided basket capable of holding up to 50 objects such as:

- wooden egg
- pastry brush
- safety mirror
- bell
- rubber plug
- fir cone
- large shell
- metal spoon
- whisk
- shoe horn
- shiny fabric
- loofah
- sponge
- ribbon
- sheepskin
- leather patch
- pumice stone

Heuristic play (both indoors and outdoors)

A collection of containers of varying sizes – plant pots, biscuit tins, plastic bottles, etc.
Collections of:

- lengths of chain
- pebbles
- corks
- fir cones
- curtain rings
- bangles
- clothes pegs
- hair curlers

Mug trees, kitchen roll holders – to hang things onto.
Sections of carpet roll inner tubes to push things through or drop things down.

The development of theories about play

Definitions and theories of play

The **continuum** of play activities ranges from totally unstructured play to more adult-led structured play. Understanding what is meant by these definitions will affect how practitioners view their role in children's play and therefore how much adult-directed activity is likely to occur within their setting.

Free flow and structured play

Structured play can be playful (as described on page 78), but the play activities are under the control of the adult. For example, the practitioner may decide on the time, space and/or resources that they make available for children's play. The practitioner may also control the engagement they have with the child during the play activity.

Free flow play is often seen as open-ended, intrinsically motivated, deeply satisfying and usually highly imaginative. It is wholly under the control of the child, allowing them to make all the decisions about where, when and how they play. Observations of children engaged in free flow play often note that the children:

- engage in multi-sensory exploration

- have absolute focus and concentration on the self-chosen activity

- set challenges for themselves

- make links to previous learning/experience

- engage In independent exploration.

The 'Playwork Principles' developed by SkillsActive UK advocate free flow play and state that:

- children need to play

- play is essential to children's health

- play must be under the control of the child

- children must be free to make their own decisions about their play.

The principles go on to assert that the role of a play worker is to:

- support and promote play

- create play spaces

- follow the principle of low intervention.

Your assessment criteria:

Learning aim C: Understand how a range of perspectives influence current approaches to play

P6 Describe **theoretical, philosophical** and other approaches to play that commonly influence provision in early years settings.

M4 Analyse the extent to which an early years curriculum/ framework has been influenced by theoretical, philosophical or other approaches to play.

D2 Evaluate the success of the application of a theoretical, philosophical or other approach to play in an early years setting.

Key terms

Continuum: *a continuous sequence in which things next to each other are not noticeably different, but the extremes are quite distinct*

Philosophical: *relating to a theory or attitude that affects behaviour*

Theoretical: *relating to a system of ideas that is used to explain something*

Children engaged in free flow play will often become deeply engrossed

Case study

Stuart is a play worker at the Bankside Out of School Club and is the key person for a small group of children aged five to eight years. He is responsible for supporting free play opportunities for the children and maintaining a safe play environment.

Using the Playwork Principles (see the SkillsActive website: www.skillsactive.com):

1. describe Stuart's role in supporting and promoting the children's free flow play

2. discuss some of the ways that Stuart could create safe, imaginative play spaces for the children to make their own decisions about play.

Research

Research Tina Bruce's work on free flow play.

Observe young children at play and note down their play behaviour.

- *How many of the features of free flow play do you see?*

- *Does this change when the children choose different play activities?*

- *Are some play activities more likely to encourage free flow play?*

Theoretical approaches to play and learning

For more than a hundred years, educational theorists have been identifying approaches to early play and learning. (See also Unit 1: Child development, pages 10–55.) The work and key ideas of these experts have had a huge influence on current early years practices, as outlined in Figure 2.8 on page 72.

Figure 2.8 Educational theorists and their influence on current early years practice

Theorist	Summary of key ideas
Jean Piaget (1896–1980)	• Had a particular interest in learning and cognitive development • The 'theory of mind' – making sense of and understanding your own mind and the minds of others • The interrelatedness of cognitive and social development • Relatively fixed stages in the development of children's thinking • Children's ability to use experience to adjust their view of the world • Children as 'lone scientists' – playing, exploring and experimenting in rich environments
Lev Vygotsky (1896–1934)	• Interactions between the child and their social environment – children proactively seek to establish relationships, interactions and engagement with key people who will support them to explore their world • Children as active partners in constructing knowledge, skills and attitudes • 'Zone of proximal development' (zpd) – the difference between what children can do with adult support and what they can do independently • Children's greatest achievements are possibly in play
Jerome Bruner (1915–)	• Developed the work of Vygotsky • Learning happens through personal discovery • 'Scaffolding' – supporting children to move their learning from where it is now to where they want to go next • 'Spiral curriculum' – continually revisiting basic ideas, making links and connections to build understanding of increasingly difficult concepts • The importance of play for learning through doing • Starting with what children know and can do
Chris Athey (1924–2011)	• Had an interest in how children 'come to know things' • 'Schemas' – repeated patterns of behaviour, through which children discover common themes and ideas and 'come to know' about the world • 'Fitting not flitting' – children fit ideas together as they explore the environment, as opposed to 'flitting' from one thing to another • The importance of early education in its own right • Awareness of children's 'cognitive concerns' – their active interest and participation in their own learning

Key terms

Curriculum: the component parts of a course of study

Interrelatedness: how things are connected to one another

Philosophical approaches to play

Great philosophers have influenced current early years practice and provision, including our approach to:

- outdoor play and learning – the importance of outdoor spaces for both physical and emotional health and as places for exploration and investigation

- adult interaction during play – the adult as facilitator not instructor

- the use of natural materials – the inclusion of real and/or natural objects to make play activities more realistic.

Some of the major philosophers in early education and their key ideas are outlined in Figure 2.9 (below and on page 74).

(below and on page 74)

Your assessment criteria:

Learning aim C: Understand how a range of perspectives influence current approaches to play

P6 Describe theoretical, philosophical and other approaches to play that commonly influence provision in early years settings.

M4 Analyse the extent to which an early years curriculum/ framework has been influenced by theoretical, philosophical or other approaches to play.

D2 Evaluate the success of the application of a theoretical, philosophical or other approach to play in an early years setting.

Figure 2.9 Major philosophers in early education

Philosopher	Summary of key ideas
Friedrich Froebel (1782–1852)	• There are distinct stages of development and education must be appropriately linked to the characteristics of each stage. • Education should be shared between parents and settings. • Learning happens best through self-chosen activity. • Play is necessary and can be highly serious and deeply significant. • It is important for early years practitioners to receive training.
Rachel McMillan (1859–1917) Margaret McMillan (1860–1931)	• The first five years are vital for children's physical and emotional health. • Outdoor play and learning are essential to promote children's health. • They founded 'nursery schools'. • Early education should aim to nurture the whole child. • They highlighted the importance of children's imagination and creativity.
Maria Montessori (1870–1952)	• Practitioners act as observers and facilitators. • The practitioner's role is to remove obstacles and provide opportunities. • 'Practical life' activities' (using real/natural objects) support concentration, attention and spontaneous self-discipline. • Children should act freely in an environment that is organised to meet their needs. • Montessori identified four distinct 'planes' (periods) of human development and proposed specific educational approaches for each plane.

Figure 2.9 Major philosophers in early education (*continued*)

Philosopher	Summary of key ideas
Rudolf Steiner (1861–1925)	• Steiner identified three 'psychological and physiological' phases of childhood. • All aspects of children's learning and development are important. • Adults should respect children's right to a secure and unhurried childhood. • Children learn through self-motivated enquiry. • Steiner highlighted the importance of creative and sensory experiences. • Children need the security of repetition and rhythm (of activities or daily routines). • Practitioners should be seen as models, not instructors.

Many of the themes that run through the approaches of these philosophers are evident in early years practice and provision today. These include:

- the importance of early childhood as a significant phase in its own right
- young children as active participants in their own learning
- practitioners who support and enable early learning and development
- a belief that children are competent and capable from birth
- the significance and necessity of play as a vehicle for early learning.

British curricula and frameworks

England, Scotland, Wales and Northern Ireland all have their own curriculum frameworks. (See also Unit 13, page 322.) Figure 2.10 lists some of the key documents (and the websites where you can find them) for practitioners working with children from birth up to the age of eight years.

Key terms

Physiological: related to the physical state of a person

Psychological: related to the mental and emotional state of a person

Research

Investigate the relevant curriculum framework for the country where you live and the age of children you are working with.

Make note of any sections or statements that seem to reflect the common themes of the early education philosophers.

Figure 2.10 The curricula of England, Scotland, Wales and Northern Ireland

Country	Document	Age range	Website
England	Statutory Framework for the Early Years Foundation Stage	birth–5 years	education.gov.uk
	National Curriculum	5–8+ years	education.gov.uk
Scotland	Pre-Birth to Three: Positive Outcomes for Scotland's Children and Families	pre-birth–3 years	educationscotland.gov.uk
	Curriculum for Excellence	3–8+ years	educationscotland.gov.uk
Wales	Framework for Children's Learning for 3 to 7-year-olds in Wales	3–7 years	wales.gov.uk
	National Curriculum for Wales (Key Stage 2)	7+ years	wales.gov.uk
Northern Ireland	Pre-school curricular guidance	3–4 years	nicurriculum.org.uk
	Northern Ireland Curriculum: Foundation Stage	4–6 years	nicurriculum.org.uk
	Northern Ireland Curriculum: Primary	6+ years	nicurriculum.org.uk

Approaches to play in current practice

Modern day approaches to play

The themes running through the philosophical approaches covered on pages 73–74 have strongly influenced modern day approaches to play around the world.

Reggio Emilia

The Reggio Emilia pre-schools get their name from their place of origin in northern Italy. Their philosophy recognises:

- learning as a **collaborative** event
- the significance of specific cultural influences
- the **interdependence** of social and individual learning.

Children are seen as full of potential and childhood as a time to explore. Creativity has particular significance and children are encouraged to express this in a variety of ways, through 'the **hundred languages of children**'.

The practitioner's role is to observe, document and partner children's learning. Practitioners develop the documentation and share it with children and their parents.

The physical and cultural environment is seen as 'the third teacher'. Real life experiences and the long-term investigation of ideas provide the context within which children can be active in their own learning.

A Reggio Emilia pre-school values childhood as a time for children to explore and engage with the world

Your assessment criteria:

Learning aim C: Understand how a range of perspectives influence current approaches to play

P6 Describe theoretical, philosophical and other approaches to play that commonly influence provision in early years settings.

M4 Analyse the extent to which an early years curriculum/ framework has been influenced by theoretical, philosophical or other approaches to play.

D2 Evaluate the success of the application of a theoretical, philosophical or other approach to play in an early years setting.

🔑 Key terms

Collaborative: *working effectively with others*

Hundred languages of children: *symbolic languages, including drawing, sculpting, dramatic play, writing and painting, used to represent children's thinking and ideas*

Interdependence: *when two or more things are dependent on each other*

Te Whāriki

Te Whāriki (meaning the woven mat) is the curriculum framework for children from birth to six years in New Zealand. The philosophy of this curriculum:

- draws on Vygotsky's 'socio-cultural' perspective (see also Unit 1, page 34)

- recognises that children learn from and with others

- acknowledges that different cultures will provide a different context and therefore different influences on learning

- recognises that effective learning results from the weaving together of children's strengths and interests and the learning experiences that happen within and beyond the setting.

It identifies a number of aspirations, including the ideas that children grow up:

- as competent and confident learners and communicators

- healthy in mind, body and spirit

- secure in their sense of belonging

- secure in the knowledge that they make a valued contribution to society.

The curriculum is based on four broad principles that are interwoven with five learning areas, as outlined in Figure 2.11.

Key terms

Aspiration: *a strong desire to achieve something*

Empowerment: *giving power, ability or control to someone*

Holistic: *seeing things as a whole, not as individual parts*

Figure 2.11 Te Whāriki priniciples and learning areas

Principles	Learning areas
• Empowerment	• Mana atua – wellbeing
• Holistic development	• Mana tangata – contribution
	• Mana whenua – belonging
• Family and community	• Mana reo – communication
• Relationships	• Mana aotūroa – exploration

The High Scope approach

The High Scope approach recognises that children construct their own learning through:

- engagement with people, ideas and materials

Design

Investigate one of the approaches covered in this section. Design a leaflet/web page for parents outlining the key ideas of this approach and its benefits for children's play, learning and development.

- the provision of environments and experiences that support learning in active and meaningful ways

- using their initiative to plan for and develop their own strengths and interests

- the 'Plan-Do-Review' routine (expressing an intention, generating a learning experience and reflecting on outcomes)

- the consistency of daily routines, learning environments and interactions with adults

- practitioners building genuine relationships with both children and their parent

- a curriculum appropriate to the child's stage of development.

The Forest School movement

The Forest School movement is an outdoor approach to play and education. It involves working in a woodland environment to support:

- the development of intrinsic motivation and social and emotional skills

- the provision of engaging, motivating and achievable activities

- learning about the natural environment

- risk management, initiative, problem solving and cooperation

- the development of child-led projects.

Influences on current practice

All of these approaches to early years education and play have had an influence on provision in British early years settings, in areas such as:

- **observation and planning** – not only how we document children's learning, but how we take note of children's strengths and interests and use that information to plan (or help the children to plan) engaging and motivating experiences

- **outdoor learning** – recognising the importance of the outdoors to children's mental, emotional and physical health, as well as the unique challenges it can offer to children's learning

- **seeing all children as competent learners** – by encouraging them to develop and extend their own ideas and projects and supporting them to see themselves as learners.

Young children enjoying Forest School activities

? Reflect

Choose one of these modern day approaches to play. Reflect on how many of its key ideas you can see in the practices and provision of your placement. Evaluate (using evidence from your observations) how successful you think the practitioner was, and talk to your supervisor and find out if he or she has been influenced by these approaches.

The benefits of adult involvement in children's play

Skilful adults

Research has shown us that a skilled adult can make all the difference to children's learning.

Adults can be involved in children's play in a variety of ways (which will be explored later in this unit). As a practitioner, your involvement can bring a multitude of benefits for children, including:

1. Building supportive relationships:

- the development and maintenance of close and caring bonds

- encouraging children to build close bonds with others

- supporting children with conflict resolution.

2. Children's physical, communication and social skills:

- scaffolding learning with language

- creating richly resourced and stimulating indoor and outdoor learning spaces

- providing creative and playful 'hands-on, brains-on' learning experiences

- sensitively joining in with children's play.

3. The acquisition of higher-level thinking skills:

- ensuring that children have sustained time to develop their own thoughts and ideas

- supporting learning through 'sustained shared thinking'

- supporting children to persevere and challenge themselves

- talking to children about their thinking and learning.

The play and learning continuum

The skills that you need in order to engage effectively with babies' and children's play will vary depending on whether children are engaged in child-initiated/free flow play or more adult-led/structured play. However, research indicates that the most successful outcomes for children come about when there is a good balance of child-initiated play that is well supported by adults, together with episodes of adult-led, playful learning to teach specific knowledge and skills.

Your assessment criteria:

Learning aim D: Understand adults' involvement in children's play

P7 Explain the benefits of adult involvement in play to babies' and children's development.

P8 Explain how adults can effectively initiate and direct play.

M5 Analyse the skills that are required by adults in early years settings for effective child-initiated play, with examples.

D3 Evaluate how skilled adults in early years settings can contribute to effective child-initiated play.

Key term

Sustained shared thinking: working together in an intellectual way to solve a problem

The involvement of a sensitive adult can make all the difference for a young child

Figure 2.12 The range of play, from unstructured to adult-directed (based on the continuum of approaches in 'Learning, Playing and Interacting: Good practice in the Early Years Foundation Stage', Department for Children, Schools and Families, 2009, page 5)

Unstructured play	Child-initiated play	Adult-initiated play	Adult-directed play
Play without any adult support	Play that is led by the child but may be influenced by adults.	Play experiences and activities that are provided by adults in response to children's interests.	Adult-led playful activities to support identified next steps in learning.

Research

Ask your placement supervisor if you can observe one of the practitioners in the setting engaged in a play activity with a child or group of children. Write down the different strategies they use to:

1. build supportive relationships

2. extend children's physical, communication and social skills

3. help children acquire higher-level thinking skills.

Using evidence from your observations, evaluate how successful you think the practitioner was. Discuss your observations with your supervisor when it is convenient.

When you are engaging with babies and children during both child-initiated and adult-initiated play, you need to use the following skills:

- observe and build on children's interests

- interpret what children are doing (as a way into their thinking)

- value and respect children's independent activities and agendas

- make sensitive decisions about interacting (or not) with children during their play

- sometimes provide brief episodes of direct teaching.

Engaging with babies and children during adult-directed play requires a different but complementary skill set. Adult-led activities provide opportunities to introduce the new knowledge, ideas and skills that may not arise naturally in children's self-directed play. Children may recognise that these activities are not 'play', but as a skilful practitioner, you can certainly make them 'playful'.

Playful activities are characterised by:

- active 'hands-on' exploration and participation for all children

- flexibility – a responsive practitioner will allow children to lead their own learning when other avenues of investigation seem more appealing

- open-endedness – when neither children nor practitioner knows where an activity will lead

- interest-led or needs-led learning – what individual children are interested in or need to do next.

Effective adult involvement in children's play

Responsive adults

To be a responsive practitioner, you need to know the children really well. In settings where the key person system is well embedded, practitioners will recognise their key children's individual needs. (See also see Unit 7, pages 182–205.) They are able to do this for the following reasons:

They are observant of children's developing interests and preoccupations, particular strengths or challenges.

They are knowledgeable about child development and best practice.

They are skilful in assessing children, in identifying children's specific needs and in applying their knowledge.

They work in partnership with colleagues, parents and other professionals and agencies to gather information about their key children.

Observing children will help you get to know them really well

Responding to individual needs

Responsive practitioners respect each child's individual rate of learning and development and ensure that the child is supported in the ways that suit them best. This can apply equally to children who are gifted and talented and to those who find some aspects of learning difficult or whose development may be delayed.

Figure 2.13 shows some of the ways in you can respond to a child's individual needs.

Your assessment criteria:

Learning aim D: Understand adults' involvement in children's play

P7 Explain the benefits of adult involvement in play to babies' and children's development.

P8 Explain how adults can effectively initiate and direct play.

M5 Analyse the skills that are required by adults in early years settings for effective child-initiated play, with examples.

D3 Evaluate how skilled adults in early years settings can contribute to effective child-initiated play.

Key term

Learning style: *the way of learning that is most suited to an individual – the most common learning styles are visual (through looking), auditory (through listening) and kinaesthetic (through movement)*

Figure 2.13 Responding to a child's individual needs

Method	Examples
Adapting activities	Differentiated expectations of learning outcomes
	Varied levels of support
	Delivering activities flexibly so children can employ their preferred learning style. (See also Unit 9: Observation, assessment and planning for play and development, page 236.)
Using additional resources	'Trainer' scissors or left-handed scissors to support children's cutting skills
	Certain colours of paper or print can aid children who are visually impaired
	New and unusual resources to stimulate creative thinking and ideas
	Specialist resources, e.g. standing frames to support children with special mobility needs to engage with the learning environment
Following advice from other professionals	Working in partnership with other agencies to deliver a programme of targeted support
	Working collaboratively with skilled professionals to enhance practice and support children with particular gifts or talents

Keeping children safe

In order for children to understand risk and challenge and how to respond to it, they need to experience – within the context of a controlled play environment – what risk or challenge feels like and what they can do to overcome or master a risky or challenging situation. For practitioners this means making sure that children are safe, 'but not too safe'. Wrapping children in cotton wool will not equip them with the capacity to be strong, resilient problem solvers.

Adults can keep children safe while also allowing them to explore by:

Ongoing risk assessments (done regularly and frequently) – as a practitioner, you will need to carry out risk assessments to determine the likelihood of an accident occurring and to assess how serious an accident could be. Practitioners use risk assessments to help them make informed judgements about an acceptable degree of challenge for children in an indoor or outdoor play space.

Supervising children involves sensitive observation and intervention. The ability to make moment-by-moment judgements about whether children are being suitably challenged or are in fact in a dangerous situation is a high-level skill. Knowing children well and being clear about developmentally appropriate next steps will help.

Advising children and discussing safety issues with them (in an age-appropriate way) can help them to understand about risk. For example, talk to children about how they feel when they challenge themselves to climb higher or jump further and what happens to their body when they do these things. This will help them to recognise when they are facing a potentially risky situation.

For more information on keeping children safe, see Unit 4, page 114.

Q | Research

In your placement or work setting, ask your supervisor if you can interview three practitioners who work with children of different ages: birth to three years, three to five years and five to eight years. Ask them all the following four questions:

1. *What is your view on 'risk and challenge' for children?*

2. *How do you carry out risk assessments in their play environments?*

3. *What is your approach to supervising children who are engaged in risky or challenging activities?*

4. *How much do you talk with children about risk and challenge?*

Reflect on their answers, looking particularly for similarities and differences across the age ranges.

Think about how their responses can help shape your practice.

Assessment criteria

This table shows you what you must do to achieve a Pass, Merit or Distinction.

	Pass	Merit	Distinction
Learning aim A: Understand the links between play and children's development			
	3A.P1 Explain how play supports the physical, cognitive, language, social and emotional development of young children.	3A.M1 Discuss the role of play in supporting the physical, cognitive, language, social and emotional development of a child at different stages.	
	3A.P2 Explain how children play at different stages of development.		
Learning aim B: Understand how a range of play opportunities and types can support children's development			
	3B.P3 Explain how types of play support the development of young children to include: • physical play • imaginative play • sensory play • creative play • construction play.	3B.M2 Analyse how selected types of play meet the needs of a child and support the child's all-round development. 3B.M3 Discuss the suitability of selected types of resources to support play and play opportunities in early years settings to meet the needs of children at different stages of development.	3B.D1 Evaluate the extent to which different examples of play and selected resources support the all-round development of children from birth up to 2 years and children from 2 up to 8 years.
	3B.P4 Explain how to differentiate play to meet the development needs of individual children.		
	3B.P5 Explain how resources can best support different types of play in early years settings.		

	Pass		Merit		Distinction
Learning aim C: Understand how a range of perspectives influence current approaches to play					
3C.P6	Describe theoretical, philosophical and other approaches to play that commonly influence provision in early years settings.	3C.M4	Analyse the extent to which an early years curriculum/framework has been influenced by theoretical, philosophical or other approaches to play.	3C.D2	Evaluate the success of the application of a theoretical, philosophical or other approach to play in an early years setting.
Learning aim D: Understand adults' involvement in children's play					
3D.P7	Explain the benefits of adult involvement in play to babies' and children's development.	3D.M5	Analyse the skills that are required by adults in early years settings for effective child-initiated play, with examples.	3D.D3	Evaluate how skilled adults in early years settings can contribute to effective child-initiated play.
3D.P8	Explain how adults can effectively initiate and direct play.				

3 | Meeting children's physical development, physical care and health needs

Learning aim A:
Understand the physical needs of children for growth and development

- The importance of meeting children's basic needs
- The importance of a nutritious diet
- The role of sleep and the importance of exercise

Learning aim B:
Understand the role of the adult in supporting children's physical development

- Your role in supporting physical development
- Selecting appropriate indoor and outdoor resources
- Providing risk-managed activities to support physical development
- Inclusive provision of indoor and outdoor activities

Learning aim C:
Understand the role of adults in meeting children's physical care needs

- The importance of care routines
- Using care routines to support all-round development

**Learning aim D1:
Know how to
recognise and respond
to children who are
unwell**

▶ Recognising illness

▶ Procedures for responding
to illness

**Learning aim D2:
Understand the
role of the adult in
supporting children
with ongoing health
conditions**

▶ Supporting children with
health conditions

The importance of meeting children's basic needs

Introduction to this unit

Physical development is now considered to be one of the most important areas of development for young children. It includes fine and gross motor skills as well as general health and wellbeing. This unit will help you to understand physical development in young children, how to cater for good physical development in the setting and how to recognise and respond to a child who is not developing well.

Your assessment criteria:

Learning aim A: Understand the physical needs of children for growth and development

P1 Explain why it is important to children's growth and all-round development to provide:

  • a nutritious diet
  • exercise
  • sleep.

M1 Discuss the relationship between how children's physical needs are addressed and their all-round development.

Children's basic needs

Children's basic needs are those that are necessary to keep a child physically alive and well, such as having good food, water, warmth, exercise and sleep. If these basic needs are not met, then the child will not develop to their full potential.

Maslow's hierarchy of needs

SELF-ACTUALISATION — Realising potential

INTELLECTUAL NEEDS
Language
Reading, writing, speaking and listening — Assessing and planning for children's learning and development

ESTEEM NEEDS
Personal, social, emotional development (PSED) — Assessing and planning for children's PSED

LOVE AND BELONGING NEEDS
Attachment relationships
Inclusive practice — Effective key person relationships

SAFETY/SECURITY NEEDS
Health and safety   Safeguarding
Routines and resources — Maintaining a safe and stimulating environment

PHYSIOLOGICAL NEEDS
Food and water   Sleep
Fresh air and exercise — Absolute basic essentials

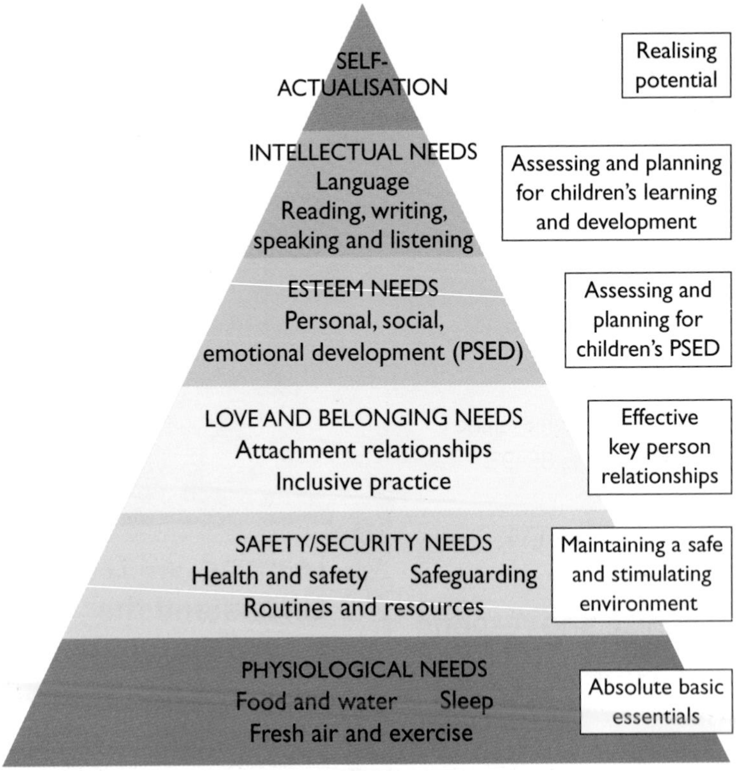

Figure 3.1 Maslow's hierarchy of needs emphasises the importance of meeting basic physical needs in order for children to achieve their full potential

In 1943, Abraham Maslow stated that for children to be able to achieve good health in any area of development, all lower levels of the hierarchy

Discuss

Think of an occasion recently when you felt ill or hungry. Discuss with your partner what effect it had on your ability to think, be a good friend and speak to and listen to others. Discuss some examples of when you have been working with children who are ill or hungry and how this affected the children.

shown in Figure 3.1 must be securely in place first. Children's basic needs are shown right at the bottom of the hierarchy pyramid. They include food, water, warmth, exercise and sleep – these are all essential for good physical health. Without them, children will fail to thrive and, in severe cases, will suffer from neglect and possibly even death. Maslow stated that the basic needs have to be satisfied before children can develop effectively at any of the higher levels.

The impact of health on growth and development

The term health is no longer used only to describe the opposite of illness. Looking holistically at children means that we must consider all the following areas of healthy development:

- physical health – the child's body is working well

- cognitive health – the child is thinking and learning well

- social health – the child is forming good relationships

- emotional health – the child can express their feelings.

It is now believed to be important to take all these different aspects into account when considering a child's state of health. In this unit the emphasis is on the physical health of children. Children who do not have good physical health will not:

- be able to think or learn effectively

- have good self-esteem

- form good relationships with others

- have the confidence to express their feelings and emotions.

Good physical health depends on eating well, having enough exercise and getting enough sleep. These will be discussed on pages 88–92.

Key terms

Health: a state of complete physical, mental and social wellbeing

Holistically: in a way that considers the whole child and all aspects of development

Your assessment criteria:

Learning aim A: Understand the physical needs of children for growth and development

P2 Explain how health impacts on a child's physical, cognitive, communication, language, social and emotional development.

Case study

Ginny is three years old. She is usually alert, inquisitive and chatty. For the last two days she has been much quieter, not interested in any of the activities and sits with adults for much of the time. Her mother has not mentioned anything unusual that has occurred in Ginny's life.

1. Use Maslow's hierarchy of needs to:

   a) explain some of the factors that might be affecting Ginny

   b) describe how you might find out why Ginny's behaviour has changed.

2. Evaluate the use of Maslow's hierarchy of needs in relation to children's wellbeing.

The reason children appear sad might not be easy to understand

The importance of a nutritious diet

Eating well

The topic of good nutrition has become very important recently, as there has been a startling increase in the number of cases of obesity in children over the last few years. Good and bad eating habits start at a very early age, so it is very important for early years practitioners to understand the need to provide a nutritious diet for the children in their care. (See also Unit 14: Food and mealtimes in the early years, pages 330–349.)

A nutritious diet must contain a balance of several essential nutrients provided in the correct proportions. Some of these are illustrated in Figure 3.2.

Your assessment criteria:

Learning aim A: Understand the physical needs of children for growth and development

P1 Explain why it is important to children's growth and all-round development to provide:

- a nutritious diet
- exercise
- sleep.

Figure 3.2 A guide to the contents of a balanced diet

Food type	Why it's important	Foods	Factors for optimum health
Protein	Growth Healing of wounds	Meat Fish Milk Beans and pulses	Many proteins are associated with high fat content, so the proteins in a children's diet need to be chosen with care.
Carbohydrates: starches	Energy	Bread Pasta Rice Potatoes	Too little can lead to hunger because children use a lot of energy. Starches release energy slowly over a long time.
Carbohydrates: sugars	Energy	Cakes Biscuits Sweets	Too much can lead to obesity and tooth decay. Sugar releases energy very quickly.

Food type	Why it's important	Foods	Factors for optimum health
Fats	Energy and digestion of some vitamins	Fried foods Red meat Butter and cream	Too much can lead to obesity, but a small amount is essential in children's diets.
Minerals	Calcium: Bone development	Milk, yoghurt	Too little may prevent normal development.
	Iron: Healthy red blood cells	Green vegetables, red meat	Too little may lead to not having adequate protection against disease.
	Sodium (salt): One of the basic elements of the body	Most foods	Too much salt in the diet can lead to high blood pressure – even in young children.
Vitamins	Vitamin A: Healthy bones, skin and eyes	Carrots, eggs, liver	
	Vitamin B complex: Healthy nervous system and growth	Meat, milk and soya beans	
	Vitamin C: Protection against infection	Citrus fruits and green vegetables	Some fruits and vegetables contain natural sugars which are good in small quantities.
	Vitamin D: Helps the body to use calcium	Dairy products, fish and natural sunlight	Take care that children are protected from too much bright sunlight.
Water	More than 70% of our body is water. Water lost by excretion needs to be replaced.	Tap water is best	Free access to drinking water is very important.
Fibre	Healthy bowel functioning	Fruit and vegetables Wholegrain cereals and bread	Insufficient fibre can lead to constipation and bowel conditions in later life.

A balanced diet

It is important to remember that most young children are very active, so they will need plenty of slowly releasing carbohydrates such as brown bread and pasta or potatoes and rice. Their needs will alter according to how active they are and so their food intake needs to be balanced with the amount of exercise they take. Good nutrition is also important to provide vitamins and minerals that help to prevent disease and promote normal physical development. The recommended daily portions are shown in Figure 3.3.

The eatwell plate (see Figure 3.3) shows how much of what children eat should come from each food group. This includes everything they eat during the day, including snacks.

So, try to ensure children eat:

- plenty of fruit and vegetables
- plenty of bread, rice, potatoes, pasta and other starchy foods (and choose wholegrain varieties whenever possible)
- some milk and dairy foods
- some meat, fish, eggs, beans and other non-dairy sources of protein
- just a small amount of foods and drinks high in fat and/or sugar.

The eatwell plate

Use the eatwell plate to help you get the balance right. It shows how much of what you eat should come from each food group.

Figure 3.3 **The recommended quantities of different foods for children**

Research

Research some of the websites that provide information about healthy eating for children under five years old. You could have a look at: www.schoolfoodtrust.org.uk and http://www.bbc.co.uk/health/treatments/healthy_living/nutrition/life_toddlers.shtml.

Make a poster for the staffroom noticeboard at your placement, showing the basic requirements of a healthy eating routine for young children.

Practitioners can check the contents of children's lunch boxes and make recommendations to parents about healthy lunches

The role of sleep and the importance of exercise

The role of sleep

The role of sleep in humans is still being researched. It is known that sleep plays an important role in allowing the body to grow and repair any damage that may have occurred. Interestingly, there is also evidence that sleep is important for reducing the risk of obesity and increasing children's memory and concentration. Together with a healthy exercise routine, getting enough sleep will contribute to the child's state of wellbeing, increasing their self-esteem, confidence and social abilities.

Some of the short-, medium- and long-term effects of sleep deprivation are shown in Figure 3.4.

Figure 3.4 The effects of sleep deprivation

Children who are often tired...	Is this effect short term, medium term or long term?
cannot control their behaviour or their emotions so well and may therefore have a reduced sense of wellbeing	short term
show signs of disrupted growth patterns	long term
gain weight	medium and long term
cannot concentrate, cannot store or retain information and therefore will not learn so well	short, medium and long term
may suffer more from illness	long term

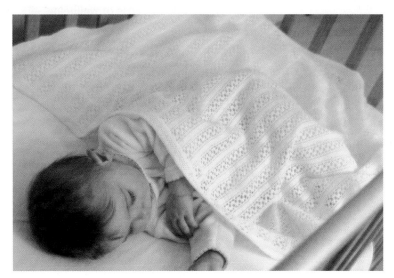

Make sure that babies' sleeping areas are quiet and dark and there is a baby alarm to alert staff when children wake up

Research

Research the effects of sleep deprivation (for example, by going to www.bbc.co.uk/health/physical_health/.../sleepdeprivation.shtml). Find out how much sleep children aged from birth to seven years need on average.

Reflect on what you learn and evaluate your role in supporting children's need for sleep.

The importance of exercise

As an early years professional, you can help minimise obesity by encouraging children to eat a healthy, nutritious diet and to be active for a large part of their day. You have a responsibility to ensure that children cultivate healthy, life-long attitudes towards fitness and activity from a very early age. This will lead to children having a strong sense of self-confidence and wellbeing that will enable them to achieve their full potential in other areas of development.

It is part of your job to provide good opportunities for children to take exercise. This includes practising physical skills, which will be described on pages 93–96.

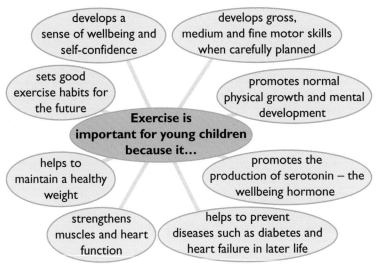

Figure 3.5 Why exercise is important for growth and development

develops a sense of wellbeing and self-confidence

develops gross, medium and fine motor skills when carefully planned

sets good exercise habits for the future

promotes normal physical growth and mental development

Exercise is important for young children because it…

helps to maintain a healthy weight

promotes the production of serotonin – the wellbeing hormone

strengthens muscles and heart function

helps to prevent diseases such as diabetes and heart failure in later life

? Reflect

It is recommended that young children get about 3 hours of physical activity a day. Think about the routine in your setting – does it allow for plenty of physical activity for the children, indoors and outdoors every day, whatever the weather? If not, what are the reasons this is not happening and how could things be improved?'

Physical activity helps children develop a sense of wellbeing

Case study

Alice and her friend Stacey are both four years old and are both overweight. The setting they attend believes that children should be free to choose what they want to do, whether inside or outside. Alice and Stacey spend most of their time inside reading, drawing and playing in the role play area.

1. Describe the possible consequences (both physical and psychological) for Alice and Stacey of not taking enough exercise each day.

2. Using the early years guidance for your country, give some examples of how you could provide opportunities for Alice and Stacey to be more active in the setting.

3. Evaluate the role of early years practitioners in providing opportunities for children's physical activity.

The nature of physical development

As well as general physical health, children need to practise and develop certain physical skills. In order to observe children's physical skills, you need to know the typical sequence of physical development and the range of normal development. (See also Unit 1, pages 16–28.)

Most children are naturally very active

Children's physical development follows certain developmental patterns:

- **simple to complex:** general, basic movements develop before specific, complicated movements

- **from head to toe:** control of the head develops before control of the legs

- **from inner to outer:** shoulder and hip movements develop before movements in the hands and feet.

It is important to understand that in order to develop fine motor skills effectively, children need to develop some middle motor skills first, such as using shoulders, elbows and wrists. Figure 3.6 gives some examples of gross and fine motor skills.

Figure 3.6 Examples of different motor skills

Gross motor skills	Fine motor skills
Running, jumping and climbing	Using small crayons and pencils
Stretching, pulling and pushing	Threading small beads
Exercises such as star jumps	Completing jigsaw puzzles
Kicking a ball	Finger painting
Swinging ribbons	Cutting fruit and vegetables with knives
Pedalling a bike	Using scissors

The role of observation

The Early Years Foundation Stage for England (2012) has placed physical development as one of the three prime areas of development for children from birth to age five. Your role in supporting individual children is to make sure that:

- children are developing and practising all physical skills

- all children are taking part in activities to develop physical skills.

In order to do this effectively, you will need to observe what children are doing and how capable they are. Good-quality observation will enable you to:

- support individual children's stage of physical development

- identify each child's specific interests

- highlight any specific needs that individual children have

- plan physical activities that are inclusive for all children.

(See Unit 9: Observation, assessment and planning for play and development, pages 222–247, for more information about observing and planning.)

(See Unit 9: Observation, assessment and planning for play and development, pages 222–247, for more information about observing and planning.)

Research

Think about the daily routine in your placement. How much time do the children get to play outside? Discuss with the staff in the setting how much emphasis is placed on planning for children's physical development.

Use the following website to discover how outdoor play areas can be improved: www.ltl.org.uk.

Key term

Observation: *the skill needed to watch and listen to children*

Adults should help children to develop physical skills outdoors as well as indoors, not just watch them play

Selecting appropriate indoor and outdoor resources

The need for resources

Children can develop many physical skills without special resources, although many skills also require specific resources, which will be described later. All physical development will be enhanced by a responsive adult and so the adults are the most important resources in any setting. Examples of activities that develop physical skills without special resources include running races, circle games, finger rhymes, games that require listening to and following instructions and stretching exercises. For all these activities, you are the most important resource, as the well-prepared practitioner who holds many activities 'up your sleeve' to introduce to the children as appropriate.

Selecting resources

When you are selecting resources, you need to consider:

- the ages and stages of development of the children
- the children's interests and individual needs
- cost and value for money
- the environment and space available
- storage facilities in the setting.

Catalogues offer a wide range of resources – choose them carefully according to the children's needs

Your assessment criteria:

Learning aim B: Understand the role of the adult in supporting children's physical development

P3 Explain how different types of indoor and outdoor activities and resources are used in early years settings to support the physical development of babies and children from birth up to 8 years.

M2 Assess the contribution of adults in an early years setting to inclusive provision in physical activities, using examples.

D1 Evaluate how adults can support a child's unique needs at different stages of their physical development.

Q | Research

Research some old-fashioned games such as 'Duck, duck, goose', 'In and out the dusky bluebells', 'Lucy Locket' and 'Ring a ring o' roses'. Practise them with your group members and prepare some to use in your placement setting.

Range of resources

Figure 3.7 gives some examples of activities and resources that you can use effectively to develop different physical skills.

Figure 3.7 Activities and resources for physical development

Large motor skills: Action	Fine motor skills: Coordination	Balance
Running races	Catching balls	Walking along a white line
Obstacle courses	Painting on paper with brushes of different sizes	Walking along a rope
Rolling down hills		Walking along a wide balance beam
Running sideways and backwards as well as forwards	Using chalks on small boards	Walking along a narrow piece of wood
Riding bikes	Threading beads	
Pushing walkers	Feeling sandpaper letters	Balancing on different parts of the body
Twirling ribbons	Sewing cards	
Stretching exercises	Buttering toast	Using a scooter
Climbing steps/on logs		
Painting walls with large brushes		
Using chalks on large boards		
Kicking balls into a goal		
Throwing balls		
Using a scooter		

Research

Using the internet or educational suppliers' catalogues, research some of the resources available for children's physical development. Reflect on the resources available at your placement setting for the physical development of children at different ages and make a list to suggest some areas for improvement.

Design

Using the Statutory Framework for the Early Years Foundation Stage, look at the expected levels of physical development for babies aged 0–12 months.

Create an illustrated poster/leaflet or web page of suitable resources to support the physical development of babies aged 0–12 months.

Twirling ribbons helps to develop shoulder and wrist muscles, which is essential before children can manipulate pens properly

Case study

During outdoor play, the practitioners at Little Gems Day Nursery have noticed that a small group of four-year-old children spend all the time sitting on the grass or in the willow shelter and talking.

1. Describe how the practitioners could encourage these children to become more active.

2. Give examples of some suitable resources for these four-year-olds to develop their gross motor skills.

Providing risk-managed activities to support physical development

Providing children with challenge

Children need to be safe and it is important that their parents have confidence that the early years setting is a safe place. However, sometimes too much emphasis is placed on safety at the expense of children learning how to assess and manage risk for themselves. Tim Gill has written about this in his book *No Fear: Growing Up in a Risk-Averse Society* (2007). The culture in early years settings is now changing to one where children are encouraged to explore, create environments and judge risk for themselves.

As a practitioner, you need to enable children to take some risks by providing them with opportunities to challenge themselves. It is your responsibility to provide and resource the environment so this exploration can happen.

Some settings regularly take children into more challenging outdoor environments, such as parks and woods. Other settings provide resources such as crates, beams, tyres, logs and large building blocks for children to create their own play environments. Of course, you need to ensure children's safety, but you also need to know when it is appropriate to trust children to manage their own risk and allow them to experiment and design their own challenges.

The key to providing children with risk-managed activities is to find the balance between the danger of accidents occurring and the benefits of allowing young children to take calculated risks.

Understanding risk

A risk assessment form will help you to find the balance between enough challenge and too much risk. It allows you to assess risks realistically and objectively. (For more on risk assessment, see Unit 4: Health and safety practice in early years settings, pages 128–129.)

Figure 3.8 on page 98 gives an example of a risk assessment used to help balance the risks involved in a visit to the park with the benefits to the children of this activity.

Your assessment criteria:

Learning aim B: Understand the role of the adult in supporting children's physical development

P4 Explain ways in which adults can provide inclusive, risk-managed activities that support varied physical development of children in an early years setting.

M2 Assess the contribution of adults in an early years setting to inclusive provision in physical activities, using examples.

Key term

Challenge: *opportunity for children to stretch their abilities*

Children need to experience opportunities where they can assess the risk themselves

Figure 3.8 A risk assessment for an outdoor activity

Activity	Probable benefits to children	Possible risks to children	How will the risk be managed?	Who will be responsible for managing this risk?
Walking to the park with a group of four-year-olds	Learning about road safety awareness Learning to walk sensibly and carefully Taking part in a social outing Experiencing a different environment Knowing their local area Being part of the community Opportunities for conversation on different topics	Children may stray into the road	An adult:child ratio of 1:3 Adult reminders of the possible dangers of the traffic	The person leading the outing All adults present will know and enforce shared rules about behaviour and expectations
		Children may run off in the park	Strict reminders about where children can play while on the outing, enforced by all adults	
		Children may need medical attention while away from the setting	Carry first aid kit and mobile phone	

With good role modelling and careful supervision, children can handle kitchen equipment safely

? Reflect

Reflect on the philosophy of your placement setting in allowing children to take risks. How do you feel about allowing children in your care to manage their own challenges and risks?

Q Research

Compare and contrast the effectiveness of different risk assessment forms from the placements of your fellow students.

Design

Describe an activity in your placement setting that might involve challenge and risk. Design a risk assessment form similar to the one in Figure 3.8 for your chosen activity to show how you would manage the possible risks involved.

Case study

Ben is a newly qualified practitioner working with a group of two- and three-year-old children in a day nursery. He is very keen to play outside with the children and loves helping them to build dens. One day, the supervisor comes outside and sees that two children are playing dangerously with some ropes intended for securing the tarpaulin for the den. It seems clear that Ben has not pointed out the dangers to the children.

1. Describe how these ropes might be dangerous for the children.

2. Explain how Ben could manage the use of ropes in order to balance safety with exploration.

3. Complete a risk assessment form for den building that will help to make this situation safer for the children in future.

Inclusive provision of indoor and outdoor activities

Using the indoor and outdoor environment

Indoor and outdoor environments have different characteristics and you can use these effectively to help support different areas of physical development. You can provide activities for most areas of physical development both indoors and outdoors, but it is important to provide variety for the children in the setting and to value the qualities of the different environments.

Many advantages of being outdoors are overlooked

Inclusive provision

The need to provide an environment that is inclusive to all children is a fundamental value for early years practitioners. It means making sure that you provide opportunities for all children to develop their skills, whatever their age, gender or culture and whatever their stage of development. If you make sure you are catering for every child's needs and interests according to their stage of development, then you will be demonstrating inclusive practice. (See Unit 10: Diversity, equality and inclusion in the early years, pages 258–263 for more information about inclusive practice.)

Babies

Babies develop physically through their senses. In order to stimulate them physically, provide as many sensory experiences as you can. Introduce **treasure baskets**, sensory rooms, light boxes and pop-up toys.

Your assessment criteria:

Learning aim B: Understand the role of the adult in supporting children's physical development

P3 Explain how different types of indoor and outdoor activities and resources are used in early years settings to support the physical development of babies and children from birth up to 8 years.

 Discuss

In a small group, discuss what you think the outdoor environment has to offer that cannot be found indoors. Describe how your placement setting uses both the outdoor and indoor environments for physical development. Evaluate how effectively the outdoor space in your placement is used for children's physical development.

Your assessment criteria:

Learning aim B: Understand the role of the adult in supporting children's physical development

P4 Explain ways in which adults can provide inclusive, risk-managed activities that support varied physical development of children in an early years setting.

M2 Assess the contribution of adults in an early years setting to inclusive provision in physical activities, using examples.

D1 Evaluate how adults can support a child's unique needs at different stages of their physical development.

As babies become more mobile, provide resources such as baby walkers, soft play blocks for climbing and play games such as 'Row row row your boat' to develop balance and a sense of movement. Babies can spend time outdoors if you make sure they are properly clothed and the environment is suitable for them.

Toddlers

As children become more mobile, provide push-along and pull-along toys and bikes without pedals (sit-and-ride toys). Sand pits with digging implements and water trays with pouring toys are all suitable for this stage of development.

Pre-schoolers

At this stage, you can encourage children to start challenging themselves and to create their own stimulating physical environment, for example by building a climbing structure with milk crates or inventing their own obstacle course.

Children with disabilities

Planning according to children's needs will include catering for children with disabilities. It is important to cater for a child's individual stage of development rather than the expected norms for their age. For example, a four-year-old child with motor difficulties may need activities and resources that you would usually provide for a two-year-old. To do this well, you will need to observe children sensitively and plan for them appropriately.

Babies will enjoy being outdoors as much as older children

 Key term

Treasure basket: a resource that provides a range of sensory experiences for babies to explore (developed by Elinor Goldschmied)

 Design

Think of a child you know quite well in your placement setting. Design a range of activities to develop their physical skills. Discuss with a partner why you have chosen these activities and what resources you would use.

Case study

In Happy Days out of school club, a group of five-year-olds like to play football outside for as long as they can. One day, Peter, who is normally part of the group, arrives in a wheelchair. The day before, he fell badly at school and broke his ankle. He is likely to be in a wheelchair for three or four weeks. A member of staff wheels Peter to watch the other children playing football and leaves him alone there for half an hour.

1. Describe the impact this might have on Peter.

2. Using some practical examples, explain how the staff could support Peter's physical developmental needs during the time he is in a wheelchair.

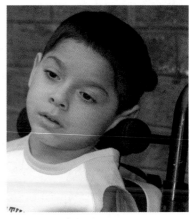

All children's physical development needs must be catered for

The importance of care routines

The need for routines

Settings need to plan **routines** in order for days to run smoothly, for staff to prepare well and for children to develop a sense of security. Yet it is important for the routines to be centred primarily on the children's needs. Allowing flexibility in the routines indicates respect for children's needs and will result in the children feeling greater control over their environment. Good settings show this responsive approach and adapt the setting to fit the children rather than the other way round. This section will look at nappy changing, toileting and sleep routines.

Working with parents

The younger the child, the more likely it is that they will have a fixed routine at home that parents will want you to carry on with in the setting. Good practice involves exchanging information with the parents about the routine in the setting and their child's care, including when their child usually eats and sleeps. A flexible setting will be able to accommodate the majority of parents' requests, especially with younger children where the ratio of staff to children is higher and the routine is fluid. If staff manage to give the children the same routines as they have at home, this will help very young children to settle easily and it will ensure consistency between home and the setting. More significant to older children is having a familiar, yet stimulating environment and consistent staff to care for them.

Nappy changing

Babies need their nappies changing regularly to prevent nappy rash. Dirty nappies always need changing immediately. There will be clear guidelines on nappy changing practice in your setting, and they will include the following essential points. The changing area must be kept:

- private from passers-by

- attractive and warm for the babies' stimulation and comfort

- clean and tidy, with each baby's nappies and cream clearly labelled

- well-stocked with disposable gloves and aprons.

Close communication with the parents is vital. Parents will tell you how they change their baby's nappy and their baby's likes and dislikes. For continuity and security during this vulnerable time, it Is best to follow the parents' routine as much as possible. However young the baby is, always give plenty of warning that you are about to change their nappy.

Key term

Routine: regular schedule for certain activities throughout the day

Parents need to be reassured that their children's personal care is important to staff

While you are working so closely with an individual child, remember that there are plenty of opportunities to develop other areas of learning. For example, you can:

- ask the baby to hold things ready for use

- comment on attractive mobiles or pictures

- sing songs or play finger rhymes

- use baby massage techniques.

Toilet training

If a child is not ready to be toilet trained, trying to force them can cause conflict and take longer, creating a traumatic experience for children and adults alike. However, being toilet trained and independent in using the toilet alone can contribute to a child's sense of wellbeing, so it is important to recognise when a child is ready. Some of the signs include:

- long periods when a child's nappy is dry

- a child's awareness that they are urinating or having a bowel movement in their nappy

- understanding and using words to say they need the toilet

- interest in other children using the toilet.

It is vitally important to work closely with parents during this time, to follow the individual needs of the child and to create a relaxed approach towards toilet training.

As children start toilet training, they should have free access to the toilets at all times. Children will develop greater independence more quickly if the toilets are freely and easily accessible and at the right height. Do not presume that young children know how to wipe their bottoms. This will need checking as the children gain independence and start using the toilet on their own. Allowing this free access and demonstrating that children are trusted with their own personal hygiene will develop children's self-confidence, independence and self-esteem.

Research

Research the toileting and nappy changing policies in your placement setting. How is information obtained from parents and where is this information kept? Compare and contrast some of the similarities and differences in procedures with others in your group.

Your assessment criteria:

Learning aim C: Understand the role of adults in meeting children's physical care needs

P6 Explain how adults in early years settings work with parents to support children's progression out of nappies.

Case study

Tim works in to toddler room at Little Oaks pre-school. He has noticed that the nappies of Anton, who is 2 years and 3 months old, have been dry most times when they have been changed.

1. Discuss what this might indicate.

2. Explain how Tim could work closely with Anton's parents to progress the development of Anton's toilet training.

Nappy changing can be a pleasant learning experience for a baby if the environment is well planned and staff interact well with the children

Using care routines to support all-round development

How routines contribute to all-round development

There are good opportunities for very close, personal communication with children during nappy changing, toileting and mealtimes and when putting a child to bed. It is important to make the most of this time to further the child's learning and development.

Mealtimes

Some of the ways that you can use mealtimes to support children's holistic development include:

- developing conversation skills

- learning about healthy eating

- learning to use knives, forks and spoons correctly

- learning socially acceptable manners

- learning to care for others and the environment.

Some settings have a fixed snack time when all the children sit and eat together with the practitioners, while other settings have a 'rolling' snack time or café system where children can help themselves to a snack whenever they want to.

Sleep routines

Sleep is important for a variety of different reasons (see page 91). As babies grow older, they need less and less sleep and it is important to communicate with parents about their child's changing needs. Some parents might ask you to keep their child awake during the day, but if a child is obviously sleepy you will have to discuss this with the parents. Babies need a separate sleeping room, but toddlers might not need this — a suitable quiet and comfortable area might be sufficient for them to relax and sometimes fall asleep in.

Many children have comfort objects for sleeping or when they are distressed, such as a dummy or a soft toy. There may be disagreements about the use of dummies and, if dummies are discouraged in your setting, you should be prepared to give parents the reasons for this.

Your assessment criteria:

Learning aim C: Understand the role of adults in meeting children's physical care needs

M3 Analyse the extent to which different care routines in early years settings contribute to children's all-round development.

D2 Assess and make recommendations for improving care routines.

Q | Research

Investigate the Voluntary Food and Drink Guidelines for Early Years Settings in England at www.schoolfoodtrust.org.uk. In small groups, create a chart to compare and contrast the advantages and disadvantages of both a fixed snack time and a 'rolling' snack time for young children in a nursery setting.

Babies often need comfort objects when they go to sleep, so ask the parents to provide one if necessary

Sudden infant death syndrome

Sudden infant death syndrome is also known as cot death and the charity Foundation for the Study of Infant Deaths produces regularly updated guidelines to prevent this happening. You can find these at www.fsid.org.uk.

Basic guidelines for minimising the risk of cot death include:

- Place your baby on the back to sleep (and not on the front or side).

- Cut smoking in pregnancy – dads too. And don't let anyone smoke in the same room as your baby.

- The safest place for your baby to sleep is in a crib or cot in a room with you for the first six months.

- Do not let your baby get too hot, and keep your baby's head uncovered.

- Never sleep with your baby on a sofa or armchair.

- It is dangerous for your baby to sleep in your bed if you (or your partner) smoke (even if you never smoke in bed or at home), have been drinking alcohol, take medication or drugs that make you drowsy, or feel very tired. It is also dangerous for your baby to sleep in your bed if your baby was premature (born before 37 weeks) or low birth weight (less than 2.5 kg or 5.5 lb).

- Settling your baby to sleep (day and night) with a dummy can reduce the risk of cot death, even if the dummy falls out while your baby is asleep.

- Breastfeed your baby. Establish breastfeeding before starting to use a dummy.

Skin protection

The use of sunscreen should form an important part of routine skin care for children, particularly during the summer months. Parents are usually asked to provide appropriate suncream for their children and to say how often it should be applied.

Sunlight is good for vitamin D production but too much is dangerous for the skin

 Discuss

Discuss with a partner how the daily routines in your setting such as snack time, toileting, hand washing and sleeping are used to promote learning and development. What improvements could you introduce?

Figure 3.9 Care routines for children's learning and development

Routine	Opportunities to develop children's learning and development
Nappy changing	Singing favourite rhymes or playing games
	Sensitive listening and responding to each other
Toileting	Boosting independence and self-esteem
	Encouraging physical hygiene
	Practising getting dressed and undressed

Routine	Opportunities to develop children's learning and development
Mealtimes	Creating opportunities for conversation between children and adults
	Learning about healthy eating
	Developing physical skills such as using cutlery or opening packets
Hand washing	Instilling good hygiene habits
	Developing independence
	Learning about the importance of hygiene
Sleep routines	Developing sense of security and wellbeing
	Sensitive adult–child interaction

Case study

Sam is a nine-month-old baby who has just started attending a day nursery for two days a week. His mum and dad both work full time and Sam spends the other three days a week with his grandma. Sam's mum has told his key person that she does not want Sam to sleep for more than half an hour in the morning and half an hour in the afternoon, and never any later than 4pm. She has also said that he usually sleeps with a favourite cloth, but that she is trying to stop that now that he has started at nursery.

After two weeks at the nursery, Sam is still not settling to sleep well and he cries when he is woken up.

1. Discuss some of the reasons why Sam might be crying when he is woken up.

2. Explain how you might discuss this with Sam's mum.

In strange settings children may need comfort objects more than they do at home

 Discuss

In a group, discuss what manners you think are important for children to develop when they are eating at a table with others. Make of list of essential good manners and desirable good manners. Does everyone in your group agree on these? Discuss how this might be resolved in a setting.

? Reflect

With your neighbour, compare the snack and meal times in your two settings. How are these times used as opportunities for children to develop social, personal and emotional skills? How do staff try to instil healthy eating habits into the children?

How are snack and meal times used as opportunities for children to develop social, personal and emotional skills?

Recognising illness

Signs and symptoms of illness

Young children are vulnerable to infection, as their immune systems are immature. As an early years practitioner, it is important for you to be able to recognise common signs and symptoms of illness in order to: treat the child quickly and reduce suffering, help prevent the spread of infection, and prevent the child becoming seriously ill.

Some of the most common signs of childhood illness are outlined in Figure 3.10.

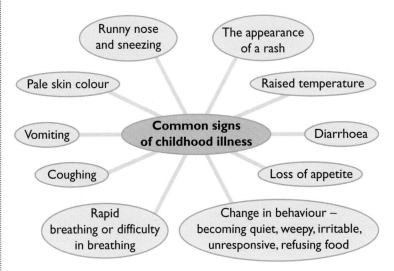

Figure 3.10 **Common signs of childhood illness**

Serious signs and symptoms

Some signs of illness in children need more urgent attention. If a child has severe difficulty in breathing, becomes unconscious, has a severe allergic reaction or develops a rash that does not disappear under pressure, then you must take emergency action. (See also Unit 4, page 130.)

Some of the most common serious conditions in children are shown in Figure 3.11 on page 107.

Research

Research the statutory guidance for dealing with sick children in early years settings at www.education.gov.uk. Evaluate how your setting's policies differ or are similar to those of your group members.

Your assessment criteria:

Learning aim D1: Know how to recognise and respond to children who are unwell

P7 Describe how to recognise signs of illness in babies and children.

Key terms

Immune systems: the parts of the body that fight infection

Signs: indications of illness that can be seen by others

Symptoms: indications of illness that are experienced by the person

Research

Research the following childhood illnesses and make a list of the signs and symptoms: common cold; chicken pox; meningitis.

Choose one of these illnesses and design an illustrated handout for early years practitioners, with information about recognising the signs and symptoms.

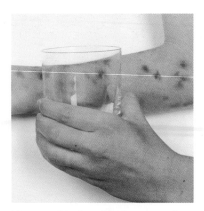

You need to be able to recognise and respond to symptoms of meningitis, as its progress is rapid

Figure 3.11 Serious conditions common in children

Condition	Signs	Action to be taken
Food poisoning	Diarrhoea and vomiting	Maintain the highest level of cleanliness. Stay with and reassure the child. Offer drinks of water to keep the child hydrated and contact the parents or carers. Seek medical advice.
Asthma attack	Difficulty in breathing; wheezing	Stay with and reassure the child. Loosen any tight clothing. Keep other children away. Sit child upright to ease breathing; use inhaler if prescribed. Seek medical advice if symptoms persist.
Diabetic coma; seizures	Unconsciousness	Place the child in the recovery position. Do not leave the child and monitor breathing and heart rate. Call an ambulance.
Meningitis	Rash that does not fade under pressure (see the photo)	Check for other signs of meningitis (e.g. neck stiffness, fever, vomiting). Contact parents and call an ambulance.
Severe allergic reaction	Swelling, rash, difficulty in breathing	Maintain an open airway. Stay with and reassure the child. Contact parents. Use prescribed medication if necessary and call an ambulance.

The importance of procedures

Your setting will have policies and procedures to follow in the case of children becoming ill. It is your responsibility to read, understand and adhere to these. Good practice will normally include:

- contacting the parents as quickly as possible

- staying with the child and giving reassurance and comfort

- if a child feels cold, covering them with a blanket

- if a child has a high temperature, putting a damp cloth on their forehead and offering cool drinks

- offering the child a favourite toy or a comfort object from home, if they have one

- administering any relevant medication that has been supplied by the parents, if necessary.

Your assessment criteria:

Learning aim D1: Know how to recognise and respond to children who are unwell

P8 Explain procedures to follow in early years settings when babies and children are unwell.

Children who are unwell need comfort and reassurance

Procedures for responding to illness

Reporting and recording illness

There are very specific guidelines relating to reporting and recording illness in early years settings. The managers of your setting must follow the governmental and Ofsted (or equivalent) requirements for developing policies and procedures. These include accident and incident records, medication records and lists of prescribed medication that can be administered. If a child is ill, you must:

- contact the parents and discuss the situation with them as soon as possible

- make a note of the signs in the relevant record book

- keep a written record of what medication has been administered to the child and inform parents

- notify some diseases (e.g. food poisoning) to the local Health Protection Agency and Ofsted (or equivalent)

- receive training to administer EpiPens if a child is susceptible to anaphylactic shock.

Other procedures will help with the management of illness in the setting. These include:

- obtaining information from the parents about a child's health requirements, dietary requirements and food allergies

- having clear policies for administering medicines – usually only those prescribed by the doctor

- maintaining good communication with the parents about the child's health.

Preventing the spread of infection

If a child becomes ill in an early years setting, there is a chance of infection spreading to other children. Minimising the spread of infection is part of your responsibility as an early years practitioner. (For more information on this topic, see Unit 4, pages 120–122.)

Nose blowing

One of the most common problems with some illnesses is children having a runny nose. Many settings now have a 'nose blowing station' consisting of a mirror, a box of tissues, some anti-bacterial fluid and a

Your assessment criteria:

Learning aim D1: Know how to recognise and respond to children who are unwell

P8 Explain procedures to follow in early years settings when babies and children are unwell.

M4 Assess how partnership work with parents could meet the health needs of babies and children.

D3 Evaluate the role of the adult in early years settings in meeting the needs of children who are unwell and those who need ongoing support, using examples.

🔑 Key terms

Accident: an unplanned event that results in injury

Anaphylactic shock: a severe allergic reaction

EpiPen: an injector used to administer adrenalin if a child has anaphylactic shock

Incident: an unplanned event that does not result in injury (but could have done)

small rubbish bin. When necessary, children can use this independently as well as being directed there by staff.

Washing hands

To help prevent the spread of infection, your setting should implement the practice of washing hands before eating or preparing food and after using the toilet.

Administering medicines

As a practitioner, you need to know, understand and adhere to your setting's policies regarding the administration of medicines to children.

Good practice includes:

- having all medications clearly labelled
- keeping all medications locked away
- administering only medicines that have been prescribed by a doctor
- receiving written instructions from parents about how and when to administer the medication
- recording all medication administered
- informing parents of what medication has been administered.

Working with parents

Over the last few years, working closely with parents has become a greater priority. Having a close and trusting relationship with parents is of particular importance in order to fully understand children's needs when they are ill. It is essential for practitioners to:

- obtain important information from parents about a child's health when they register at the setting
- maintain regular communication with parents about their child's health
- keep accurate records
- contact parents immediately if their child becomes ill in the setting.

It is important to wash your hands regularly, and to encourage children to do so too

It is imperative that all medicines are clearly labelled and stored in a locked cabinet

? Reflect

In your setting, ask to look inside the medicine cabinet. Ask about how the medicines are stored and labelled and whether any children have any serious conditions. Make a poster showing a medical cabinet and annotate this with good practice guidelines for other new students.

Discuss

Take some time at your setting to ask a member of staff about how they know about the health of their key children. Notice how much time a child's key person has to chat with the child's parent of carer on arrival and departure. Discuss with your group how important this communication is yet how difficult it seems to be sometimes.

Case study

Maya is six months old and has attended Rainbow nursery for one month. One day, she arrives and does not settle as well as usual. She finds it difficult to sleep, has a slightly raised temperature and is unusually 'grizzly'.

1. Describe the course of action that Maya's key person in the nursery should take.

2. Describe how working in partnership with Maya's parents could help to meet her health needs.

Supporting children with health conditions

Asthma

Asthma is a condition that affects children's ability to breathe. There are differing levels of the condition and different triggers for attacks, including dust, pollen and animal fur. Children who suffer from asthma will usually come to the setting well prepared with an asthma inhaler, which can help to control the condition and prevent an asthma attack from occurring. Very young children may need to use a spacer device or a nebuliser, which parents will help you to use. Inhalers all look alike so they must be labelled with the child's name.

As a practitioner, you need to know about children's specific triggers and to stay with a child who is having an asthma attack, in order to monitor their condition and provide reassurance. If the child's prescribed inhaler does not reduce the symptoms of an asthma attack, always call an ambulance.

Very young children may need to use a spacer device

Eczema

Eczema is an irritable skin condition that causes red, itchy rashes and swelling. Medication usually prevents itchiness and helps to reduce the swelling and to hydrate the skin. Parents will supply the required medication and demonstrate how to apply it if necessary while the child is in the setting.

You need to be aware of any specific irritants that may affect the child's eczema (such as sand) and you should try to prevent children from scratching in order to minimise the risk of infection. If children need to have cream applied, help them with this in private so as not to draw extra attention to their need.

Your assessment criteria:

Learning aim D2: Understand the role of the adult in supporting children with ongoing health conditions

P9 Explain how adults in early years settings support children with asthma, eczema and diabetes.

Key terms

Asthma attack: *a sudden worsening of asthma symptoms, with extreme wheezing, coughing and breathlessness*

Hyperglycaemia: *too much sugar in the blood*

Hypoglycaemia: *too little sugar in the blood*

Nebuliser: *a device used to dispense medication in the form of a mist inhaled directly into the lungs*

Pancreas: *a large gland behind the stomach that produces insulin and digestive enzymes*

Spacer device: *a specialised inhaler designed for very young children with asthma*

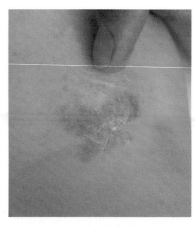

An eczema rash might look like this

Diabetes

Diabetes in children is a condition in which the pancreas does not produce the hormone insulin, which converts sugar into energy. The child needs regular injections of insulin in order to maintain a healthy blood sugar level. The condition can result in high blood sugar levels leading to hyperglycaemia (a condition that can result in a coma). More common in children is hypoglycaemia, caused by low blood sugar levels. If this occurs, the child will become confused, distant and can appear to be asleep. The only way to treat hypoglycaemia is to give the child some sugar such as a sweet, soft drink or chocolate as quickly as possible. It is important to communicate with parents about their child's specific needs, including exercise and activity, maintaining a balanced diet and how to recognise the signs and symptoms of hypoglycaemia. You should always stay with the child if they have a hypoglycaemic attack to monitor their condition and reassure them when they come round.

Supporting children with ongoing health conditions

When children have ongoing health conditions, working closely with their parents is an essential part of their daily care. You need to be informed about the child's condition, their individual needs and treatment requirements. It is important that children are not made to feel different in any way, and you must be sensitive to both their emotional and physical needs. You may have to change routines to accommodate individual children's needs, and private areas of the setting might be needed for specific treatments. Observation and record keeping are extremely important in caring for children with ongoing health conditions. You may also need to work closely with other professionals; for example, a nutritionist may provide advice on diet for a child with diabetes.

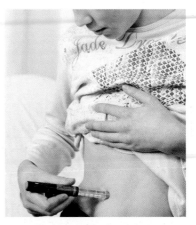

Parents will provide specific instructions about how to care for a child with diabetes

Case study

Penny is a four-year-old girl who has just been diagnosed with diabetes. Her parents have been into the setting to show staff how and when they give Penny her injections. They also informed staff that Penny often starts to slur her words if she is becoming hypoglycaemic and that a sugar solution is the best thing to give her to prevent her losing consciousness.

1. As Penny's key person, describe the measures you would take to meet Penny's ongoing health needs.

2. Describe how you would work in partnership with Penny's parents in the management of her diabetes.

3. Evaluate the role of the adult in caring for a child with diabetes in an early years setting.

🔍 | **Research**

Using relevant websites such as www.asthma.org.uk, www.eczema.org and www.diabetes.org.uk, research more about asthma, eczema and diabetes. Make notes on aspects of best practice for supporting children with these conditions when they are in your care.

Assessment criteria

This table shows you what you must do to achieve a Pass, Merit or Distinction.

Pass	Merit	Distinction
Learning aim A: Understand the physical needs of children for growth and development		
3A.P1 Explain why it is important to children's growth and all-round development to provide: • a nutritious diet • exercise • sleep.	3A.M1 Discuss the relationship between how children's physical needs are addressed and their all-round development.	
3A.P2 Explain how health impacts on a child's physical, cognitive, communication, language, social and emotional development.		
Learning aim B: Understand the role of the adult in supporting children's physical development		
3B.P3 Explain how different types of indoor and outdoor activities and resources are used in early years settings to support the physical development of babies and children from birth up to 8 years.	3B.M2 Assess the contribution of adults in an early years setting to inclusive provision in physical activities, using examples.	3B.D1 Evaluate how adults can support a child's unique needs at different stages of their physical development.
3B.P4 Explain ways in which adults can provide inclusive, risk-managed activities that support varied physical development of children in an early years setting.		

Pass	Merit	Distinction
Learning aim C: Understand the role of adults in meeting children's physical care needs		
3C.P5 Explain how adults use care routines in early years settings to support children's physical care needs.	3C.M3 Analyse the extent to which different care routines in early years settings contribute to children's all-round development.	3C.D2 Assess and make recommendations for improving care routines.
3C.P6 Explain how adults in early years settings work with parents to support children's progression out of nappies.		

Learning aim D:

1   Know how to recognise and respond to children who are unwell

2   Understand the role of the adult in supporting children with ongoing health conditions

Pass	Merit	Distinction
3D1.P7 Describe how to recognise signs of illness in babies and children.	3D1.M4 Assess how partnership work with parents could meet the health needs of babies and children.	3D.D3 Evaluate the role of the adult in early years settings in meeting the needs of children who are unwell and those who need ongoing support, using examples.
3D1.P8 Explain procedures to follow in early years settings when babies and children are unwell.		
3D2.P9 Explain how adults in early years settings support children with: • asthma • eczema • diabetes.	3D2.M5 Discuss how adults in early years settings can best support children with an ongoing health condition.	

4 | Health and safety practice in early years settings

Learning aim A1:
Understand the importance of complying with relevant health and safety legislation and regulations

- Legal requirements for early years settings
- Health and safety practice in early years settings

Learning aim A2:
Understand how to prevent the spread of infection

- How infection spreads
- Infection control in an early years setting

**Learning aim B:
Understand how to
prevent accidents and
incidents and carry
out risk assessments**

- ▶ Common hazards and how to
  prevent accidents, incidents
  and injuries

- ▶ Supervision and resources to
  prevent accidents

- ▶ Carrying out risk assessments

**Learning aim C:
Understand how
to respond to
emergencies**

- ▶ Procedures for responding
  to accidents

- ▶ Procedures for responding to
  other emergencies

Legal requirements for early years settings

Introduction to this unit

Parents want their children to be safe and well when they leave them in someone else's care. They also need reassurance that early years practitioners know exactly what to do in the event of an emergency. In this unit, you will learn about preventing the spread of infection and how to deal with emergencies in an early years setting. You will also learn how to create safe environments, both indoors and outdoors, while still allowing children to explore and take risks. The knowledge from this unit provides an introduction to a paediatric first aid course, which is required for work in most settings.

Legal requirements for practitioners

Understanding and complying with health and safety legislation is one of the most important aspects of working with young children. Parents and carers need to know that their children will be safe in your care and you are legally obliged to follow the guidance set out in health and safety regulations. Young children are very vulnerable and depend on you to keep them safe from harm. It is therefore very important to have a sound working knowledge of the legal requirements for health and safety.

Health and safety legislation

The law relating to health and safety varies in the four home countries of the UK and it is important that you are familiar with the relevant legislation for the country in which you work. The health and safety legislation for all four countries includes guidance for practitioners relating to:

- promoting the good health of children by preventing accidents and dealing with emergencies

- preventing the spread of infection by maintaining strict hygiene practices and infection control procedures

- carrying out risk assessments and maintaining a safe, secure environment, both indoors and outdoors

- keeping up to date with legislation relating to health and safety and undertaking regular training.

Some of the main legislation and regulations relating to health and safety are summarised in Figure 4.1 on page 117.

Figure 4.1 on page 117.

Your assessment criteria:

Learning aim A1: Understand the importance of complying with relevant health and safety legislation and regulations

P1 Describe how legal requirements affect practice in early years settings using examples relevant to the home country:

- to promote the good health of children

- to prevent the spread of infection

- for risk assessment

- for organisation of the environment.

M1 Discuss reasons why early years settings must comply with legal requirements for health and safety.

Health and safety statement
Health and safety at Work etc Act

This is the Health and Safe...

It is important for practitioners to have a sound working knowledge of health and safety legislation

 Key terms

Health and Safety Executive (HSE): national independent watchdog for work-related health and safety issues

Health Protection Agency (HPA): the organisation responsible for protecting public health

Figure 4.1 Health and safety legislation relevant to early years settings

Legislation	Impact on early years practice
The Health and Safety at Work Act 1974 (Great Britain) The Health and Safety at Work (Northern Ireland) Order 1978	Outlines the responsibility of individual employees for maintaining health and safety in the workplace.
Childcare Act 2006	Focuses on improving outcomes for children in the early years through the 'five outcomes' of Every Child Matters (including 'being healthy' and 'staying safe'). Introduced the Early Years Foundation Stage in 2008 (including the welfare requirements for promoting health and safeguarding children).
Manual Handling Operations Regulations 1992	Provides guidance for lifting and carrying children, including correct techniques and procedures for risk assessment.
Control of Substances Hazardous to Health Regulations 2002 (COSHH)	Protects children from dangerous chemicals (including cleaning substances and medicines), including regulations about storage and usage.
Reporting of Injuries, Diseases and Dangerous Occurrences Regulations 1995 (RIDDOR)	Outlines the procedures for reporting accidents, injuries and infectious diseases such as TB and meningitis to the Health and Safety Executive (HSE) and the Health Protection Agency (HPA).
The Food Hygiene (England) Regulations 2006 (similar legislation in Scotland, Wales and Northern England)	Provides guidance on the preparation, storage and cooking of food and the requirements for staff training in food hygiene.
Statutory Framework for the Early Years Foundation Stage 2012 (England)	The safeguarding and welfare requirements outline the legal responsibilities for providers in promoting children's health, safety and wellbeing (ages 0–5 years).

Organisation of the environment

The statutory safeguarding and welfare guidance in the Early Years Foundation Stage (2012) include the legal requirements for organising the setting in order to meet the health and safety needs of children from birth to five years old. In registered settings, the indoor premises must be large enough for the number of children in the setting. The provider must also ensure that, so far as is reasonable:

- the facilities, equipment and access to the premises are suitable for children with disabilities

- there are suitable hygienic facilities for changing any children who are in nappies

- there is an adequate number of toilets and hand basins available.

Q | Research

Investigate the safeguarding and welfare requirements of the Early Years Foundation Stage 2012. Reflect on how it affects your practice in placement and make a list of some of the reasons why it is important to comply with the legal requirements in the following areas:

- promoting children's good health

- preventing the spread of infection

- organisation of the environment in your setting.

Health and safety practice in early years settings

Complying with legislation

As an early years practitioner, it is your responsibility to understand how health and safety legislation applies to your own practice in the workplace setting. Complying with health and safety legislation is extremely important in order to:

- protect children, staff and others from accidents, injuries and illness
- promote children's health and wellbeing
- provide reassurance for parents and carers and inspire their confidence in the setting
- maintain a safe working environment for children, staff and visitors
- meet the requirements for registration with Ofsted (the Office for Standards in Education) in England or other regulatory organisations: Estyn in Wales, Education and Training Inspectorate in Northern Ireland and Education Scotland.

Professional practice

You will need to undertake regular training in areas such as first aid and food hygiene and will also be responsible for keeping up to date with changes in legislation and regulations. Some aspects of professional practice in health and safety are summarised in Figure 4.2.

Your assessment criteria:

Learning aim A1: Understand the importance of complying with relevant health and safety legislation and regulations

P1 Describe how legal requirements affect practice in early years settings using examples relevant to the home country:

- to promote the good health of children
- to prevent the spread of infection
- for risk assessment
- for organisation of the environment.

M1 Discuss reasons why early years settings must comply with legal requirements for health and safety.

D1 Assess the ways in which legislation and procedures in early years settings contribute to children's health and wellbeing.

Figure 4.2 Professional practice in health and safety

Professional practice	Example
Take care of your own health and safety.	Avoid lifting heavy objects on your own or without the appropriate training.
Follow health and safety policies and procedures in the setting.	Know the emergency procedures for fire and evacuation of the setting. Keep fire exits clear. Make sure that medicines and other harmful substances are stored safely.
Follow strict hygiene guidelines.	Maintain strict hygiene practices when preparing food or drinks for children and when carrying out toileting or nappy changing procedures. Maintain the cleanliness of the environment, toys and play materials.
Conduct risk assessments.	Check the safety of the environment, equipment and play resources. Assess risks for planned activities and outings.
Encourage children to follow health and safety procedures and hygiene policies.	Carry out regular hand washing routines. Supervise the safe use of toys and play equipment.

Professional practice	Example
Wear protective clothing when necessary.	Use aprons and disposable gloves when changing nappies.
Report accidents, incidents, injuries and illness.	Complete accident reports. Notify the relevant authorities. Communicate with parents and carers when necessary.

Health and safety information

There are many organisations that provide information and guidance on all aspects of health and safety. These include:

- **Health Protection Agency (HPA):** an organisation responsible for protecting public health through the provision of support and advice to the National Health Service, local authorities, emergency services and the Department of Health

- **Health and Safety Executive (HSE):** a national independent watchdog for work-related health and safety issues, responsible for acting in the public interest to reduce work-related death and serious injury

- **Food Standards Agency (FSA):** an independent government department responsible for food safety and food hygiene across the UK

- **British Safety Council:** a UK charity that works with businesses to improve their health, safety and environmental management

- **Child Accident Prevention Trust (CAPT):** a UK charity working to reduce the number of children killed, disabled or seriously injured In accidents.

Always follow hygiene guidelines when changing nappies

 Key term

Regulatory: *having authority and responsibility to enforce regulations*

 Research

Investigate the procedures in your placement or workplace setting for:

- *reporting accidents and notifying childhood illnesses*

- *food hygiene procedures when preparing snacks for children*

- *storage of medicines and cleaning substances.*

Using additional information from the Health and Safety Executive (www.hse.gov.uk), create a health and safety report that explains the ways in which these procedures contribute to children's health and wellbeing.

Case study

Cheryl has just been promoted to the position of deputy manager at Little Rascals Day Nursery, a registered setting that provides places for children aged six months to five years. The manager has asked Cheryl to review and update the health and safety policies at the nursery.

1. Describe the health and safety policies you would expect to be in place at Little Rascals Day Nursery.

2. Explain why it is important for early years settings to review and update their health and safety policies on a regular basis.

3. List some of the health and safety organisations that Cheryl might consult, and give examples of the information she might obtain from each one.

 Design

Investigate one of the organisations listed in this section. Design an information leaflet or web page for new employees, providing guidance on the work of the organisation.

How infection spreads

The spread of infection

Most infections are caused by harmful organisms such as bacteria or viruses (these are both often referred to as 'germs'). These organisms can easily spread from person to person through the process of cross-infection and this can happen in a variety of different ways. Figure 4.3 outlines the different ways in which infection spreads and how to prevent this from happening.

Your assessment criteria:

Learning aim A2: Understand how to prevent the spread of infection

P2 Explain why it is important to control the spread of infection in an early years setting.

M2 Analyse how procedures in early years settings prevent the spread of infection.

Figure 4.3 Ways in which inspection spreads and how to prevent this

Method of spread	Example	Prevention
Airborne or droplet (breathing in)	Infection is spread through the air by coughing or sneezing (e.g. the common cold).	Cover the mouth when coughing or sneezing. Use tissues and dispose of them appropriately. Have good ventilation in the setting.
Direct contact (skin to skin)	Infection is spread by touching (e.g. cuddling or shaking hands).	Frequent, thorough hand washing procedures, particularly after using the toilet, before handling food and after touching animals
Ingestion (swallowing)	Infection can be spread by eating contaminated food (food poisoning), by touching food with dirty hands (e.g. not washing hands after using the toilet) or by putting dirty hands in the mouth (e.g. after playing outside).	Strict food hygiene procedures. Thorough hand washing, particularly after using the toilet and outdoor play. Regular cleaning and disinfection of equipment, toys and play materials
Body fluids (blood, urine, vomit)	Some infections can spread from one person to another by direct exchange of body fluids (e.g. hepatitis, HIV and AIDS).	Always use the Standard Infection Control Precautions when dealing with blood and other body fluids. Wear disposable aprons and gloves. Dispose of nappies, blood-soaked dressings and other used first aid materials appropriately. Cover your own cuts with waterproof, adhesive dressings.
Vectors (animals)	Some infections can be spread by insects and animals (e.g. flies or ticks).	Keep food covered. Try to keep flies out of the setting. Encourage children to wash hands frequently, particularly after handling animals or playing outdoors.

Preventing the spread of infection

Young children are vulnerable to infection, as their immune systems are still developing. Policies and procedures to prevent the spread of infection are extremely important for protecting children from illness and promoting good health. In settings where there are groups of children together, infection can easily spread from one child to another. Early years practitioners have a responsibility to follow strict procedures in order to prevent infection from spreading.

One of the main ways to prevent the spread of infection in early years settings is through the practice of frequent hand washing, by children, staff, other adults and visitors to the setting.

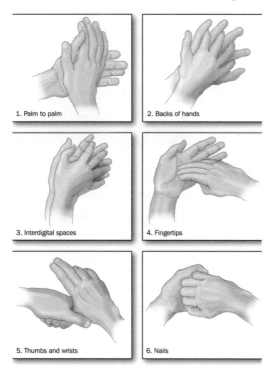

1. Palm to palm
2. Backs of hands
3. Interdigital spaces
4. Fingertips
5. Thumbs and wrists
6. Nails

Figure 4.4 The Health Protection Agency (HPA) recommended hand washing procedure; practise using this method until it becomes your routine way of washing your hands

Health and safety equipment and resources

Another important way to prevent the spread of infection in an early years setting is by using appropriate equipment and resources. For example, you should use disposable gloves and aprons, appropriate waste bins for hazardous waste (including dirty nappies), disposable tissues and paper towels or hand dryers. The spread of infection can be minimised if all staff follow guidelines, use equipment correctly and encourage children to do the same.

Infection control in an early years setting

Professional practice in controlling the spread of infection

There are many ways for practitioners to control the spread of infection in early years settings. Some of the ways in which you can do this are summarised in Figure 4.5.

Figure 4.5 Measures used to control the spread of infection

Measure	Examples of good practice
Policies and procedures	Make sure you are familiar with the policies relating to infection control, e.g. food hygiene and dealing with illness.
Personal hygiene	Wash your hands frequently. Keep your fingernails short and tie back long hair. Cover your mouth when coughing or sneezing. Cover any cuts with waterproof, adhesive dressings.
Changing nappies and toileting routines	Wear aprons and disposable gloves. Wash your hands before and afterwards. Dispose of used nappies in an approved waste unit.
Hand washing	Always wash your hands thoroughly, following the procedure recommended by the Health Protection Agency (see Figure 4.4 on page 121.)
Handling food	Follow strict hygiene procedures when preparing, storing or cooking food, as outlined by the Food Standards Agency.
Disposal of waste	Follow guidance for waste disposal, including nappies, chemicals and other hazardous waste, glass and other sharp materials, as outlined by the Department of Health.
Dealing with body fluids	Follow the Department of Health Standard Infection Control Precautions for dealing with blood and all other body fluids (including urine and vomit). Wear disposable gloves, wash hands thoroughly and dispose of waste materials (including used first aid dressings) in approved clinical waste units.
Cleaning procedures	Always clean up spillages immediately. Use an approved disinfection solution to clean surfaces, equipment and play materials. Machine wash soft toys and dressing up clothes regularly. Keep the outdoor environment clear of animal faeces, broken glass and other debris.

Make sure you clean and disinfect surfaces, equipment and play materials on a regular basis

Design

Design a poster that could be displayed in your staffroom, providing guidelines for staff in preventing the spread of infection.

Research

Investigate how different kinds of waste are disposed of in your placement or work setting (e.g. dirty nappies, first aid materials and broken glass). Make sure you know how to do this correctly.

Research

Go to the Health Protection Agency Website at www.hpa.org.uk and investigate the methods of spread, incubation and infectious periods for the following diseases: chicken pox, meningitis, rubella.

Record keeping and reporting procedures

Accurate record keeping can help practitioners take appropriate precautions to control the spread of infection. Records must be easily accessible, although confidential information about children must be held securely (according to the requirements of the Data Protection Act 1998).

Information held about each child in the setting should include:

- full name, date of birth, address and emergency contact details for parents or carers

- immunisation records and medical history (including details of medical conditions such as diabetes or asthma)

- any allergies (e.g. specific foods, bee stings or other allergies that could result in a medical emergency).

Parents or carers of infected children should always be notified immediately. The parents of the other children in the setting should be informed by phone, letter, email or other communication methods.

It is important for parents to understand that they should not bring ill children into the setting. The setting should advise parents to contact their GP or other health professional if they are concerned about their child's health. Most infectious diseases have a specific incubation period and children should be isolated throughout the infectious period of the illness.

Notifying relevant authorities

Most cases of infectious diseases in early years settings must be reported to Ofsted (or the equivalent regulatory organisation – see page 118). The outbreak of some infectious diseases (such as meningitis) must be reported to the Health Protection Agency (HPA). In some cases, this may lead to the closure of the setting for a period of time. It is very important to report and record all information accurately and to provide clear information and reassurance for parents. (See also Unit 3: Meeting children's physical development, physical care and health needs, pages 108–109.)

Research

Investigate where children's records are kept in your placement or work setting.

How is confidential information kept securely?

Compare the procedures in your placement with those of others in your group and make a note of the similarities and differences.

Key terms

Data Protection Act (1998): *the UK law that protects the privacy of individuals, and ensures that information about them is kept securely and is processed fairly*

Incubation period: *the time between exposure to a disease and the appearance of symptoms*

Infectious period: *the time during which an infected person can transmit the infection to another*

The incidence of some infectious diseases must be reported to the Health Protection Agency

Research

Investigate the procedures in your placement or work setting for notifying parents about infectious diseases in the setting.

Design a fact sheet that could be used to inform new parents about the procedures in your placement.

Common hazards and how to prevent accidents, incidents and injuries

Recognising and reporting hazards

Hazards can be present in many different forms in an early years setting and Figure 4.7 gives some examples.

All of these hazards can pose a risk to the children, staff and other adults in the setting, so it is important to make regular checks in both the indoor and outdoor environments. Most settings, including home-based care with childminders, will have an established system for recognising and reporting hazards in order to minimise the risk and initiate an action plan for improvement. This will vary depending on the type of setting, the age and stage of development of the children and the layout of the environment – Figure 4.6 gives examples of the daily checks that typically need to be carried out.

Your assessment criteria:

Learning aim B: Understand how to prevent accidents and incidents and carry out risk assessments

P4 Explain common hazards and how adults could prevent accidents to babies and children in an early years setting to include:

- selecting appropriate resources

- adequate supervision of children.

M3 Analyse the role of adults in early years settings in preventing accidents to babies and children, with examples.

Figure 4.6 Daily checks in an early years setting

Indoor environment: daily checks	Comments/ Action
Fire escapes are clear	
Electrical sockets are covered	
All chemicals are out of reach (e.g. medicines and cleaning materials)	
All toys and equipment are clean and in good working order	
Specialised safety equipment is in place (e.g. safety stair gates or fireguards in a home setting)	
Radiator heat is controlled and radiator guards are in place (if necessary)	
Ventilation is available	
Refrigerator temperature is within the approved range	
Toilets are clean	
Windows and doors are secure	
Outdoor environment: daily checks	
Play equipment, outdoor toys or games are in good repair	
Outdoor play surfaces, exterior fencing and exterior gates are in good repair and secure	
No dog faeces, broken glass or other potentially dangerous debris in the outdoor play area	
No poisonous plants in the garden or outdoor area	
No damage to exterior security or access systems	
Staff initials	

Figure 4.7 Hazards in early years settings

Physical objects (e.g. faulty or unsafe play equipment)

Fire (e.g. from faulty electrical equipment)

Hazards in early years settings

Food safety (e.g. unhygienic food preparation)

Security (e.g. unauthorised personnel entering the setting)

Key terms

Hazard: any object or situation that has the potential to cause injury or ill health

Risk: the chance that somebody could be harmed by a hazard

The role of the adult in preventing accidents

Parents need to know that their children will be safe in your care, so you have an important responsibility to prevent accidents to babies and children in the setting. Some of the ways you can do this are:

- providing adequate supervision of children at all times
- role modelling safe practice and behaviour
- checking for hazards, both indoors and outdoors
- following reporting and recording procedures
- conducting regular risk assessments
- understanding children's development, capabilities and individual needs
- carrying out routine observations of children
- communicating with parents and carers
- selecting appropriate resources for children's age and stage of development
- using appropriate safety equipment when necessary.

Common injuries to children

Accidents can result in a wide range of injuries to children of different ages, for example:

- burns and scalds from boiling water, hot drinks or unguarded fires
- cuts from knives, broken glass or other sharp implements
- poisoning from medicines, cleaning substances or plants in the outdoor area
- falls from play equipment, which can result in broken bones, sprains or head injuries.

You have a responsibility to prevent injuries to children by being vigilant, following safety procedures and ensuring that equipment is in a good state of repair.

Make sure you use specialised safety equipment when necessary

Research

Research the Health and Safety Executive website at www.hse.gov.uk and examine the information about risk management.

Investigate the procedures in your placement or work setting for recognising and reporting hazards. Make a list of the daily checks that are made to ensure children's safety in the setting, both indoors and outdoors.

Reflect on the importance of early years staff carrying out these daily checks and write a report for parents that explains how these checks help to prevent accidents to babies and children in the setting.

Case study

Anya is a childminder who provides care in her own home for three children, aged 14 months, two years and four years. Her home has a large garden, with a sand pit and a swing, and an indoor playroom where she keeps a variety of toys.

1. Describe some of the daily checks that Anya should make in order to prevent accidents occurring to the children in her care.

2. Analyse Anya's responsibilities as a childminder to ensure the safety of the children in her care, using examples.

Supervision and resources to prevent accidents

Selecting appropriate resources

Children are curious and love to investigate. This can lead to all kinds of situations that could result in accidents occurring. As an early years practitioner, you need to have a thorough understanding of child development and children's capabilities. You need to be able to select equipment, toys and play materials that are suitable for children's age and stage of development. Some examples are shown in Figure 4.8.

Safety equipment

A wide range of safety equipment and other resources are available to help practitioners to keep children safe indoors, outdoors and on outings away from the setting. The choice of safety equipment used will depend on a variety of factors, including the age and stage of development of the children, the type of setting and the nature of the potential risks involved. For example, safety gates, socket covers and fireguards make the home environment safer for toddlers, while playground surfaces, secure fencing and CCTV cameras help to maintain a safer environment for children in group care.

All equipment used with babies and children, such as toys and play materials, electrical items and outdoor equipment, needs to meet the relevant health and safety standards.

These items should display a product-safety logo, such as the CE mark, to show that they meet European health and safety standards.

Your assessment criteria:

Learning aim B: Understand how to prevent accidents and incidents and carry out risk assessments

P4 Explain common hazards and how adults could prevent accidents to babies and children in an early years setting to include:

- selecting appropriate resources
- adequate supervision of children.

M3 Analyse the role of adults in early years settings in preventing accidents to babies and children, with examples.

School-age children need challenging activities within safe limits

Figure 4.8 Selecting appropriate resources for children

Age range	Development and capabilities	Examples of resources
Babies (0–1 year)	Very dependent on adults Can easily choke on small objects	Choose toys and play materials with no loose or small parts.
Toddlers (1–2 years)	Love to climb and explore Much more mobile but have little sense of danger	Use stair gates, fireguards, and window and cupboard locks.
Pre-school children (2–4 years)	Enjoy being independent More coordinated but lack self-control	Choose resources that encourage independence safely, e.g. safety scissors and knives.
School aged children (4–7 years)	Enjoy investigating and testing their abilities More mature but still require supervision	Provide challenging activities within safe limits, e.g. stabiliser wheels on bicycles and safety helmets.

Supervision of children

Children should be supervised in the setting at all times. They must never leave the setting unsupervised and should only be released into the care of individuals who have been notified to the provider by the parents. In addition, the Statutory Framework for the Early Years Foundation Stage also prescribes the number of staff that must be available to supervise children in the setting at all times. The mandatory (compulsory by law) staff to child ratios are outlined in Figure 4.9.

The CE mark indicates that toys and other items meet European safety standards

Figure 4.9 Minimum staff to child ratios in early years settings

Age of children	Staff/child ratio for group care	Comments
0–2 years	1 member of staff for every 3 children	At least half of all the staff must have received training that specifically addresses the care of babies.
2 years	1 member of staff for every 4 children	
3 years and over (in registered settings operating from 8am to 4pm)	1 member of staff for every 13 children	Where a person with Qualified Teacher Status (QTS) or Early Years Professional (EYP) status is working directly with the children
3 years and over (in registered settings operating from 8am to 4pm *and additional extended hours*)	1 member of staff for every 8 children	Where a person with Qualified QTS or EYP is not working directly with the children
5 years and over (within the relevant school year)	1 member of staff for every 30 children	Infant class size is regulated by the Education Act 2002.
Childminders		
At any one time, childminders may care for a maximum of six children under the age of eight. Of these six children, a maximum of three may be young children, and there should only be one child under the age of one.		

Extra attention should be paid to staff to child ratios when taking children on visits or outings away from the setting

 Key term

CE mark: a symbol that shows that a product complies with European health, safety and environmental legislation

 Research

Investigate the safety advice for babies and young children by the Child Accident Prevention Trust at http://capt.org.uk.

Carry out a check and make a list of the equipment and resources that might help to prevent accidents in your placement or work setting.

Carrying out risk assessments

The process of conducting risk assessments

Most things in life carry some element of risk. Young children need to learn how to take risks safely and this requires a realistic approach and a certain amount of common sense. If children are constantly 'wrapped up in cotton wool', they are denied the opportunity to practise risk taking.

A health and safety risk assessment is the process of identifying risk and considering measures to reduce the risk to a safe level. The formal risk assessment process generally involves the steps shown in Figure 4.10.

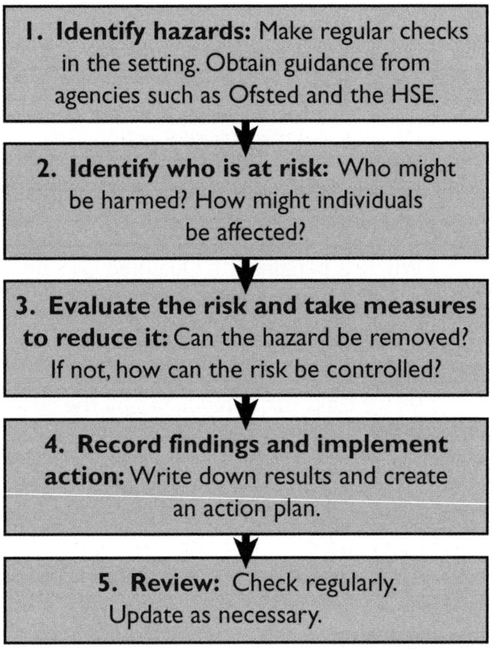

1. **Identify hazards:** Make regular checks in the setting. Obtain guidance from agencies such as Ofsted and the HSE.

2. **Identify who is at risk:** Who might be harmed? How might individuals be affected?

3. **Evaluate the risk and take measures to reduce it:** Can the hazard be removed? If not, how can the risk be controlled?

4. **Record findings and implement action:** Write down results and create an action plan.

5. **Review:** Check regularly. Update as necessary.

Figure 4.10 The risk assessment process

For another example of a risk assessment, see Unit 3, page 98.

Recording risk assessments

The practitioners in early years settings should carry out risk assessments on a regular basis. These should include checks on the premises, equipment and planned activities, as well as outings away from the setting. Each risk assessment should assess the potential hazards, identify who is at risk and the level of risk involved, the action to be taken and a date for review. This should be recorded on a risk assessment form. The form used will vary according to the type of setting, but will always include some main sections, as shown in the example in Figure 4.11 on page 129.

For another example of a risk assessment, see Unit 3, page 98.

Your assessment criteria:

Learning aim B: Understand how to prevent accidents and incidents and carry out risk assessments

P3 Explain how to undertake risk assessments in an early years setting.

D2 Evaluate the extent to which risk assessment contributes to effective early years practice in a selected early years setting.

Research

Carry out an audit of the equipment and resources for preventing the spread of infection in your placement or work setting. Make a list of everything that you find.

Research

Download the document 'Risk Assessment of Children's Play Areas' from the Royal Society for the Prevention of Accidents (www. rospa.com). Investigate the process for conducting risk assessments in your placement or work setting. Examine the forms used for recording risk assessments. Write a report that evaluates how the risk assessment process contributes to effective early years practice when supervising a group of children playing outside.

Figure 4.11 A risk assessment for an outdoor activity

Area/activity	Hazards	Risks (to children, staff and parent helpers) Level of risk (H/M/L*)	Evaluation/action plan
Children planting bulbs outside in the nursery garden	1. Children will be using gardening tools and digging in soil. 2. Children will be exposed to the weather, insects, potentially dangerous objects (broken glass, poisonous plants, dog faeces). 3. Children's security is more vulnerable outdoors.	1. Injury (L) 2. Infection (L) 3. Sunburn (L) 4. Bee/wasp stings or insect bites (L) 5. Wandering off the premises (L)	1. Check the garden and outdoor area for any hazards and remove if necessary. Check the security of fencing and locks on gates and make secure. Encourage the children to practise using gardening tools beforehand (e.g. in their play). 2. Ensure that the children wash their hands thoroughly after the activity. 3. Check the weather: apply sunscreen and supply sunhats or supply rainwear, as necessary. 4. Check staff's and children's health records for any bee or wasp allergies. Take necessary precautions. 5. Ensure there are enough staff members present to supervise the children at all times.

* Level of risk: H = high, M = medium, L = low

Safety on outings

There are different risks involved when taking children out of the setting. For example, the outing may involve travelling on public transport, a different environment or children being involved in different activities.

Practitioners must follow the policies and procedures for safety on outings and take all the necessary precautions to prevent accidents and incidents from occurring. A full risk assessment must be completed, to include:

- the required adult to child ratios for supervision (this will usually require more adults than the normal ratios)

- the hazards that may be present and the precautions that staff will take

- the weather conditions and how staff will accommodate these

- any specific, individual needs of the children (such as allergies and special dietary requirements)

- the times of departure and return to the setting

- a register of all the children attending.

Your assessment criteria:

Learning aim B: Understand how to prevent accidents and incidents and carry out risk assessments

P5 Describe policies and procedures which must be followed when taking children on outings from an early years setting.

Practitioners must follow safety procedures when taking children on visits outside the setting

Procedures for responding to accidents

Policies and procedures for accidents and incidents

Emergency situations can create shock and panic in early years settings. Policies and procedures provide a framework to support practitioners in these situation and help them to use best practice, following health and safety guidance. Most early years settings will have policies and procedures for a number of emergency situations, including:

- responding to an accident, calling for emergency help (including an ambulance) and reporting and recording procedures

- basic first aid procedures

- responding to a missing child

- evacuating the setting, for example in the case of a fire or bomb scare.

How to respond to accidents

Accidents in early years settings may involve falls, sharp or dangerous objects, poisonous substances, fire or water and can result in injuries such as cuts, burns, broken bones and shock. It is very important that you know exactly what to do in response to an accident. The children involved will be frightened and will rely on you to remain calm.

Principles of first aid

Every early years setting must have at least one designated first aider who is trained in the principles of first aid for young children and who is responsible for attending to first aid situations. Their duties will include recognising and responding appropriately to:

- bleeding injuries
- choking
- shock, including anaphylactic shock and electric shock
- lack of pulse and breathing (including resuscitation procedures).

- burns and scalds
- unconsciousness

If an accident occurs, the calm and prompt attention of a trained first aider can save a child's life. The main principles of first aid are as follows:

- Check if the child is breathing and has a pulse – if not, begin resuscitation immediately.

- If necessary, telephone 999 (or 112) for an ambulance.

Make sure you know where the first aid box is kept

Check if the child is conscious – if not, make sure their airway remains open by placing the child in the recovery position.

- Check for signs of bleeding, head injury, broken bones or shock.

- Do what you can to manage any injuries, using the setting's first aid kit.

- Reassure the child and try to keep them calm.

The recovery position

When to call an ambulance

A child's condition can deteriorate very rapidly following an accident and this can put their life at risk. It is very important for you to know when emergency medical help may be needed. You should always seek urgent medical attention or call an ambulance if a child in your care has any of these symptoms:

- a very high temperature (39 °C or above)

- breathing difficulties

- a convulsion or seizure

- becomes unconscious

- severe bleeding, burns or scalds.

Accident and incident reports

It is vital that staff record any accidents or incidents with children. Early years settings have a legal duty to report any incidents and should complete the special forms for this purpose. The first aider or practitioner involved should take great care to record all the information about the incident clearly and accurately and to sign and date the record.

Key terms

Anaphylactic shock: an extreme and sometimes life-threatening allergic reaction, usually to certain foods, drugs or insect stings

Convulsion: violent, uncontrollable contractions of muscles, sometimes known as a seizure or a fit

Recovery position: a position used in first aid that enables an unconscious casualty to breathe and prevents choking

Resuscitation: also known as CPR: manually keeping a person's heart and lungs working when their heart has stopped beating and they are not breathing

Research

In your placement or work setting, find out:

- who the designated first aider is

- where the first aid kit is kept and what it contains.

Make a list of the contents of the first aid kit in your placement.

Research

Investigate the regulations for carrying out risk assessments in the Safeguarding and Welfare requirements of the Early Years Foundations Stage at: http://www.education.gov.uk.

Investigate the accident forms in your placement or work setting.

What information is included on the form?

Procedures for responding to other emergencies

Missing children

Children do occasionally go missing from early years settings, although it is relatively rare. This is a particular concern when taking children on outings away from the setting. The security measures in place should ensure that children are safe at all times. However, if a child does go missing, it is very important that you know how to respond. The procedure should include the following:

- inform the manager of the setting (or person in charge)

- immediately begin an organised search, checking all areas of the setting

- make sure that staff members communicate with each other (e.g. using mobile phones)

- supervise all the other children and make sure they are safe

- if the missing child is not found immediately, inform the parents or carers and the police

- make a full written report of the incident

- inform the relevant authorities (e.g. Ofsted).

Evacuating the setting

There are many different reasons why an early years setting may need to be evacuated, for example a bomb scare, fire, gas leak or intruder(s) on the premises. All early years settings are required to have procedures for evacuating children safely. Staff should practise the routine during regular drills so that everyone knows exactly what to do. It is extremely important that you remain calm. You should reassure the children and explain to them what is happening, using clear and simple language. The person in charge should direct everyone to the assembly point and take a register to check that everyone (children and adults) has been safely evacuated. No one should leave the assembly point or return to the building until the person in charge has authorised them to do so.

In case of fire

If the setting has to be evacuated because of fire, the procedure should be as follows:

- Raise the alarm by telephoning 999 (or 112).

Your assessment criteria:

Learning aim C: Understand how to respond to emergencies

P6 Describe procedures in an early years setting for:

- responding to an accident

- responding to a missing child

- evacuating the setting

- calling for emergency help.

 Key term

Assembly point: *a designated place where people should gather after evacuating a building in the event of an emergency*

Research

Have you been involved in a fire drill in your placement or work setting?

Investigate the procedure and make sure that you know what to do in case of a fire.

Compare your notes with a colleague and discuss the importance of an effective evacuation policy in helping to protect children's health and safety in an early years setting.

- If possible, close all windows and doors as you leave the building, to minimise the spread of the fire.

- Remain calm and reassure the children.

- Evacuate the children from the building, following the procedure of the setting, including specific procedures for infants or children with special needs.

- Do not return to the building until authorised to do so.

Calling for emergency help

Emergency situations often cause panic and can affect the judgement of the people involved.

As an early years practitioner, you must remain calm and professional in emergency situations. If emergency services are required, you should do this by telephoning 999 (or 112) and communicating the following information clearly and accurately:

- which emergency service is required (ambulance, police and/or fire and rescue service)

- a contact telephone number

- the exact location of the incident

- the type and seriousness of the incident

- the number and approximate ages of any casualties involved, if possible.

The importance of policies and procedures

The consequences of accidents and other emergencies can be life-threatening and practitioners have a responsibility to follow health and safety guidelines and legislation. Settings must have policies and procedures in place to deal with emergencies and they must be able to produce these as evidence that the setting is fulfilling statutory requirements, such as those set out in the Early Years Foundation Stage (2012).

All early years settings must have procedures for evacuating children safely

Your assessment criteria:

Learning aim C: Understand how to respond to emergencies

M4 Discuss the importance of policies and procedures for prevention of incidents and emergencies in a selected early years setting.

D3 Evaluate the extent to which policies and procedures for response to emergencies in early years settings contribute to children's health and safety.

Make sure you know how to contact the emergency services

Case study

Adam is the playwork supervisor at Young Explorers Out of School Club. He works with children aged four to eight years. He is reviewing the procedures for evacuating the premises and is planning to organise a fire drill next week.

1. Describe the key elements of the evacuation procedure that should be in place at Young Explorers.

2. Discuss the importance of having fire and evacuation procedures to support children's health and safety.

Assessment criteria

This table shows you what you must do to achieve a Pass, Merit or Distinction.

	Pass	Merit	Distinction

Learning aim A:
1   Understand the importance of complying with relevant health and safety legislation and regulations
2   Understand how to prevent the spread of infection

Pass	Merit	Distinction
3A1.P1 Describe how legal requirements affect practice in early years settings using examples relevant to the home country: • to promote the good health of children • to prevent the spread of infection • for risk assessment • for organisation of the environment. **3A2.P2** Explain why it is important to control the spread of infection in an early years setting.	**3A1.M1** Discuss reasons why early years settings must comply with legal requirements for health and safety. **3A2.M2** Analyse how procedures in early years settings prevent the spread of infection.	**3A.D1** Assess the ways in which legislation and procedures in early years settings contribute to children's health and wellbeing.

Learning aim B: Understand how to prevent accidents and incidents and carry out risk assessments

Pass	Merit	Distinction
3B.P3 Explain how to undertake risk assessments in an early years setting. **3B.P4** Explain common hazards and how adults could prevent accidents to babies and children in an early years setting to include: • selecting appropriate resources • adequate supervision of children. **3B.P5** Describe policies and procedures that must be followed when taking children on outings from an early years setting.	**3B.M3** Analyse the role of adults in early years settings in preventing accidents to babies and children, with examples.	**3B.D2** Evaluate the extent to which risk assessment contributes to effective early years practice in a selected early years setting.

Pass		Merit		Distinction	

Learning aim C: Understand how to respond to emergencies

3C.P6	Describe procedures in an early years setting for: • responding to an accident • responding to a missing child • evacuating the setting • calling for emergency help.	3C.M4	Discuss the importance of policies and procedures for prevention of incidents and emergencies in a selected early years setting.	3C.D3	Evaluate the extent to which policies and procedures for response to emergencies in early years settings contribute to children's health and safety.

5 | Collaboration with parents, colleagues and other professionals in early years

Learning aim A1:
Understand the impact of parental rights, views and experiences on collaborative work with them in early years settings

- ▶ Parental rights and responsibilities

- ▶ Parents' enduring relationship with their children

- ▶ The impact of parental views and parenting styles

- ▶ The impact of parents' own experiences

Learning aim A2:
Understand how to work with parents

- ▶ Building professional relationships with parents

- ▶ Effective communication with parents

- ▶ Working within your limitations as a practitioner

Learning aim B1: Understand the role of other professionals in families' lives

▶ The role of other professionals

Learning aim B2: Understand collaborative working in early years settings

▶ The benefits and difficulties of collaborative working

Parental rights and responsibilities

Introduction to this unit

As parents are their child's first and most important educators, it is in the best interests of the children in our care to form as close relationships as possible with them. This unit explores the importance of working with parents and suggests ways that settings and individual practitioners can do this on a daily basis. Practitioners also have to work closely with other staff in their setting and other professionals who may be involved with the children they care for. This unit illustrates who some of these people may be, and encourages students to consider relating this to their setting and their own practice.

Your assessment criteria:

Learning aim A1: Understand the impact of parental rights, views and experiences on collaborative work with them in early years settings

P1 Describe how concepts of parental rights and responsibilities affect the care of children in early years settings.

M1 Discuss the impacts arising from parental rights and parenting for the care of children in early years settings.

Parents' rights

The Children Act (1989) established the important principle that partnerships between practitioners and parents must be active, valued and treated with respect in order to have the greatest positive effect on children. In 2007, the Parents, Early Years and Learning (PEAL) project was launched and focused on this partnership to support parents 'long before compulsory schooling starts'. The PEAL project stated that 'parents are children's first and most enduring educators', and encouraged practitioners and parents to work together to have a positive impact on children's development and learning.

As their child's first and most enduring educators, parents have legal **rights** to choose how they look after their child. Figure 5.1 shows some of the different decisions that are the rights of parents.

Q | Research

Research the PEAL project (www.peal.org.uk).

In a small group, discuss ways of including young children in the decisions that affect them.

Figure 5.1 Choices regarding their children's upbringing that are the rights of parents

Families will differ in many different ways, even if they come from the same ethnic and religious group

How children are cared for will differ from family to family, including how they spend their leisure time

Parental responsibility

Parental responsibility is a term introduced in the Children Act 1989. It means that a parent's rights must be balanced by their responsibility to ensure the welfare of their child. Importantly, the child's rights, as stated in the United Nations Convention on the Rights of the Child (UNCRC) (1989) can overrule those of the parents, especially if the parents fail to provide adequate care.

In most cases, the mother has parental responsibility for a child. This responsibility is usually shared with the father, but not always. In some cases, other adults as well as the parents might have parental responsibilities for a child, such as someone who is a named guardian. It is because of the importance of this parental responsibility that practitioners must work as closely as possible with the parents of children in their care. As a practitioner, you have a **duty of care** to the children you work with, but the person (or people) with parental responsibility maintains overall responsibility. (See also Unit 8, page 218.)

Key terms

Duty of care: the commitment to do everything we can to keep the children in our care safe from harm

Parental responsibility: the legal responsibility of the person or people who care for a child to ensure the welfare of the child

Rights: entitlements that are protected by law and agreed upon by society as fair and just expectations

Case study

Ellie is a two-year-old girl whose parents both have parental responsibility for her. Ellie's mum works nights and her dad brings her to nursery each day with a lunch box he has prepared. The lunch box contents (which are vegetarian, as specified by the parents) are not providing a balanced diet, as they consist mostly of sweets, crisps and chocolate.

1. Describe how you would discuss Ellie's lunches with her parents, showing respect for their choice of food but also informing them of the nursery policy about healthy eating for children.

2. Reflect on the difficulties of balancing respect for the views of parents with a duty of care for young children.

Parents' enduring relationship with their children

Parents' relationships with their children

In the vast majority of cases, there is a strong emotional bond between parents and their children. This **attachment relationship** is extremely important for the child's sense of wellbeing, self-esteem and self-confidence (see also Unit 1, page 38). Parents who are mentally and physically available for their children and who are sensitive and responsive to their children's needs will ensure a strong attachment with their child.

As a practitioner, you need to be responsive to the needs of each child in your care and form a strong attachment relationship with them. However, you need to realise that this relationship can never replace the strength of the enduring bond between the parents and the child.

Secure attachments promote good mental health

Children's interests

Parents who are sensitive and responsive to their children's needs and interests will also understand how best to look after them, physically and mentally. As an early years practitioner, you will need to be open and involved with parents so that you can tap into their knowledge in order to meet the needs of the children in your care. Parents are also responsible for the long-term interests of their child. Establishing what the child's long-term interests are through discussion with the parents will help you to provide the best possible care for the child.

Your assessment criteria:

Learning aim A1: Understand the impact of parental rights, views and experiences on collaborative work with them in early years settings

P1 Describe how concepts of parental rights and responsibilities affect the care of children in early years settings.

P2 Explain how children's needs and behaviours and the role of adults in early years settings are affected by parenting styles and the effectiveness of parenting.

M1 Discuss the impacts arising from parental rights and parenting for the care of children in early years settings.

Key term

Attachment relationship: *the strong, emotional bond between a child and another significant person in their life*

Research

In a small group, research and discuss attachment theory. Analyse the importance of attachment theory for early years practitioners.

Adults as role models

The influence and importance of adult role models in children's lives has been well researched by Albert Bandura (see Unit 1, pages 30 and 40). The attitudes and behaviours modelled by parents are the most important influences on young children. Parents' attitudes and behaviours may differ from those of the practitioners within the setting or from the settings' policies. Where there are differences, you may need to discuss them with parents. You will need to show them respect and discuss the differences sensitively and objectively.

Parental effect on children's learning

In 2004, the government published the Effective Provision of Pre-school Education (EPPE) report. The report presented the results of a wide-reaching research project, which studied the early experiences of 3000 children aged three to seven years in England over a period of five years, and compared these experiences with the children's educational outcomes. One of the main conclusions of the research was that: 'For all children, the quality of the home learning environment is more important for intellectual and social development than parental occupation, education or income. What parents do is more important than who parents are.' It is your responsibility as a practitioner to work closely with parents to ensure that home learning is optimised.

Parents' emotional response to their children

A variety of influences can lead to parents being emotionally unavailable to their children. These include:

- Parents' own upbringing: this can influence their parenting style and relationship with their children.

- Parents' culture: habits and conventions within the cultural group may affect the way childhood and education are viewed.

- Parents' education: parents may lack understanding of good parenting skills, the nature of childhood and how to nurture children.

- Parents' mental health: mental health problems could lead to poor attachment and emotional unavailability.

- Family circumstances: factors such as poverty, poor housing, illness, depression and divorce may result in parents' inability to meet their children's needs.

 Reflect

Who is a good role model to you at the moment? The children will see you as a role model. Think about what it is about certain people that makes children choose them as a role model in your setting. Reflect on how important your modelling is to the children in your care.

Parents can play a vital role in their children's learning and development

Discuss

In a small group, discuss the different influences that can affect parents' emotional response to their children. Reflect on how you think each of these influences might affect the parents' relationship with their child. Can you suggest any other possible influences?

Discuss how you were brought up and what influences there might have been on your parents' or carers' styles of parenting.

The impact of parental views and parenting styles

Different views of parenting

The way in which parents were brought up themselves will affect how they behave as parents to their own children. Different parenting styles are partly influenced by different views about the nature of childhood. These views will have been formed by the parents' own experiences as children. Figure 5.2 gives some examples of attitudes towards childhood that have been important in the past. These examples represent extremes and most parents would not use these expressions today. However, they still play a part in influencing and determining parents' views of childhood.

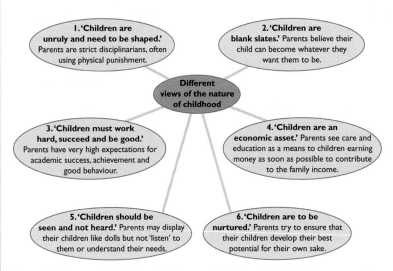

1. 'Children are unruly and need to be shaped.' Parents are strict disciplinarians, often using physical punishment.

2. 'Children are blank slates.' Parents believe their child can become whatever they want them to be.

Different views of the nature of childhood

3. 'Children must work hard, succeed and be good.' Parents have very high expectations for academic success, achievement and good behaviour.

4. 'Children are an economic asset.' Parents see care and education as a means to children earning money as soon as possible to contribute to the family income.

5. 'Children should be seen and not heard.' Parents may display their children like dolls but not 'listen' to them or understand their needs.

6. 'Children are to be nurtured.' Parents try to ensure that their children develop their best potential for their own sake.

Figure 5.2 Some of the historical views of childhood that still play a part in today's attitudes

Parenting styles

Partly as a result of these different views of childhood, there are many different parenting styles. The four main styles that are recognised today are illustrated in Figure 5.3. The diagram shows the relationship between support and control in the different parenting styles.

In practice, most parents use a range of parenting styles depending on the circumstances and the age and stage of development of their children. The parent–child relationship is a dynamic, two-way process and the characteristics of the child will also affect the parenting style. The factors influencing parental styles are covered on pages 144–145.

on pages 144–145.

Your assessment criteria:

Learning aim A1: Understand the impact of parental rights, views and experiences on collaborative work with them in early years settings

P2 Explain how children's needs and behaviours and the role of adults in early years settings are affected by parenting styles and the effectiveness of parenting.

M1 Discuss the impacts arising from parental rights and parenting for the care of children in early years settings.

🔑 Key terms

Authoritarian parenting: *a parenting style with many rules and little support*

Authoritative parenting: *a parenting style with rules and much support*

Permissive parenting: *a parenting style with few rules and much support*

Uninvolved parenting: *a parenting style with few rules and little support*

Knowing about a family's values, beliefs and habits can help you to care better for the children

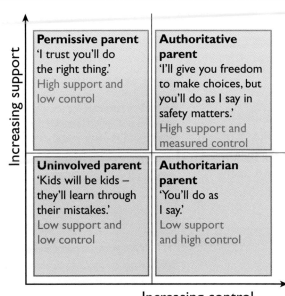

Figure 5.3 Parenting styles

Authoritative parenting style

Authoritative parenting is often described as 'firm but fair' and is widely regarded as the most successful style of parenting for children's overall development. Parents who use this parenting style set clear rules and boundaries, which they explain to their children and apply consistently. There is good communication, warmth and responsiveness between parents and children.

In general, children raised with an authoritative parenting style:

- are frequently given praise and affection
- are expected to behave maturely
- are more likely to be confident, independent and sociable
- conform more readily to disciplinary measures
- achieve better outcomes than children raised with other parenting styles.

Case study

Charlie is a four-year-old boy with two older brothers aged six and eight. In the nursery, Charlie is very physical, he has a lot of energy and often engages in rough and tumble play with other children, who don't like this. His dad has said to the staff, 'Well, boys will be boys. Anyway, he's got to be able to protect himself in today's world.'

1. Describe how the staff at Little Stars nursery should address these comments from the parent.

2. Evaluate why it is important for the staff to respect different parenting styles, while maintaining support for children's rights and welfare in the setting.

Building professional relationships with parents

Professional relationships

Children's outcomes improve when practitioners and parents work closely together, as was demonstrated in the EPPE project (see page 141). However, this relationship is not always easy.

As a practitioner, you play an extremely important role in the care, education and development of the children you work with, but the parents' role is even more important. Developing a professional relationship is important so parents can:

- trust the practitioners in the setting

- ask for advice and give advice when they feel they need to

- feel confident that practitioners are acting in the best interests of their child

- exchange knowledge about the child's interests, development and wellbeing

- be sure there is maximum continuity of care

- learn from practitioners about how best to help their children learn and develop at home

- feel supported through traumatic events such as separation or bereavement.

Professional relationships with parents are characterised by:

- the practitioner having good knowledge of childcare and development, objectivity and honesty

- the parents having a strong emotional attachment and thorough knowledge of their child.

Parents' emotional attachment

A strong emotional attachment between parents and children is a necessary feature of good parenting that contributes to positive outcomes for children. However, this strong emotional attachment can mean that parents show a less objective view of their child. Some parents might:

- overestimate or underestimate their child's abilities

- be very protective about their child's health and safety

Key term

Professional: demonstrating skill, knowledge and integrity in the work that you do

Design

Make an illustrated booklet to stress the meaning of the word 'professional' in the context of early years. Give examples of good professional behaviour as if it was a message to staff about their conduct.

- be very anxious about their child taking risks

- have strong opinions about what is best for their child

- be adamant about certain fixed routines in their child's day.

It is rare to find parents who do not have their children's best interests at heart, but in order to build a good relationship, it is essential for both the practitioner and the parent to show respect for the other's opinions, however different they are. Parents' emotional attachment to their children as well as their own previous experiences will lead to a wide variety of different ideas about how they want their children to be cared for and educated. For smooth relationships between parents and staff, there must be a mutually respectful approach to these differences. Figure 5.4 shows some of the concerns that parents might have when their child starts pre-school.

Figure 5.4 Parents' concerns

Discuss

Think about your own placement or work setting. In your groups (with due respect for confidentiality), discuss the following questions:

- *What are some of the concerns of parents?*

- *How do staff show respect for parents' ideas and concerns?*

- *How much flexibility does the setting have to accommodate parents' ideas?*

Compare and contrast the concerns of parents from the different settings in your group.

Research shows that practitioners and parents working closely together improves children's outcomes

Case study

Penny is an Early Years Professional student working at a day nursery. For her qualification, she has decided to work on ways in which her setting could improve communication with parents. She sent a questionnaire to the parents and from it she has learned that the parents would like:

- more information about the learning and development requirements for their children

- clearer information about their children's progress

- more say in the flexibility of the daily routine in the baby room.

Describe some of the ways that Penny could:

1. provide more information for parents about the learning and development requirements for their children

2. provide clearer information for parents about their children's progress

3. give parents more input into the planning of the daily routine in the baby room.

Effective communication with parents

What is meant by good communication?

Positive relationships with parents do not necessarily happen automatically and it is your responsibility as a practitioner to initiate, foster and develop these relationships in your setting. One of the most important and reliable methods of building a strong relationship with parents is to make sure there is effective communication. Relationships that you develop and maintain through good communication will be secure. Without good communication, a professional relationship will not exist.

Consistent, positive non-verbal communication marks the start of a trusting relationship and maintains this on a daily basis. Examples include smiling and demonstrating open body language. This is particularly important when you are working with parents whose first language is not English. The wider the range of communication styles you use, the more likely it is that you will be able to share meaningful information with parents.

Your assessment criteria:

Learning aim A2: Understand how to work with parents

P4 Examine how different forms of communication affect working with parents in early years settings.

M2 Analyse how different ways of building professional relationships with parents can be used effectively in early years settings.

Figure 5.5 The different methods of communication

Method of communication	Advantages	Disadvantages	Examples of positive communication in the setting
Non-verbal communication (including gestures, body language and eye contact)	Positive non-verbal messages are reassuring and convince parents of our true feelings.	It can be difficult to hide negative feelings and these can be transferred very easily.	Do staff welcome all children and their parents with eye contact and a smile?
Verbal communication (including telephone)	It is spontaneous and instant.	It is sometimes difficult for staff to give their full attention to a conversation when they are busy.	Can the setting organise routines so that staff can talk if parents want to? Do parents know how to make appointments if they need to? Does the setting have a private area for confidential discussions?
Written communication (including texts, email and other computer-based communication, newsletters, noticeboards, policies and procedures, children's records)	It provides a permanent record. Parents can take more time to absorb the information.	It is less spontaneous. Some parents might not read well, especially if their first language is not English.	Does the setting have written information in other languages? Does the setting allow time for staff to discuss children's progress records with the parents? Does the setting seek the opinions of parents regarding policies and procedures?
Visual communication (including photographs, videos, DVDs, digital recordings, wall displays)	It is attractive and easily absorbed.	Equipment and printing can be costly.	Well-annotated photographic records in children's developmental records are powerful evidence of what the children have been doing.

Two-way communication

Really effective communication means a two-way dialogue. As well as giving parents information about their children, you must also ask for information about the children at home. It is good practice to encourage parents to become active in the setting's decision-making processes. Areas of practice that will benefit from good communication with parents are:

- the setting's policies and procedures, philosophy and achievements
- accidents or incidents
- information about special events or celebrations
- children's progress, interests and health.

Parents will have a valid contribution to make about all of these. You also need to show genuine interest in your communication with parents, for example by:

- displaying warmth and sincerity
- showing sensitivity to parents' feelings and opinions
- **active listening**.

These skills are called **empathy** and are crucial to forming truly responsive interactions with parents.

You will need to be able to work in partnership with parents to support their children

 Key terms

Active listening: *a communication technique in which the listener feeds back what they hear to the speaker to confirm that they both understand what is being said*

Empathy: *the ability to read and respond sensitively to other people's moods and feelings*

Case study

Read the letter below, which was sent from a parent to the manager of an early years setting.

Dear Sue,

I was upset to see that Sam's sun hat was obviously not used yesterday, as his face was very red when he came home. I asked Hailey yesterday morning to make sure Sam was protected against the sun, but I have to say I was disappointed that she seemed distracted and not really interested in what I was telling her. Please can you make sure Sam wears his hat at all times outdoors, whether it's sunny or not?

Sincerely,

Mrs Andrews

1. Analyse some of the communication problems that have occurred in this situation.

2. Discuss how the manager might deal with the issues raised in Mrs Andrews' letter.

Research

Investigate your setting's policy about working together with parents.

How involved are parents in their children's learning and development and the way the setting is run?

Can you suggest any ways of involving parents in areas where there is little parental input?

Barriers to effective communication

Sometimes your best intentions to promote positive relationships with the parents of the children you work with will not produce close working partnerships. Figure 5.6 gives some of the reasons why these relationships might not succeed.

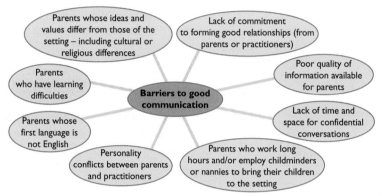

Figure 5.6 Barriers to effective communication

Strategies to overcome barriers

Strategies settings can use to overcome these barriers include:

- provide information in a wide range of styles, formats and in languages appropriate for your setting, for example texts, emails and telephone calls, as well as newsletters and noticeboards

- ask parents how they would prefer information conveyed to them

- keep information up to date and attractively displayed

- impress on parents and all staff how children's outcomes are promoted when parents and practitioners work well together

- provide a private space to meet with parents

- explain the setting's philosophy to parents so they can make an informed choice about the setting

- ensure **key person** allocations are sensitive to the personality of the child and the parents

- provide information about daily activities that parents and children can take home.

Confidentiality

Early years settings must treat all information shared with and by the parents of the children in their care as confidential. This is one of the most important features of a professional relationship and settings will

 Discuss

Make a list of all the different forms of communication you use every day. Discuss with a partner how effective these are for communicating different types of messages.

All families will need to access information about the setting's provision

have a confidentiality policy. The Data Protection Act (1998) states that individuals have the right to know what information is held about them, can refuse to give certain information and must have access to their data at all times. Therefore, all records about children must be kept securely but with easy access for staff or parents to view them at short notice. (See also Unit 9, pages 227–228.)

Parental consent

Parents must give their permission for certain aspects of their children's care when in the setting. Parents' permission is always required for:

- keeping certain information about children, such as written observations
- making observations of children's development
- taking photographs or videos of children
- sharing information about children with other professionals
- giving medicine or applying sun cream
- taking children on trips outside of the setting.

Case study

Anita receives an invitation from the local primary school for the nursery children to attend the school's harvest festival service at 10am the next day. She decides to take all the four-year-olds. This means a five-minute walk across the road to the school hall. The next day a mum complains to Anita that the nursery had not informed her about this trip.

1. Discuss the justification of this parent's complaint and outline some of the concerns that the manager's decision raises.
2. Describe the procedure that Anita should have followed.

The key person approach

The statutory framework for the EYFS in England (2012) states that each child must be assigned a key person. A good key person will:

- provide a consistent point of contact and communication for the parents about their child
- form a secure attachment relationship with each of their key children
- get to know the child's individual needs and interests
- respond sensitively to the child's needs
- observe, assess and plan for the child's needs.

(For more on the key person approach, see Unit 7, pages 186–187.)

Working within your limitations as a practitioner

Practitioners' limitations

It is impossible for everyone to know everything about childcare. There are many other professionals with various specialities to whom you must signpost parents if the need arises. Part of your knowledge as a practitioner must be when, where and how to signpost parents to services that cater for other aspects of childcare.

If you do not know the answer to a parent's question, you must say so and refer the parent to someone who does know. There is no shame in not knowing everything. It is far worse to pretend you know and give the parent wrong information. Figure 5.7 gives some examples of occasions when signposting is most effective.

Figure 5.7 Signposting to other agencies

Situation	Other agencies
Suspicion of a learning delay	The local authority special educational needs coordinator (SENCo)
Possible language delay	Speech and language therapist
Possible hearing difficulties	Doctor or health visitor
Behaviour problems at home	Family outreach workers at the local children's centre

Factors affecting parental participation

Most parents will want to find out about their children's progress and how they can help them to develop, or express concerns they may have. Many parents will have the confidence to initiate conversations, but there will be some parents who find this difficult. Figure 5.8 gives some of the possible reasons why parents might find participation difficult and suggests strategies you can use to overcome these difficulties in order for children to benefit from the relationship you have with the parents.

Figure 5.8 Factors affecting parental participation

Factor	Strategies
Language	Display welcome posters in a variety of languages and in plain English. Provide information in a variety of languages. Provide access to translators.

Key term

Signpost: point parents in the direction of other helpful professionals

Make sure phone calls to other professionals about children in your care are private and cannot be overheard

Factor	Strategies
Lack of confidence	Visit the family at home.
	Provide a private place for discussions.
	Use telephone/text/email communication.
	Provide help in reading and filling in forms.
	Greet families with a smile and engage all parents in conversation.
Parents in full-time employment	Provide alternative dates and times for meetings.
	Use email/web-based communication.

Research

In your own area, find out how to contact the organisations listed in the table below. Copy and complete the table. Can you add any other organisations in your local area that can provide useful information and resources?

Name of organisation/ person	Contact details (phone number, website address)
Nearest hospital (with emergency services)	
Local health visitor	
Local doctor	
Social services department	
Local Sure Start Children's Centre	
Local safeguarding officer	

Case study

Susan is the manager and owner of a small private day nursery. She has been qualified for 35 years and has owned her setting for 30 years. During that time, Susan has changed very little about the way that she provides information for parents. She hosts an open day every year and sends out an information newsletter every term. A new Sure Start Children's Centre has opened in the town, offering a wide range of services for children and their families. The manager of the Sure Start Centre has approached Susan to explore ways of working together, but Susan is not very keen on this idea.

1. Describe some of the ways that Susan could signpost parents to the services at the new Sure Start Centre.

2. Evaluate some of the advantages for children and families if Susan works in partnership with the new Sure Start Centre.

Sure Start Children's Centres cater for families with a variety of needs

The role of other professionals

Other professionals supporting the child and family

From birth, all children and their families have a range of different professionals working with them to provide support and ensure that children thrive and develop well. It is important for you to understand the roles of other professionals and to work collaboratively with them to benefit the children in your care and their families.

Service provision is organised differently in the various regions of the UK, but in general, the main areas of support include education services, health services and family care. In some local authorities, the different services for children are referred to as integrated children's services.

Education
- Pre-schools
- Schools
- Educational psychologists
- Counsellors
- Special needs teams
- Advisory teachers

Health
- Doctors
- Child psychiatrists
- Midwives
- Health visitors
- Speech and language therapists
- Dieticians
- Child development clinics

Family care
- Social workers
- Police family liaison officers
- Family support workers
- Mental health officers
- Family information

Figure 5.9 Services in family care, education and health

Family care and health services

Several groups of professionals work specifically with children and families, with the aim of supporting parents and improving outcomes for children. Some of these are shown in Figure 5.10 on page 155.

Your assessment criteria:

Learning aim B1: Understand the role of other professionals in families' lives

P6 Explain the role of other professionals in the lives of families with babies and children.

Key term

Integrated: all services involved with children working together

Research

Research Sure Start Children's Centres and how they operate at www.education.gov.uk.

Ask if you can arrange to visit a Sure Start Children's Centre near you or arrange for a representative to visit your group. Make a note of the services they offer to cater for the needs of parents in your setting.

Research

Choose one of the roles mentioned in Figure 5.10 that particularly interests you. Research the role and the responsibilities it carries. Prepare a slide presentation and a handout to share with your peers.

Figure 5.10 Professionals who work with children and their families

Professional	What they do
Social workers	Social workers are employed by the local authority's social care department and are involved with the welfare and safety needs of children. They work with families in their own home and often with other agencies to ensure that children's basic needs are met. Social workers are also involved with children in the care system (looked after children) and with adoption and fostering services.
Police family liaison officers	Police family liaison officers are trained to work with families if there has been a death or other traumatic event in the family that has involved the police. They facilitate care and support for the family and help the family contribute to the investigation.
Family support workers	Family support workers are usually based in Sure Start Children's Centres. They provide parenting support through home visits and specialised groups. They help parents with issues such as behaviour management, healthy eating and home safety and often signpost the family to other services where they can obtain further help.
Health professionals	A variety of health professionals will provide support for children and families, both in hospital and in the community. Health services include doctors, nurses, dentists and school health services. Midwives provide care for mothers during pregnancy and monitor the baby's health after birth. Health visitors provide developmental assessments and health screening services for children. In many areas, there is now a close link between the Sure Start Children's Centres and the health visitors – this facilitates the referral process and helps to introduce families to other services available through the children's centre.
Speech and language therapists	Speech and language therapists are employed by the health service. Their role is to work with children to support their speech and language development. The Every Child a Talker (ECaT) programme supports the building of close relationships between early years practitioners and the speech and language teams. (For more on speech and language therapists, see Unit 6: Supporting children's communication and language, page 178.)
Dieticians	As the incidence of childhood obesity is increasing, there is more need for the involvement of dieticians from the health service. They advise families on healthy lifestyles and healthy eating habits, including the type and quantity of food that is offered to young children.
Child psychiatrists	Child psychiatrists focus on children's mental health and wellbeing. They help children with disorders such as hyperactivity, autism, conduct disorder and depression in order to improve their ability to learn, express their emotions and form good relationships with others.

Education professionals

A wide range of education professionals provide support for children and their families. As an early years practitioner, you need to be aware of the different services available, especially for children with special educational needs.

Educational psychologists

These professionals are employed by the local authority but also operate privately. They are concerned with helping children who are experiencing emotional or learning difficulties in the educational setting and they also work with teachers, parents, social workers and others involved with the child.

Counsellors and therapists

When children have experienced some trauma, such as a bereavement or abuse, they often need help to understand how it has affected them and how to deal with their feelings. This might involve play therapy or discussion with a counsellor to help the child come to terms with their experiences and emotions.

Special needs teams

Your local authority will employ a variety of specialists to work with children who have special educational needs. Their work will involve assessment, strategies and early intervention programmes. The special educational needs services in local authorities are usually coordinated by a specialist adviser and all early years settings must have an appointed SENCo.

Specialist teams are trained to work with children with special educational needs

Your assessment criteria:

Learning aim B1: Understand the role of other professionals in families' lives

P6   Explain the role of other professionals in the lives of families with babies and children.

Educational psychologists work with children with behavioural and learning difficulties

Key term

SENCo: special educational needs coordinator

Design

Find out how the special needs team in your area works. Make a flow chart of the process that is normally followed in your setting if a child is suspected of having a developmental delay. Identify all the people involved. This activity will help you appreciate how important it is for you to be able to communicate with a wide variety of different people.

Advisory teachers

Each local authority will provide advisory teacher support for early years settings. This provision will vary in different regions of the UK. Advisory teachers give advice on good practice, support settings in maintaining high standards of care and early education, and provide training for practitioners.

Research

Research the role of one of the following: educational psychologist, health visitor, speech and language therapist or physiotherapist. Make a small booklet describing their work with young children for parents. Find out how to contact this specialist in your area and add this information to your booklet.

Case study

The Benedict family lives in housing association accommodation, on the fifth floor of a block of flats. The dad is in prison. The mum is living alone with three children under the age of five and suffers from depression. The children do not attend pre-school or any activities at the local Sure Start Children's Centre. Their mum is struggling to cope with shopping, feeding her children and managing their behaviour.

1. Identify the different professionals who may be able to provide support for the Benedict family.

2. Give examples of the kind of support that could be provided.

3. Evaluate how professional support for this family could improve the outcomes for the children.

Reflect

Imagine that have just started working with a three-year-old child with Down's syndrome. In your group, draw a spider diagram to show how you might access information about Down's syndrome on your own. For example, which people would you approach to find out about Down's syndrome, and which people could help you to understand the needs of this child in particular?

Case study

Harry is three years old and recently started attending Pink Elephant pre-school, which is attached to the local Sure Start Children's Centre. When Harry's mother completed his registration form, she did not provide any information about other professionals or agencies involved with their family.

Harry's key person, Sunita, is worried about how well Harry has settled into the pre-school and she has also noticed that his mum rarely speaks directly to Harry when she leaves him and when she picks him up at the end of the session. When Sunita tries to speak about her concerns, Harry's mum dismisses them as not important.

One morning, Sunita notices that Harry and his mum are attending a Let's Play session at the Children's Centre so she speaks to the staff about Harry. She finds out that his mother is severely depressed and that the family has regular support from the family support worker and health visitor.

1. Discuss why it is important for Sunita to be aware of the other professionals involved with Harry's family.

2. Analyse some of the ways that Sunita could work together with the other professionals involved with Harry's family.

157

The benefits and difficulties of collaborative working

The need for collaborative working

In February 2000, an eight-year-old girl called Victoria Climbie was murdered by her two guardians in London. Her death was investigated through a serious case review and in 2003, the Laming Report of the inquiry was published. Different agencies had intervened in the family many times before Victoria's death, and the Laming Report attributed part of the blame for Victoria's death to a lack of communication between the different professionals involved. The Laming Report advocated the need for multi-agency collaborative working. This led to a green paper entitled Every Child Matters (2003), which subsequently led to the Children Act 2004.

The benefits of collaborative working

Research has shown that it is possible for a child and their family to have seen as many as 20 professionals by the time the child is five years old. General practitioners and health visitors might be the first to hear of parental concerns or to recognise developmental delays. This can lead to the involvement of professionals such as speech and language therapists, psychologists and medical specialists. In some cases, social care departments will assess the family's needs and, as the child approaches school age, more education-related professionals may be introduced. The family may also be involved with voluntary organisations and support groups. With so many people involved, it is vitally important for them to communicate clearly, otherwise families become confused and service provision is disjointed.

Each professional working with a child and family brings a different, specialist view and working together will benefit children, families and professionals, as outlined in Figure 5.11.

Professionals come together in case conferences to act in the best interests of the child

Your assessment criteria:

Learning aim B2: Understand collaborative working in early years settings

P7 Review the purpose of working collaboratively with other professionals for work in early years settings.

P8 Explain why difficulties may arise in working collaboratively with other professionals in early years settings.

P9 Explain how information sharing could be managed in early years settings to support collaborative working.

M4 Discuss, using examples, ways in which working collaboratively with other professionals benefits children and families.

M5 Discuss how the potential difficulties in sharing information with other professionals could impact on outcomes for children.

D2 Evaluate the extent to which collaborative work with colleagues and other professionals in early years settings could impact on outcomes for children.

 Key terms

Collaborative working: professionals from different specialities working together

Green paper: a document that sets out government proposals for new policy and legislation

Serious case review: an inquiry conducted when a child dies or is seriously harmed as a result of abuse or neglect

Problems with collaborative working

The findings and recommendations of the Laming Report seem to be common sense and it might appear unnecessary to publish a report to highlight the need for different agencies to communicate with each other. In reality, however, sharing information is not always easy. There are several issues that can result in information not being shared effectively or quickly enough. These are outlined in Figure 5.11.

Research

Investigate the Victoria Climbie Inquiry Report at www.dh.gov.uk. Evaluate how and when the different agencies could have communicated with each other.

Figure 5.11 The benefits and difficulties of collaborative working

Benefits	Difficulties
Helps all professionals to understand the child and to coordinate support	Poor communication between professionals – finding time to meet
Makes finding a cause and a solution to a problem clearer	Poor coordination between services – arranging meeting times and places
Saves time and costs when information is shared	Misunderstandings about the meaning of the need for confidentiality
A holistic approach can be taken to address the child's needs	Use of different vocabulary and jargon in different services
Helps professionals understand each other's work	Different priorities in different services
Improves the child's life chances and promotes positive outcomes, including preventing injury and even death	Lack of trust, respect or understanding of other services
Develops trust in parents as the child is better understood	Poor record keeping by professionals

Information sharing

So that different services share information effectively, the Childcare Act (2006) outlines a procedure, including the following requirements:

- formal communication channels so that each service knows who, how and when to pass on concerns or refer to another service

- all partners must be committed to maintaining confidentiality of each other's information once it has been shared

- parents must give their consent for information concerning their child to be shared

- the Data Protection Act (1998) must be followed.

The **Common Assessment Framework (CAF)** was introduced in England in 2005 as a standardised framework for assessing the needs of children and their families. The completion of a CAF can lead to a multi-agency meeting, where all professionals meet together with the family to discuss the best way to provide support.

Key term

Common Assessment Framework (CAF): a standardised process for assessing the needs of children and families and identifying the support required from different professionals

Research

Ask about information sharing in your setting. Is there specific paperwork to be completed and are there restrictions on who can be given information?

Assessment criteria

This table shows you what you must do to achieve a Pass, Merit or Distinction.

	Pass	Merit	Distinction
Learning aim A:			
1 Understand the impact of parental rights, views and experiences on collaborative work with them in early years settings			
2 Understand how to work with parents			
	3A1.P1 Describe how concepts of parental rights and responsibilities affect the care of children in early years settings.	3A1.M1 Discuss the impacts arising from parental rights and parenting for the care of children in early years settings.	3A.D1 Evaluate how effective professional relationships with parents in early years settings can impact on outcomes for children.
	3A1.P2 Explain how children's needs and behaviours and the role of adults in early years settings are affected by parenting styles and the effectiveness of parenting.		
	3A2.P3 Explain the importance of building a professional relationship with parents in early years settings.	3A2.M2 Analyse how different ways of building professional relationships with parents can be used effectively in early years settings.	
	3A2.P4 Examine how different forms of communication affect working with parents in early years settings.	3A2.M3 Assess the likely impact on the relationship with parents of not recognising own limitations when giving advice.	
	3A2.P5 Explain, using examples from early years settings, the limitations in own role when giving advice to parents.		

Pass	Merit	Distinction
Learning aim B:		
1 **Understand the role of other professionals in families' lives**		
2 **Understand collaborative working in early years settings**		
3B1.P6 Explain the role of other professionals in the lives of families with babies and children.	3B.M4 Discuss, using examples, ways in which working collaboratively with other professionals benefits children and families.	3B.D2 Evaluate the extent to which collaborative work with colleagues and other professionals in early years settings could impact on outcomes for children.
	3B.M5 Discuss how the potential difficulties in sharing information with other professionals could impact on outcomes for children.	
3B2.P7 Review the purpose of working collaboratively with other professionals for work in early years settings.		
3B2.P8 Explain why difficulties may arise in working collaboratively with other professionals in early years settings.		
3B2.P9 Explain how information sharing could be managed in early years settings to support collaborative working.		

6 | Supporting children's communication and language

Learning aim A1: Understand the role of communication and speech in children's overall development

Learning aim A2: Understand how research into language development supports good practice

▶ The development and use of communication and language

▶ The links between communication and language and overall development

▶ Theories of language development

▶ The impact of theories on professional practice

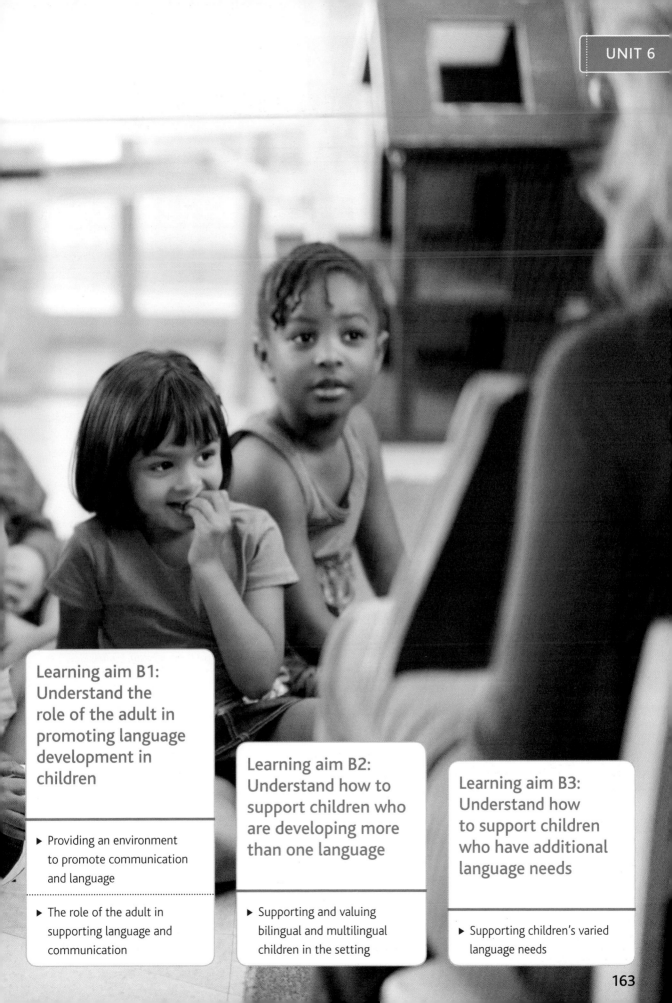

Learning aim B1:
Understand the role of the adult in promoting language development in children

▶ Providing an environment to promote communication and language

▶ The role of the adult in supporting language and communication

Learning aim B2:
Understand how to support children who are developing more than one language

▶ Supporting and valuing bilingual and multilingual children in the setting

Learning aim B3:
Understand how to support children who have additional language needs

▶ Supporting children's varied language needs

The development and use of communication and language

The earliest exchanges between babies and their caring adults will be mostly non-verbal

 Key terms

Linguistic: relating to language

Non-literal: not in the strict sense of the words, e.g. in phrases such as 'don't let the cat out of the bag' (in contrast to 'literal', which means in the strict sense of the word)

Pre-linguistic: the stage in communication development before the use of recognisable language

Language and development

The range of verbal and non-verbal communication skills

Communication is about conveying messages. It relies on the ability to express and receive information and is usually made up of both verbal and non-verbal behaviours.

Verbal communication, such as speech and written text, is based on words. Non-verbal communication relies on expressions and gestures, for example eye contact, body language and facial expressions.

Stages in the acquisition of speech and communication

Children will develop speech and communication skills in their own individual way, and some will develop more rapidly than others. However, most children will follow the same pattern of development, which includes both the pre-linguistic and linguistic phases, as outlined in Figure 6.1.

Figure 6.1 Stages in the acquisition of speech and communication

Pre-linguistic phase	
Age	**Typical speech and communication behaviours**
0–11 months	Locates and responds to interactions from others by smiling, looking and moving.
	Uses babbling and speech-like sounds to communicate with others. (At around 7 months, these sounds will become more typical of the home language they will come to use.)
	Uses non-verbal behaviours such as gestures, eye contact and facial expressions.

Linguistic phase	
Age	**Typical speech and communication behaviours**
8–20 months	Imitates and experiments with words and sounds. Begins to understand single words. Begins to understand turn taking during interactions with others.
16–26 months	Knows and uses the names of some familiar and everyday objects. Demonstrates listening by joining in with simple rhymes and actions. Begins to link two words together, but some sounds are not yet clear. Asks simple questions.
22–36 months	Speech is becoming clearer. Recognises, listens with interest and responds to familiar adults and sounds. Understands action words, simple concepts and simple questions. Asks a greater variety of questions. Uses a rapidly expanding vocabulary, often learning several new words a day.
30–50 months	Speech is mostly grammatically correct. Uses more complex sentences. Language is used more creatively to recall and retell events and experiences. Listens to and joins in with familiar rhymes and stories.
40–60 months	Uses different types of language for different purposes. Speech is fully intelligible. Continues to extend vocabulary. Listens attentively and can follow complex instructions.
5–8 years	Identifies words that rhyme. Uses the correct form of verbs. Understands non-literal meanings. Uses a range of sentence types and constructions. Understands and uses longer or compound words.

The components of speech

A variety of words are used to describe the different components of speech. These include:

Phonology: The way in which separate sounds (phonemes) are organised and combined to make words.

Syntax: The rules that govern how we construct sentences.

Semantics: The study of meaning: the relationship between signs, symbols, words, phrases or gestures and what they stand for.

Expressive language: Using words and gestures in a way that others will be able to understand.

Receptive language: Understanding the words and gestures that others use in their communications.

Research

Investigate the Statutory Framework for the Early Years Foundation Stage (DfE, March 2012) at www.education.gov.uk. Look at the strands of Language and Communication and consider some of the age-appropriate ways that you might support children in your placement to develop their:

- *listening and attention skills*
- *understanding of language and communication*
- *speaking skills.*

Compare your notes with others in your group.

The links between communication and language and overall development

Factors affecting communication and language development

Learning language is a complex task that is influenced by many factors. Understanding these factors will help you to ensure that your practice and provision promote those factors that enhance development and to seek (where possible) to limit those that inhibit development. Examples of both types of factors are outlined in Figure 6.2.

Figure 6.2 Factors affecting communication and language development

Factors that can support development	Factors that may hinder development
A 'language-rich' environment with stimulating interactions, activities and experiences 'Tuned in' adults who use varied language and respond positively to children's communication	An environment with high levels of background noise, e.g. television, radio A lack of adult stimulation and support The presence of a recognised condition, e.g. conductive hearing loss Structural or physiological conditions, e.g. cleft palate Developmental delay or learning difficulties caused by neurological factors, e.g. brain damage, or genetic factors, e.g. Down's syndrome

The importance of early identification and intervention

Once you know and understand the typical stages of language and communication development and are 'tuned in' to the unique children you are working with, you will be able to:

- track the progress that children are making

- ensure the early detection of problems

- refer children to other professional agencies, if appropriate

- provide appropriate support to children and their parents or carers.

Providing timely interventions, sometimes in collaboration with other agencies, will have a positive impact on the child's language and communication outcomes. It will also have a positive effect on the child's immediate wellbeing and future life chances.

Key terms

Conductive hearing loss: *a problem conducting sound waves through the outer ear, the eardrum or the middle ear*

Genetic: *as a result of genes or heredity*

Holistic: *seeing things as a whole, not as individual parts*

Interrelated: *each part is connected to all the other parts*

Neurological: *of the nervous system*

Physiological: *the structures, functions, activities and processes of the body*

The links between communication and language and other areas of development

Language and communication are at the centre of children's learning and development and have close links with both emotional and social development and cognitive development.

By providing rich linguistic experiences and environments, skilled practitioners demonstrate that they recognise the interrelated and holistic nature of children's learning and development, as summarised in Figure 6.3.

 Discuss

When you are in placement, talk to your supervisor about any children who have difficulties with language and communication. Find out what their difficulties are. Ask if the child is receiving any additional language support and, if so, what form it takes.

Make a note of the different types of language support that are used in the setting.

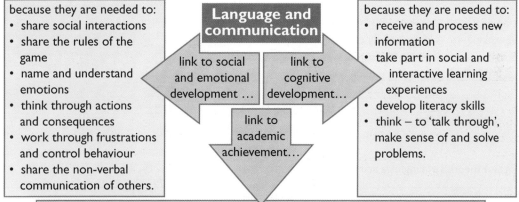

because they are needed to:
- share social interactions
- share the rules of the game
- name and understand emotions
- think through actions and consequences
- work through frustrations and control behaviour
- share the non-verbal communication of others.

Language and communication

link to social and emotional development …

link to cognitive development…

link to academic achievement…

because they are needed to:
- receive and process new information
- take part in social and interactive learning experiences
- develop literacy skills
- think – to 'talk through', make sense of and solve problems.

because children who can communicate and use language effectively and confidently are more likely to achieve academic success.
- Language and communication are key skills for accessing and benefiting from new learning experiences.
- Speaking and listening skills are the foundations for reading and writing.
- Access to the full curriculum is dependent on the spoken, signed or written word.

Figure 6.3 The links between language and communication and other areas of development

Case study

Alex works in a day nursery with children aged between two and four years and is the key person for Cara, aged three years and four months. Cara is very talkative but her speech is difficult to understand, and Alex has noticed that the other children are avoiding playing with her. Alex has also observed that Cara is losing the confidence to initiate conversations with adults.

1. Describe the impact that this language difficulty could have on Cara's social and emotional development.

2. Give some examples of the strategies that Alex and the staff team could use to support Cara's language development in the nursery.

3. Explain how Alex could work with Cara's parents to support Cara's language development.

Children with immature or delayed speech may have difficulty forming relationships

167

Theories of language development

Theories and ideas of language acquisition

The main theories of language acquisition reflect the nature–nurture debate, which influences much of our thinking about child development. Language learning appears to be a combination of:

- having a human brain that is biologically pre-wired for language acquisition (the 'nature' element)

- experiences that are shaped by the particular language environment in which a child is brought up (the 'nurture' element).

While no single explanation is likely to fully explain the acquisition of this complex skill, it is worth knowing the significant ideas of the major theorists. Some of these are outlined in the Figure 6.4.

Figure 6.4 Important theories of language acquisition

Theorist and theory	Description
Noam Chomsky **Nativist perspective**	Human beings are biologically programmed to learn language. He originally proposed that babies are born with a 'language acquisition device' (LAD): an innate capacity to acquire and produce language. He later proposed 'principles and parameters': all languages have grammatical rules or principles, but their use is constrained by the parameters unique to the particular language being spoken. Children are able to produce an infinite number of utterances by applying these rules.
B. F. Skinner **Behaviourist theory** (sometimes also known as **learning theory**)	Language, like any other behaviour. is learned through selective reinforcement. Adults shape children's language by reacting to the babbling that sounds most like words. Sounds that are not 'like words' are ignored and thus not reinforced. When an adult understands and rewards a child, the child's understanding of that word is reinforced.
Jerome Bruner **Interactionist theory**	Language acquisition is dependent on both biological and social factors, and on collaborative learning with older or more able language users. LASS (Language Acquisition Support System) refers to the social network, which supports innate mechanisms to encourage or suppress language development. Language acquisition comes from an innate human desire to communicate with others.

Roger Brown's observations of speech patterns in young children led to him identifying five stages of language development based on the 'mean length of utterances' (MLU), which means the average length of the phrases and sentences that children use. He found that the complexity of language structures that children use develops along very predictable lines, and is a better indicator of their stage of language development than their chronological age.

The five stages provide guidelines that help us to understand and predict what typical language development will usually look like. The five stages are summarised In Figure 6.5.

Figure 6.5 The five stages of language learning

Stage	Age in months	MLU range (measured in morphemes)	Characteristics and example
1	12–26	1 – 2	Nouns and verbs: 'See dog!'
2	27–30	2 – 2.5	Plurals and tenses: 'Cars go fast!'
3	31–43	2.5 – 3	Questions and negation: 'Where is Dad?'
4	35–40	3 – 3.75	Embeds sentences: 'Baby mummy bought me!'
5	41–46	3.75 – 4.5	Sentences and prepositional relationships: 'I want baby on top!'

Children learn language by using language

❓ Reflect

Think about your experience of working with children in your placement or work setting. Reflect on what you have noticed about:

a) the different ways that babies communicate from the moment they are born

b) the variety of ways that toddlers are able to put words and sentences together

c) how often young children imitate the language of others.

🎨 Design

Design a poster for the staffroom at your setting that outlines the many different ways that children communicate in the first years of life.

Supporting and valuing bilingual and multilingual children in the setting

Supporting multilingual and bilingual children

Many children are bilingual or multilingual and these children need to develop and use their home language. It plays a significant part in developing a self-concept and supports positive family and community relationships. The cognitive skills involved in using one language are transferable to learning new languages, giving children knowledge about how language works and supporting their developing skills in English.

Valuing home languages

You can show that you value the home languages of individual children in the setting by:

- finding out about the language(s) that children use at home and using this information to support your planning and to show parents that the home language is valued in the setting

- using displays, resources, books and stories, songs and rhymes, and by using the home language yourself

- reassuring family members who do not speak English, or who speak English only a little, that they can continue to play a significant part in their child's learning and development.

The key person

A child's key person will play a significant role in supporting the child's emerging use of English. It is important that the key person supports young children to 'tune in' to the language of the setting. Otherwise, this seemingly incomprehensible noise could become something irritating and irrelevant that the child ignores. To ensure that this happens, the child's key person needs to engage sensitively with the child and provide activities and opportunities that have rich language-learning potential. (For more on the role of the key person, see also Unit 7, page 186.)

Children who are new to the English language

The impact of being introduced to English in the setting will vary from child to child, but it is likely to show itself in the linguistic and emotional behaviours that children exhibit, particularly if there is no one with whom they can use their home language.

Your assessment criteria:

Learning aim B2: Understand how to support children who are developing more than one language

P4 Explain how to support children in an early years setting who are developing more than one language.

M4 Discuss how to plan for and give support to children with varied language and communication needs.

D2 Evaluate the extent to which adults in early years settings contribute to the language and communication development of children with varied needs.

Key terms

Bilingual: able to speak two languages fluently

Multilingual: able to speak several languages with ease

Many children speak more than one language

Figure 6.10 Some of the behaviours that children new to English are likely to demonstrate

Behaviour	Why?
A continued use of the home language	Communicating their needs using their home language has always worked before.
A silent/non-verbal period (perhaps accompanied by withdrawn behaviours or outbursts of frustration)	Communicating becomes too difficult and the child needs to work out another strategy.
Play with repetitive or familiar language	The words and phrases of familiar routines are useful for getting needs met.
The use of more complex or productive language	The innate need to communicate drives children to engage with others, which in itself promotes further language development.

The adult role in supporting children who are new to the English language

As a sensitive, responsive practitioner, you need to:

- surround children with good role models throughout the day
- increase the use of mime, actions and gesture
- develop visual signs and symbols
- support the child through use of the home language
- continue talking even if the child does not respond
- provide interesting experiences that the child will want to talk about
- support non-verbal communication and praise every effort
- allow time for a response (verbal or non-verbal)
- include other children.

You will need to adopt a wide range of strategies to support children who use English as an additional language

Case study

Margy works in a children's centre and is the key worker for Zeynab, aged three years and seven months. Zeynab's family have recently arrived from Pakistan, and English is not spoken in their home. Zeynab is very chatty as she arrives and leaves with her mum, but is finding it very difficult to communicate in the setting, where no other children or adults speak her home language.

1. Describe how Margy can ensure that the emotional and physical environments in the setting support Zeynab's communication.

2. Give examples of specific strategies that Margy can use to help Zeynab learn English.

Supporting children's varied language needs

Supporting children with additional language needs

For many children, their additional language needs will be temporary. With the right support, they will 'catch up' with their peer group. A small number of children will have more severe or permanent needs which may require the involvement of a range of professionals and some children will need to use enhanced methods of communication such as signing or using symbols. Whatever the child's needs, practitioners must:

- recognise and respond to any warning signs that the child may have additional language needs

- work to recognise and remove any barriers that are preventing the child's full participation in the setting

- provide appropriate challenge and support.

Working closely with parents

Parents are supporting their children's communication and language all the time. They will have the single biggest impact on the child's developing language skills. A positive professional relationship between parents and practitioners provides the context for:

- a two-way flow of information about the child and his or her particular needs

- the sharing of good practice

- celebrating successes and sharing concerns

- consistency of practice.

(For more on building professional relationships with parents, see Unit 5, pages 146–151.)

Working closely with speech and language therapists

Working collaboratively with speech and language therapists is likely to result in the best outcomes for the child. Speech and language therapists can provide:

- expertise on the identification of specific language needs or disorders

- advice on a range of strategies and practices

- reassurance and support for both parents and practitioners

Your assessment criteria:

Learning aim B3: Understand how to support children who have additional language needs

P5 Explain how to support children in an early years setting who have additional language needs.

M4 Discuss how to plan for and give support to children with varied language and communication needs.

D2 Evaluate the extent to which adults in early years settings contribute to the language and communication development of children with varied needs.

🔑 Key terms

Peer group: a group of people who have similar characteristics and are about the same age

Sensori-neural: a type of hearing loss caused by damage to the inner ear or the sound-processing part of the brain

Support for children with additional language needs will have a positive effect on their social and cognitive development

- signposting to additional sources of information

- specific programmes of support.

(See also Unit 5, page 155.)

Providing quality interactions

Becoming a skilful communicator in your practice will help you to provide quality interactions by:

- modelling and promoting good speaking and listening skills

- giving children plenty of time and space to respond

- 'recasting' children's utterances (see Figure 6.7 on page 171)

- adapting the complexity of your own speech to match the abilities of the child

- providing opportunities for real conversations

- modelling and valuing non-verbal conversation.

Using visual cues and props will enable children to take a more active role in interactions by giving them additional information. It will also help children be more independent.

Working with children with hearing loss

Children's hearing loss can be:

- **sensori-neural** or conductive

- temporary or permanent

- mild through to severe.

When working with children with hearing loss, you will be most effective if you:

- understand the nature and extent of the hearing loss

- know which services are already involved or which could be helpful

- work collaboratively with other agencies

- understand the use of any 'aids'

- minimise background noise

- give children plenty of time to process both verbal and visual information

- support interactions by using non-verbal communication and by fully facing the child.

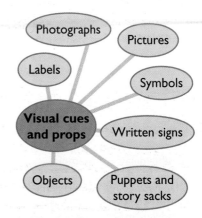

Figure 6.11 Visual cues and props you can use to support children's language needs

Research

Try to talk to a speech therapist about their work with young children.

Research

Use the internet to research causes of hearing loss and find out about strategies for supporting children with hearing loss.

Research

Research the work that the charity 'I Can' does to support children with speech, language and communication needs (SLCN) at www.ican.org.

Working with children with language delay

Children with language delay may have difficulty understanding language (receptive language) or sharing their thoughts and experiences (expressive language). Language development follows the typical sequence of development but more slowly. In order to provide timely and appropriate intervention, it is important to recognise the signs of possible delay. For example:

- babies may not babble as much as expected

- toddlers may be slower to use words

- it may take the child longer to speak in full sentences.

If you are working with children with language delay, you can help by:

- being interested and responsive when children are talking

- role modelling language to describe everyday things

- adding commentary to the things you do together

- using books and songs to introduce new vocabulary

- reinforcing non-verbal language

- always replying – rewarding the child for talking

- giving time and space for a response.

Children with language delay will often develop their communication skills more slowly than others in their peer group

Case study

Mattie is four years old and has just started in the reception class of her local primary school. Her understanding of language and her use of speech do not correspond with her chronological age. No other agencies or professionals are currently supporting Mattie or her family. Rubi is the classroom assistant in Mattie's reception class and she has expressed some concerns about Mattie's speech and language.

1. Describe the first steps you would expect Rubi to take in this situation.

2. Give examples of some specific strategies that might help to support Mattie in the reception class.

3. Discuss how Rubi could involve Mattie's parents in supporting Mattie's speech and language.

Assessment criteria

This table shows you what you must do to achieve a Pass, Merit or Distinction.

Pass	Merit	Distinction
Learning aim A:		
1 Understand the role of communication and speech in children's overall development		
2 Understand how research into language development supports good practice		
3A1. Explain how communication and language development can affect social and emotional development.	3A1.M1 Analyse how communication and language development affect the overall development of children using examples from early years settings.	3A.D1 Evaluate the relative worth of a theory of language development in relation to the overall development of children.
3A2.P2 Explain how theories of language development apply to early years practice.	3A2.M2 Discuss how theories of language development have contributed to effective practice in an early years setting.	
Learning aim B:		
1 Understand the role of the adult in promoting language development in children		
2 Understand how to support children who are developing more than one language		
3 Understand how to support children who have additional language needs		
3B1.P3 Describe how to provide an environment in an early years setting that promotes language development.	3B1.M3 Analyse the role of the adult in providing appropriate environments to support children's language and communication in early years settings, using examples.	3B.D2 Evaluate the extent to which adults in early years settings contribute to the language and communication development of children with varied needs.
3B2.P4 Explain how to support children in an early years setting who are developing more than one language.	3B.M4 Discuss how to plan for and give support to children with varied language and communication needs.	
3B3.P5 Explain how to support children in an early years setting who have additional language needs.		

7 | Supporting children's personal, social and emotional development

Learning aim A1:
Understand how the key person approach supports children's personal, emotional and social development

- ▶ The importance of attachment relationships

- ▶ The role of the key person

Learning aim A2:
Understand how to support transitions

- ▶ Preparing children for transitions

- ▶ Supporting transitions

Learning aim B1:
Understand the role of the adult in supporting children's personal, emotional and social development

- ▶ Developing relationships with children

- ▶ Supporting the development of social skills

Learning aim B2:
Understand the
role of the adult in
supporting children's
positive behaviour

▶ Factors that influence
behaviour

▶ Promoting positive behaviour

The importance of attachment relationships

Attachment theory: influences on current practice

John Bowlby developed attachment theory in the 1950s, and it remains one of the most significant theories about children's emotional development in use today. Attachment theory was further developed through the work of Mary Ainsworth. (For more information about attachment theory, see Unit 1: Child development, page 38.)

Attachment theory underpins many aspects of current early years practice, including the key person approach, settling in procedures and helping children to deal with separation and transitions.

In the 1950s, James and Joyce Robertson studied young children in hospital who were separated from their parents for long periods of time. They observed the children's reactions to being separated from their parents and the negative effect this had on the children's emotional development. The work of Bowlby, Ainsworth and the Robertsons has helped us to understand how important children's relationships with their parents or main carers are, as well as the fundamental significance of these relationships for children's emotional security.

Impact on children's development

A strong attachment relationship provides a firm foundation for all other areas of a child's development. Children who feel secure and confident also develop resilience, which supports their ability to deal with stress and the general ups and downs of life. Secure children are also much more sensitive to the needs and feelings of others and have a greater capacity to show empathy. Some of the main ways that a strong attachment can influence children's all-round development are outlined in Figure 7.1 on page 185.

Securely attached children are more trusting and self-confident in making relationships with others

Key terms

Empathy: the ability to understand and be sensitive to the thoughts and feelings of others

Key person: a practitioner who has a special responsibility for individual children in an early years setting

Resilience: the ability to deal with the ups and downs of life and the capacity to recover from setbacks

Transition: the process of changing from one state or condition to another

Figure 7.1 The impact of a strong attachment relationship on children's all-round development

Area of development	Influence of a strong attachment
Physical	Children are more confident, keen to explore and to take risks.
Cognitive	Children are more self-assured, with better concentration and motivation and have an improved disposition to learn.
Communication	Children have well-developed self-esteem, which supports their confidence in communicating with others.
Emotional	Children are secure and more resilient to stress, with an increased capacity for empathy.
Social	Children are more trusting and self-confident in making relationships with others.

Nurturing children

Research has shown that specific, **nurturing** behaviour can positively influence strong attachment relationships between children and their main carers.

Physical contact is particularly important in supporting strong attachment relationships. Warm, nurturing physical touch is extremely important for children's emotional development. It results in the production of the chemical **dopamine** in the brain, which is an important **neuro-transmitter** associated with feelings of enjoyment and motivation. Babies need to be cuddled, toddlers need physical comfort and even older children need a reassuring pat on the back to help them feel calm and secure at times. Naturally, the physical contact provided needs to be age appropriate and should always be respectful of the individual child.

Figure 7.2 The key features of nurturing behaviour

Warm, nurturing physical touch is extremely important for children's emotional development

🔑 Key terms

Dopamine: a chemical that helps to control emotional responses

Neuro-transmitter: a chemical substance that is released at the end of a nerve fibre and transmits impulses from one nerve cell to another

Nurturing: the act of encouraging, nourishing and caring for someone

❓ Reflect

Reflect on how you feel about physical contact. Are you a 'touchy-feely' kind of person? Or are you protective of your own personal space? What about other members of your family?

185

The role of the key person

The role of the key person in early years settings

It is a requirement of the Statutory Framework for the Early Years Foundation Stage (EYFS), 2012, that all children in registered settings have a key person. The role of a key person is to:

- ensure that every child's care is tailored to meet their individual needs

- help the child become familiar with the setting

- offer a settled relationship for the child

- build a relationship with their parents.

Different settings

The role of a key person will vary slightly in different settings. For example, in a nursery setting, the key person is usually responsible for a small group of key children, meeting their individual needs, monitoring their development and communicating with their parents. With babies, this will usually involve individual personal care such as nappy changing and feeding. In home-based care, a childminder is the key person for all the children and is responsible for building a relationship with each child and their parents.

Some settings offering care for older children, such as out of school clubs, also use a key person approach. This sometimes involves organising the children in 'family groups' of mixed ages and being responsive to the needs of children at different stages of their development.

Strong attachments with the key person

A strong attachment relationship with a key person is very important for children's personal, emotional and social development. It provides the child with a secure base, which helps them to feel safe, builds their self-esteem and creates a defence against stress and trauma.

Some factors that indicate a strong attachment are outlined in Figure 7.3 on page 187.

Your assessment criteria:

Learning aim A1: Understand how the key person approach supports children's personal, emotional and social development

P2 Explain the role of the key person in early years settings in meeting children's personal, emotional and social developmental needs.

P3 Explain how the key person approach can be applied in different types of early years settings.

The key person has a special responsibility for individual children in an early years setting

Research

Research the role of the key person in the EYFS Statutory Framework.

Investigate the key person approach at your placement or work setting. Make a list of the main areas of responsibility for the key person role.

Key term

Secure base: a child's key attachment figure with whom they feel safe

Figure 7.3 Factors that indicate a strong attachment relationship

The child	The key person
'Checks in' frequently with their key person (seeks them out either visually or physically).	Keeps the child 'in mind' (frequently referring to them by name, even when they are not directly engaged, for example: 'I can see you over there, Amy.')
Prefers to be with their key person and will often refuse to go to other practitioners in the setting.	Responds sensitively to the child's demands, using soothing voice tones and nurturing touch
Will appear to be content when they are with their key person and distressed when separated from them.	Regularly engages in playful interactions with the child, using smiles, laughter and warm, physical contact

Relationships with parents and carers

Parents need to know that their child's individual needs will be met. Being able to trust a special person to do this is very important for their own peace of mind and their confidence in the setting. Equally, practitioners need to know about anything that may affect the child during their time at the setting, for example a change in routine or events in the family such as the arrival of a new baby. This helps the key person to support the child and plan relevant activities. For example, a child's key person might help the child adjust to a new baby in the family using activities involving bathing dolls. Communication between parents and the key person is therefore an important two-way process.

Your assessment criteria:

Learning aim A1: Understand how the key person approach supports children's personal, emotional and social development

M1 Analyse how relationships with parents impact on the role of the key person in an early years setting.

Research

In your placement or work setting, observe a key person with one of their key children.

Make notes on what you observe about their relationship and highlight some of the key points that would be important to share with parents or carers.

Case study

Jamilla is four years old and has just started at Apple Tree Nursery. Her family have recently moved into the area from Pakistan. Jamilla and her siblings all speak English, although Urdu is the language spoken in their home. Fiona will be Jamilla's key person in the nursery.

1. Explain why is it important for Fiona to develop a strong attachment relationship with Jamilla.

2. Describe how the attachment relationship with Fiona could help to support Jamilla's personal, emotional and social development.

3. Analyse how Fiona's relationship with Jamilla's parents could impact on her role as Jamilla's key person.

Research

Investigate the Foundation Years website (www.foundationyears.org.uk) and explore the information about effective communication in working with parents.

Communication between parents and the key person is a two-way process

187

Preparing children for transitions

The effects of different transitions

Children will experience many different transitions throughout their lives. Some transitions will affect most children, for example starting school, but other transitions will only affect some children, for example parental divorce or the death of a close family member.

Children and young people respond to transitions in different ways, and this can affect their development both positively and negatively. Transitions can be extremely stressful for children. Some of the negative effects of transitions on children's all-round development can include:

- physical problems, such as food refusal, encopresis or sleep disturbances, including nightmares

- communication problems, such as stuttering or selective mutism

- cognitive problems, such as lack of concentration, learning difficulties or depression

- changes in behaviour, such as becoming withdrawn or clingy, aggressive or attention-seeking

- regression, such as bed wetting or 'baby talk'.

How to prepare children for transitions

When children are facing changes in their lives, they need support to help them prepare for the experience. It is very important for practitioners to discuss transitions with parents beforehand. This helps parents feel more confident and enables them to share important information with practitioners in the setting. It is also less confusing for the child if parents and practitioners are working together to maintain consistency.

Some of the strategies you can use to help to prepare children for transitions are described in Figure 7.4 on page 189.

Some of the strategies you can use to help to prepare children for transitions are described in Figure 7.4 on page 189.

? Reflect

Think about some of the major transitions in your own life. Create a timeline to show when the transitions happened.

Reflect on how these transitions affected you.

Transitions can be extremely stressful for children

Figure 7.4 Strategies to help prepare children for transitions

Strategy	Example
Providing information	Explain what is going to happen and what that might mean for the child. Answer children's questions honestly and acknowledge their feelings. With young children, use simple language and don't provide too much information at once.
Listening	Allow plenty of time for children to process information and to respond. Listen sensitively to children and treat their concerns seriously.
Books and stories	Sharing books with children, for example about the arrival of a new baby or starting school, helps provide reassurance about new situations.
Photographs	Using photographs, for example of their new school or new childminder, helps to familiarise children with changes in their lives.
Imaginary play	Imaginary play can provide opportunities for children to explore different ideas and express their feelings. For example, they could play at doctors and nurses in preparation for going into hospital. Puppets, painting, small world play and sand play can all help children to understand and come to terms with changes in their lives.
Preparatory visits	Visiting a new place in advance of the transition can help some children feel more comfortable with the change. For example, children could visit a new pre-school or a different room within the nursery setting.

Key terms

Encopresis: *the inability to control defecation (bowel movements)*

Regression: *going back to the development or behaviour of an earlier stage*

Selective mutism: *a communication disorder in which a child who is capable of normal speech does not speak in some social situations or to some people*

Reflect

In your placement or work setting, think about how you support children who are experiencing different types of transitions. Design an illustrated leaflet for parents to inform them about strategies they can use to help prepare children for different types of transitions.

Case study

Marek is four years old and lives with his mum, dad and two older sisters. He attends a local pre-school group every morning, where Kay is his key person. Marek enjoys imaginary games and playing outdoors with a small group of friends. Marek's mother is expecting a new baby in two months' time and she is anxious that Marek is well prepared for and supported through this exciting event in their family.

1. Explain why it is important for Marek to be prepared for the arrival of the new baby.

2. Give examples of some of the ways that Kay could help to prepare Marek for the new baby's arrival.

Developing relationships with children

Personal, social and emotional development (PSED)

Personal, social and emotional development (PSED) is one of the three 'prime areas' of the Statutory Framework for the Early Years Foundation Stage (EYFS), 2012. As an early years practitioner, you have a responsibility to support children's wellbeing and help children develop social skills, form positive relationships and develop respect for others.

Theory of mind

Young children are egocentric, which means they are very self-centred with no regard for the thoughts and feelings of other people. Developmentally, young children are incapable of understanding that other people have thoughts and feelings that are different from their own. However, as children mature, they become less egocentric and develop what researchers call 'theory of mind'; that is, the ability to understand that other people have different thoughts, feelings and beliefs from their own. This is a significant stage in children's development, which enables them to interact with and respond more effectively to others and begin to develop empathy.

Positive relationships

A positive relationship is important for children's personal, social and emotional development because it helps children feel valued, builds their self-esteem and promotes a positive outlook.

Theories about the development of self-esteem have been discussed in Unit 1: Child development (see pages 36–38), including the importance of positive relationships between children and practitioners.

There are many different factors involved in developing positive relationships with children. These are summarised in Figure 7.5 on page 193.

Your assessment criteria:

Learning aim B1: Understand the role of the adult in supporting children's personal, emotional and social development

P7 Explain how to develop relationships with children in early years settings to support their personal, social and emotional development.

🔧 **Key term**

Egocentric: *thinking only of oneself without regard for the thoughts or feelings of others*

A positive relationship is important for children's personal, social and emotional development

Figure 7.5 Developing positive relationships with children

Factor	Examples
Communication: using verbal, non-verbal and active listening skills	Comforting a crying baby
	Laughing and singing with a toddler
	Providing reassurance for an anxious pre-school child
Consistency: always responding in a reliable, dependable way	Implementing a consistent key person approach
	Developing and agreeing reliable rules and boundaries
Showing respect and courtesy: keeping professional boundaries and empowering children	Not taking advantage or dominating situations with children
	Sensitivity when carrying out personal care routines
	Offering choices and involving children in decision making
	Respecting children's own views
Valuing and respecting individuality: acknowledging and appreciating individual differences	Being responsive to children's individual likes, dislikes, interests and needs
	Understanding different attitudes and beliefs; welcoming and celebrating diversity
Interactions with parents: to identify children's individual needs and share information	Using positive body language and sensitive communication (particularly with parents whose home language is not English)
	Maintaining strict confidentiality with personal information

Supporting wellbeing and resilience

A sense of wellbeing involves feeling good about yourself and having a positive outlook on life. Resilience is the ability to deal with the ups and downs of life and the capacity to recover from setbacks. It is based on secure early attachments and positive relationships. As a practitioner, you can support the development of wellbeing and resilience with children in many different ways, including the following:

- Praise and encourage children's efforts and achievements.

- Celebrate every small step they take towards independence.

- Include children in decision making and provide choices so they can feel in control.

- Listen to children with respect and interest.

- Respond to children with warmth and patience.

- Respect children's right to have their own opinions.

- Give them opportunities to achieve and to do things they feel proud of.

- Provide children with routines and consistent boundaries so they know what is expected of them.

Professionalism

Although you need to be approachable and playful in your relationships with children, it is extremely important to maintain professional boundaries at all times. This requires a clear understanding about the appropriateness of physical contact and use of language with children, as well as following strict guidelines about sharing information about your personal life. You should always refer to the policies and procedures of your setting and seek advice from your manager if you are not sure.

? Reflect

In your placement or work setting, how well do you:

1. *welcome children into the setting every day?*

2. *use facial expressions and positive body language to show you are listening actively?*

3. *show respect for children's ideas and allow them to make their own decisions?*

Make notes of ways you could improve your own practice.

Case study

Cameron is three years old and today is his first day at nursery. Vikki will be his key person and has visited Cameron at home. She has found out that he enjoys dancing to music and imaginative play with his action figures. Cameron arrives at the nursery with his mother and seems very anxious. He is not crying, but looks very upset and clings to his mother's coat as they enter the nursery. Vikki approaches Cameron and his mother as they enter the room.

1. Describe how Vikki can start to build a positive relationship with Cameron in the nursery.

2. Explain why it is important for Vikki to build and maintain a positive relationship with Cameron and his mother.

It is important to maintain professional boundaries in your relationships with children and their parents

Supporting the development of social skills

Developing social skills

An important part of children's social development is learning to get along with each other. Friendships are very important for children's all-round development and help to support confidence and self-esteem. However, making friends can be a challenging process for young children, who are still very egocentric and focused on their own thoughts and feelings. Young children do not fully understand that other people have thoughts and feelings that are different from their own and therefore find it difficult to show empathy in their relationships with other people.

The role of observation

Regular, ongoing observation can be a very useful tool for practitioners in supporting children to develop personal, emotional and social skills. Figure 7.6 gives some of the ways in which you can use observation.

...monitor changes in children's behaviour (becoming withdrawn, aggressive, attention-seeking, etc.)

...assess children's progress in developing social skills (interactions with others, sharing, cooperating, turn taking, etc.)

Use observation to...

...plan further experiences and activities to support the child's developing social skills

...recognise signs of bullying (isolation, tearfulness, angry outbursts, etc.)

...be aware of developing friendships between children and take note of any difficulties (quarrels, conflict, falling out, etc.

...observe children who are dealing with transitions (separating from their parents, changing rooms within the setting, coping with change within the family, etc.)

Figure 7.6 Uses of observation

(For more information about observation, see Unit 9, pages 222–247.)

Techniques to support a child's personal, emotional and social development

In addition to regular observations, you can support children's personal, emotional and social development in the ways shown in Figure 7.7 on page 196.

Your assessment criteria:

Learning aim B1: Understand the role of the adult in supporting children's personal, emotional and social development

P9 Explain how observations can be used in early years settings to support children to develop social skills.

M3 Assess the success of particular techniques or approaches being used to support a child's personal, social and emotional development in relation to early years practice.

D2 Evaluate the techniques and approaches adults take in supporting a child's personal, social and emotional development in an early years setting.

🔍 Research

In your placement or work setting, observe a child in a group situation with other children. Watch closely how the child communicates, plays and interacts with the other children.

Make a note of some of the child's developing social skills.

Figure 7.7 Supporting children's personal, emotional and social development

Technique	Example
Being a good role model through your own communication and behaviour	Always being polite and respectful
Supporting effective, respectful communication between children	Encouraging friendships and helping to resolve disputes fairly
Promoting the importance of listening to each other	Using a talking stick at group or circle time
Encouraging sensitivity between children and the development of empathy	Acknowledging each other's feelings or using empathy dolls
Encouraging and appreciating individual differences and diversity	Using inclusive practices
Providing consistent rules and boundaries about social interaction and behaviour	Developing policies in the setting
Being vigilant for signs of bullying (e.g. becoming withdrawn, stammering, lacking confidence, becoming distressed and anxious, or aggressive and unreasonable) and helping children to be aware of bullying	Sharing books and stories about bullying
Communicating effectively with parents	Sharing information as a two-way process and valuing parent contributions

Circle time can help to promote the importance of listening to each other

Key terms

Empathy dolls: special dolls used at circle or group time to support children in developing empathy

Talking stick: an object that children hold when it is their turn to speak during circle or group time

Research

Investigate the benefits of circle time for children's developing social skills at www.circle-time.co.uk.

Evaluate the benefits of this approach in supporting children's personal, social and emotional development, and make a note of some of the strategies you could use in your placement or work setting

Research

Investigate the 2010 NSPCC report about bullying at: www.nspcc.org.uk/inform/research/briefings/school_bullying_pdf_wdf73502.pdf

Research some of the books that can help young children become aware of bullying, for example at: www.booktrust.org.uk/books-and-reading/children/booklists/127/

Select one of these books and assess how effective you think it would be in supporting children who are dealing with issues related to bullying.

Keep a list of the titles for future reference.

Factors that influence behaviour

Influences on behaviour

There are many different factors that can influence children's behaviour, some are relatively short-lived, but others can have more serious consequences. As a practitioner, you need to understand some of these influences in order to have realistic expectations and respond appropriately to children's behaviour.

Cultural influences

Different cultural influences can affect children's behaviour, for example in relation to behaviour at mealtimes, social greetings or educational achievement. Equally, there can be different gender expectations regarding behaviour in some cultures, for example where boys are expected to be more dominant.

Social influences

Children's behaviour will also be influenced by social factors, both within and outside the family, including parenting style, family structure, educational experience and the wider community. These factors can include the child's position in the family, the influence of siblings or extended family members, parental role modelling, influences from peers and wider social groups, and social experiences within the child's own community. (For more information about this, see the explanation of Bronfenbrenner's ecological systems theory in Unit 1: Child development, page 39.)

Expectations about age and stage of development

As a practitioner, you need to have a sound understanding of child development in order to have realistic expectations about children's behaviour, particularly the links between children's language, their cognitive development and their behaviour. For example, it would be unrealistic to expect a baby to understand the danger of touching a hot iron or to imply that a toddler is being 'naughty' when they refuse to share their toys. This knowledge and understanding will help you to have realistic expectations and to implement appropriate strategies to support positive behaviour. Some of these important links are explained in Figure 7.8 on page 198.

Your assessment criteria:

Learning aim B2: Understand the role of the adult in supporting children's positive behaviour

P10 Describe different factors that may affect children's behaviour.

? | **Reflect**

Think about the cultural and social influences on your own life and how they have shaped your own behaviour.

Share your experiences with colleagues in your class.

Figure 7.8 Links between age/stage of development and expectations for behaviour

Age/stage of development	Language and cognition	Expectations for behaviour
0–1 year	Pre-linguistic stage: babies cannot express themselves verbally Starting to become mobile and explore their environment, but unsteady and uncoordinated Exploring objects in their mouth Enjoys casting (throwing) toys and objects	Exploring their environment: curious and impulsive, not 'naughty' Babies do not understand the meaning of 'no' or the consequences of their actions Distraction is the best way of dealing with inappropriate behaviour
1–3 years	Becoming more verbal and independent Want to do things for themselves and becoming more independent Limited understanding of right and wrong Very egocentric Much more mobile and curious to explore Attachment relationships very important	Temper tantrums are a normal expression of frustration Understands the word 'no' and more responsive to simple instructions Limited concentration: cannot sit still for long periods of time Difficulties with sharing and cooperating Exploring and experimenting is normal (e.g. 'getting into everything') Will become distressed when separating from main carer
3–5 years	More able to express their needs verbally Have more understanding of right and wrong and the consequences of their actions Thinking is still very concrete and egocentric More physically coordinated and independent	Starting to understand rules and norms of social behaviour, but will still express feelings through actions and behaviour More able to share, cooperate and take turns, but still very self-centred More able to cope with transitions, but may still become distressed when leaving main carer Can do more things independently, e.g. going to the toilet
5–7 years	Can use language to express their feelings Starting to think more logically and understand the consequences of their actions Much more independent and enjoys responsibility	Friendships are very important Enjoy being part of a group Will conform to rules (especially if involved in creating them)

Young children are very egocentric and can have difficulties with sharing

Short-term factors that may affect behaviour

Many factors can influence children's behaviour in the short term. The effects will be short-lived and are not usually serious, but you need to be aware of the signs to recognise. Some of these factors include:

- If children are tired or hungry then they will be lethargic and lack concentration.

- Children who are bored will often exhibit immature or attention-seeking behaviour.

- Illness can affect children's behaviour in a variety of different ways, including being withdrawn or clingy (particularly to their key person) and uncooperative in group situations.

- Children who are being bullied will often seem anxious or distressed, but can also show aggressive behaviour in stressful situations.

The impact of transitions has already been discussed on pages 188–191 of this unit. This process can also cause changes in the child's behaviour, for example becoming withdrawn or clingy, aggressive or attention-seeking. Some children experiencing transitions may also display signs of regression, for example in their play behaviour or by communicating using 'baby talk'.

Long-term factors that may affect behaviour

Some of the long-term factors that may affect behaviour can be more serious and can have long-lasting effects on the child's future health and development. These factors include:

- Chronic illness such as asthma can restrict children's ability to participate in activities and may also result in repeated hospital admissions. This can affect children's ability to develop friendships and interact in social situations, and their behaviour may appear to be withdrawn or isolated and uncooperative in group activities.

- Children who are suffering from anxiety or depression, perhaps as a result of difficult or traumatic family situations, may appear to be apprehensive, fearful or worried, particularly in new or unfamiliar situations.

- Abuse can affect children's behaviour in a wide variety of ways, including a lack of confidence, regression, repetitive, nervous behaviour (e.g. rocking back and forth) and inappropriate aggression. (See also Unit 8: Child protection, page 208.)

Design

Design a web page for an online parenting magazine that describes some of the short-term and long-term factors that can affect children's behaviour.

Discuss

Discuss some of the rules that you think are most important for children's behaviour in an early years setting. Create a list of five 'golden rules' that could be displayed for the children in your placement.

Children suffering from anxiety or depression may appear fearful or worried in new or unfamiliar situations

Promoting positive behaviour

Positive behaviour

Positive behaviour is often described as behaviour that is acceptable or appropriate, which means that it conforms to expected values and beliefs. Young children need to learn how to behave appropriately and they need adult help to do this. Social learning theory emphasises the importance of adult role modelling in promoting positive behaviour with young children, and this has particular significance for practitioners in early years settings. (For more on social learning theory, see Unit 1: Child development, page 30.)

Adult role modelling is very important in promoting positive behaviour with young children

Positive reinforcement

Praise is extremely important in encouraging positive behaviour. When children or young people feel that they have been rewarded for their behaviour, it encourages them to behave in that way again. This is called positive reinforcement and is linked to Skinner's theory of operant conditioning (see Unit 1: Child development, page 30). Rewarding positive behaviour supports children in learning about what is acceptable and appropriate, it helps them to feel valued and builds their self-esteem. The most important reward of all is positive attention from caring adults, and most children will respond extremely well to smiles and encouraging words. There are many other ways to reward positive behaviour, including stickers, star charts and special badges.

Your assessment criteria:

Learning aim B2: Understand the role of the adult in supporting children's positive behaviour

P11 Explain how early years settings support children's positive behaviour at different ages and stages of development.

? | Reflect

Think about your own behaviour with children in your placement or work setting.

- *Are you always polite?*

- *Do you model appropriate language?*

- *How do you model appropriate behaviour for the children in your setting?*

Share your ideas with others in the group and make a list of ways you could improve your own practice.

Star charts can be very effective in rewarding children's positive behaviour

There are both advantages and disadvantages to this method of supporting children's behaviour, as summarised in Figure 7.9.

Figure 7.9 Advantages and disadvantages of operant conditioning and positive reinforcement

Advantages	Disadvantages
Children learn that they receive a reward for acceptable behaviour, so they are more likely to repeat this behaviour.	Rewards need to be immediate, otherwise the child will soon forget the behaviour.
Children learn that unacceptable behaviour does not result in a reward, therefore their unacceptable behaviour diminishes.	It can be more challenging for practitioners to remember to praise a child whose behaviour is acceptable than reacting negatively to a child whose behaviour is unacceptable.
Star charts, stickers and other visual prompts are very useful for promoting positive behaviour with children who have special needs.	Some children can become more focused on getting the reward, rather than on their own behaviour, and may constantly demand rewards. Practitioners need to use rewards with discretion.

Supporting positive behaviour in the setting

As an early years practitioner, you have a very important role in promoting positive behaviour with young children. Some of the ways you can achieve this in the setting include:

- being a good role model: having a positive attitude and demonstrating appropriate behaviour

- giving positive attention: using lots of praise and encouragement and positive reinforcement

- use positive language: tell children what you want them to do, rather than what you don't want them to do (for example, 'Remember that the blocks are for playing with', rather than 'Don't throw the blocks')

- being consistent: providing constant messages and reliable boundaries

- giving choices: supporting children to make their own decisions

- providing stimulating activities: keeping children engaged with a variety of interesting activities to reduce the likelihood of inappropriate behaviour through boredom

- having inclusive behaviour policies: clearly outlining staff roles and responsibilities, as well as expectations for the children

- collaborating with parents and carers about children's behaviour and expectations.

 Key terms

Operant conditioning: the process by which an individual's behaviour is shaped by reinforcement or punishment

Positive reinforcement: a technique that encourages appropriate behaviour by using rewards

Social learning theory: the theory that learning occurs through observation and imitating the behaviour of others

? Reflect

In your own placement or work setting, think about the different ways that you support positive behaviour with children.

Do you use positive reinforcement?

What kind of rewards have you seen being used to promote positive behaviour with children?

How effective do you think these are?

Share your ideas with others in the group.

Strategies to support positive behaviour

Positive reinforcement is a very important approach for supporting behaviour. However, other strategies can also be effective, depending on the age and stage of development of the child. Very young children will often respond to simple distraction, whereas older children may react more positively to reasoning and reflecting on their own behaviour. Some useful strategies are outlined in Figure 7.10.

Q | Research

Investigate the behaviour policies at your placement or work setting. List some of the expectations for children's behaviour and compare your notes with colleagues. Discuss how effective you think behaviour policies are in supporting children's personal, social and emotional development in early years settings.

Figure 7.10 Strategies for supporting positive behaviour

Strategy	Description	Example
Distraction	Helpful with infants and very young children.	Distracting a child's attention away from a potentially dangerous situation and engaging them in a safer, more appropriate activity.
Communication	Eye contact, facial expressions and tone of voice can be very effective in expressing both approval and disapproval of a child's behaviour.	Saying the child's name, with the right verbal intonation, can act as an effective warning, just as a warm smile conveys positive approval.
Boundary setting	Helps children to understand expectations on their behaviour. Involving children in making the rules helps them take more ownership of their behaviour.	Reminding children that 'we don't hurt each other'.
Giving choices	Involving children in making decisions about their own behaviour is empowering. This will vary depending on the child's age and stage of development.	With young children: 'Would you like to put your coat on or me to help you put it on?' This gives the child some degree of choice, although the final result will be the same (the coat is put on). With older children: 'What do you think would be the best way to play together on the bikes?'

Policies and procedures

Policies and procedures provide a framework for setting standards about behaviour. They make sure that everyone knows the rules and is treated fairly. Behaviour policies should include clear guidance about what is expected of children and should be consistent with the accepted values and beliefs of the setting and society as a whole.

Using observations to monitor behaviour

Observing children can help you to develop a more complete picture of children's behaviour in order to understand it. It can be a useful tool for both supporting positive behaviour and dealing with inappropriate behaviour. For example, ongoing observation of children's play behaviour

Your assessment criteria:

Learning aim B2: Understand the role of the adult in supporting children's positive behaviour

P11 Explain how early years settings support children's positive behaviour at different ages and stages of development.

D2 Evaluate the techniques and approaches adults take in supporting a child's personal, social and emotional development in an early years setting.

can help you to identify children's social skills in playing cooperatively together or squabbling over toys or play materials.

Equally, observation can help to identify the trigger for inappropriate behaviour, such as snatching toys or refusing to share, and this can help you to implement an appropriate strategy. A useful method for recording observations on children's behaviour is time sampling. This method prompts practitioners to observe and record children's behaviour at regular intervals over a period of time and can be particularly useful for highlighting behaviour patterns or difficulties. For example, you could use this method to observe a child's behaviour during settling in or to monitor social interactions when a child is playing in a group. Figure 7.11 provides an example of a time sampling recording sheet.

Figure 7.11 Observation recording sheet: time sample

Name of child:	Date of birth:	
Key person:	Observation completed by:	
Date of observation:	Time sample observation: Behaviour	
Time	**Behaviour observed**	**Comments**
9am		
9.15am		
9.30am		
9.45am		
10am		
Notes for supporting behaviour:		
Comment from parent:		

Your assessment criteria:

Learning aim B2: Understand the role of the adult in supporting children's positive behaviour

M4 Analyse the extent to which observation can be used in an early years setting to support children's positive behaviour, using examples.

Key terms

Time sampling: a method of observation that involves recording observations at specific intervals over a set period of time

Trigger: a stimulus that causes something to happen

Research

In your placement or work setting, carry out a time sample observation to record a child's behaviour over a period of time. Share your findings with your placement or workplace supervisor and discuss how your observations could be used to develop a strategy for monitoring the child's behaviour.

Research

Investigate the 'Development Matters' sections of the Early Years Foundation Stage at www.education.gov.uk and explore the prime area of PSED. Use this information to write a brief report about the importance of observation in supporting children's positive behaviour in early years settings.

Observation can help to identify the trigger for children's inappropriate behaviour

Assessment criteria

This table shows you what you must do to achieve a Pass, Merit or Distinction.

	Pass	Merit	Distinction
Learning aim A: **1 Understand how the key person approach supports children's personal, emotional and social development** **2 Understand how to support transitions**			
	3A1.P1 Explain the importance of attachment to children's development.	3A1.M1 Analyse how relationships with parents impact on the role of the key person in an early years setting.	3A.D1 Evaluate the extent to which a key person in an early years setting can support children through transitions.
	3A1.P2 Explain the role of the key person in early years settings in meeting children's personal, emotional and social development needs.		
	3A1.P3 Explain how the key person approach can be applied in different types of early years settings.		
	3A2.P4 Explain how children may be affected by different transitions.	3A2.M2 Assess the contribution of adults in early years settings in supporting children through different transitions.	
	3A2.P5 Explain how to prepare children in early years settings for different transitions.		
	3A2.P6 Describe how an early years setting manages the settling in process for different transitions.		

	Pass	Merit	Distinction

Learning aim B:
1   **Understand the role of the adult in supporting children's personal, emotional and social development**
2   **Understand the role of the adult in supporting children's positive behaviour**

3B1.P7 Explain how to develop relationships with children in early years settings to support their personal, social and emotional development.	3B1.M3 Assess the success of particular techniques or approaches being used to support a child's personal, social and emotional development in relation to early years practice.	3B.D2 Evaluate the techniques and approaches adults take in supporting a child's personal, social and emotional development in an early years setting.
3B1.P8 Explain ways of supporting children's wellbeing and resilience in early years settings.		
3B1.P9 Explain how observations can be used in early years settings to support children to develop social skills.		
3B2.P10 Describe different factors that may affect children's behaviour.	3B2.M4 Analyse the extent to which observation can be used in an early years setting to support children's positive behaviour, using examples.	
3B2.P11 Explain how early years settings support children's positive behaviour at different ages and stages of development.		

8 | Child protection

Learning aim A:
Understand types and indicators of child abuse

▶ Types and indicators of abuse

▶ The effects of abuse on children

Learning aim B:
Understand how to respond appropriately to concerns that a child has been abused

▶ Responding to concerns

▶ Reporting and recording procedures

▶ Best practice in child protection

Learning aim C:
Understand the
role of the effective
practitioner in child
protection

▶ Duty of care and empowering
children

9 | Observation, assessment and planning for play and development

Learning aim A:
Understand the importance of observation and assessment in work with children

▸ The importance of observing and assessing

▸ Using observations and involving parents

Learning aim B:
Be able to present records of observations of children

▸ Methods of recording observations

▸ Selecting appropriate recording methods

Learning aim C1:
Be able to draw valid conclusions from observations of children

▸ Using information from observations

▸ Relating observations to theories of play

**Learning aim C2:
Understand the
importance of
planning to support
children's play and
development**

▶ The importance of planning

▶ The planning process

**Learning aim D:
Be able to create,
implement and
review activity plans
for children**

▶ Creating and reviewing plans
to support children's play
and development

The importance of observing and assessing

Observation

The time that children spend in pre-schools, day nurseries or with childminders has to be carefully planned according to children's interests and stages of development in order for them to develop well. Traditionally, this planning has been solely in the hands of the practitioners, but modern thinking involves the children themselves to a much greater extent. The only way that practitioners can find out about children's interests and stages of development is through good-quality observation of what the children are doing.

What to observe

In order to know as much about children as possible, you will need to watch them carefully and listen to what they are saying. This is a very important part of your work as an early years practitioner and is a skill that takes practice to perfect. Figure 9.1 shows some of the things you learn about children through careful observation.

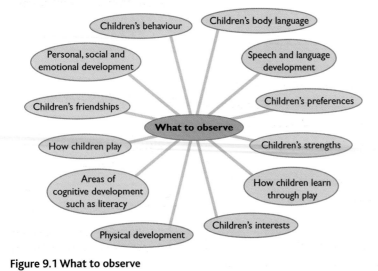

Figure 9.1 What to observe

 Key term

Observation: closely watching and listening to children

By watching children play on their own or with others, you can learn about their likes and dislikes and their stages of development

Why observation is necessary

The main reason for observing children is to get to know them so that you can plan a stimulating environment in which they can develop. This includes finding out about children's individual needs and interests, what they are capable of doing and their stage of development. The main reasons why practitioners observe and assess children's development are summarised in Figure 9.2.

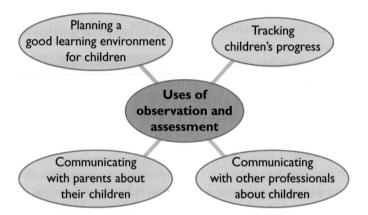

Figure 9.2 The reasons for observing and assessing children

Knowing children well

As an early years practitioner, there are four main methods you can use to help you get to know children well:

- watching children closely

- listening to what children are saying to each other

- asking children questions and listening to their answers

- asking children's parents about what their children do at home.

Assessment

Good observation is only part of the process that leads to planning appropriate activities for children and sharing information with parents and other professionals involved with the child. Practitioners need to record their observations and then compare them with the expected development for the child's age group. This is called assessment. It is only when this has taken place that practitioners can determine children's stage of development and plan what they might be learning next.

There are two main types of assessment: formative assessment and summative assessment. These are described on page 226.

These are described on page 226.

Children learn from each other

Relating observations to theories of play

Theories about play and development

Current knowledge of best practice in early years education has developed over many years. Relating theory to practice will give you a greater understanding of how the children you care for are developing and learning. One of the best times to do this is when you are observing children in play. It is useful to relate what you see and hear to these theories to help you understand and plan for the ways in which children learn. As well as increasing your own understanding, it will help you to plan further activities for the children.

Figure 9.12 summarises the theories of how children learn by playing. (For more information about theories of children's play and development, see Unit 1, pages 10–55, and Unit 2, pages 56–83.)

Children learn most when they become interested enough to 'wallow' in their play. – Tina Bruce

Children learn from 'role modelling' by those they respect. – Albert Bandura

Children learn by watching and imitating adults and more mature peers. – Lev Vygotsky

Children learn by a mixture of experimenting on their own and adult input. – Janet Moyles

How children learn by playing

Children learn when adults 'scaffold' their next steps. – Jerome Bruner

Children learn ways to behave through 'positive reinforcement'. – Burrhus Skinner

Children demonstrate particular favourite ways of playing called 'schemas'. – Jean Piaget and Chris Athey

Figure 9.12 Theories of how children learn and develop by playing

Your assessment criteria:

Learning aim C1: Be able to draw valid conclusions from observations of children

P5 Describe the observed behaviour making use of relevant theories of development.

M4 Discuss the relevance of theories of development to what has been observed about a child's progress.

D2 Evaluate how observation, assessment and planning have contributed to the observed child's progress in relation to theories of development.

🔍 Research

With permission, observe a group of children when they are playing together. Try to find out how the children are learning new things. Is it by watching someone else, by experimenting with new ideas, by becoming engrossed in what they are doing, or by receiving praise and encouragement from others? Try to link these observations to the theorists mentioned on this page.

Observing children will help you to plan further activities for them

Research

- Choose one of the theorists from the table below and research their approach.

Theorist	Key words for children's learning
Albert Bandura	The importance of role models
Jerome Bruner	Scaffolding
Tina Bruce	Wallowing in play
Janet Moyles	The play spiral
Jean Piaget	The importance of practical experience and schemas
Burrhus Skinner	Positive reinforcement
Lev Vygotsky	The importance of adults and more mature peers

- Make a handout or class presentation to summarise your chosen approach for the rest of your group.

- Copy the table and make a mix and match game to test your knowledge of which theory matches which theorist.

When you are observing children in the setting, it is useful to relate what you see and hear to theories about play and development

Case study

Background

Dean is two years old and he attends Rainbow House nursery two days a week. He plays alongside the others in the group quite normally for his age and is developing good language skills. He lacks some confidence in physical development, particularly gross motor skills. Dean always greets his mum or grandma with pleasure at the end of the day.

A recent observation of Dean in the setting

Dean has just woken up and is sitting at the table to have a drink. When offered milk or water, Dean asks for 'Mulk' and takes the jug with milk in it, trying to pour it into a cup. An adult steadies his hand and he pours enough to fill the cup and the adult says, 'Good pouring, Dean'. He says, 'My mulk' when about to drink from the cup. Afterwards, Dean gets down from the table and chooses to play at the sandpit with two other children. He picks up two beakers and tries to pour sand from one to the other but the sand falls between the two cups. He tries to take a cup from another child, saying 'Want cup', but the other child does not give it to him. With adult help, Dean manages to pour sand from a shovel into the cup until it is full, then he pours the sand into the sand pit.

1. Identify the different ways that Dean is learning through his play.

2. Describe the different theories about children's learning that relate to this observation.

3. Evaluate the importance of understanding the theoretical background when observing children's development.

Pouring their own milk develops children's physical skills and encourages them to become independent

The importance of planning

Using observations to inform planning

You can use information from observations and your knowledge about children's interests and stages of development to plan exciting and stimulating activities for children's play, learning and development. (For more information about the different types of play activities, see Unit 2: Play in early years settings, pages 56–83.) An example of using a child's interests to plan activites is given in Figure 9.13.

The role of planning

The Statutory Framework for the Early Years Foundation Stage (2012) in England states, 'Each area of learning and development must be implemented through planned, purposeful play and through a mix of adult-led and child-initiated activity.' Even more importantly, it also states, 'Practitioners must respond to each child's emerging needs and interests, guiding their development through warm, positive interaction.' It is important to note that spontaneous reactions to children's needs are considered as important as any pre-planned activity, and they should often take precedence.

Without good planning, there is no guarantee that children will make progress towards achieving positive outcomes. In the worst cases, there would be no structure and no idea of what children need or like. Planning will take different forms in different settings, but a good setting will make sure that the environment and activities are planned according to observations of children's interests and stages of development.

Design

Using the records of observations you made of children in your setting earlier in this unit and the early years guidance for your country, plan activities to help the children in your setting make progress in their play and development.

Figure 9.13 Using observations to inform planning

Observations of Philip 36 months old	Ideas from Philip and his family	Suggested ideas for Philip's learning and development
Philip has enjoyed being in the book corner more recently, sometimes with an adult's input but at other times on his own. Philip was telling a practitioner about his recent visit to the zoo.	Philip told me that he has a new puppy at home and that it is making a mess everywhere. He said he was a bit frightened of it.	• Provide books for Philip about different types of animals to capture his interest and to develop his knowledge. • Provide stories for Philip about children who have pets at home. • Encourage Philip to represent his puppy, e.g. drawing, play dough, modelling. • Talk to Philip about how his puppy will grow up, get older and be better behaved. • Talk to Philip's mum about his fear and agree on a strategy to reduce it.

Planning does not need to be overly time-consuming or based on lots of paperwork. Many settings use ongoing planning formats in order to respond to the individual needs of the children. The key functions of planning are summarised in Figure 9.14.

A good setting environment will be organised in line with the children's interests and stages of development

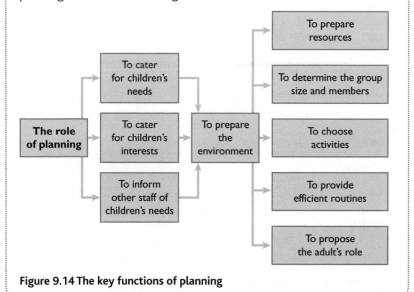

Figure 9.14 The key functions of planning

Case study

Ellie is a four-year-old girl who attends a day nursery every morning. Her parents have decided to defer Ellie's entry to school this year, as she is quite immature socially, still playing alongside other children and initiating conversation only with adults.

Ellie's parents do not agree with the day nursery's practice of planning adult-led activities every moment of the day, as they want their daughter to become independent in her choice of activities and be less directed by adults.

1. Assess the advantages and disadvantages of planning adult-led activities for Ellie's play, learning and development.

2. Describe some of the ways that child-initiated activities could provide opportunities for the nursery staff to observe Ellie and plan for her further progress.

 Discuss

Using the early years guidance for your country, discuss with your group what it says about:

- *the need for planning*
- *the difference between adult-led and child-initiated activities.*

Discuss possible difficulties in planning for:

- *a large group of children*
- *other members of staff*
- *child-initiated activities.*

The planning process

Starting to plan

Before starting to make any plans for the children, you need to ask yourself the following questions.

- Have I carried out observations of the child?
- Have I assessed the child's stage of development?
- Have I identified the child's likes, dislikes or special interests?
- Have I consulted the relevant early years guidance?
- Have I taken the child's own ideas into account?
- Have I consulted and involved the child's parents?

Planning methods

Effective planning should contain as much information as possible based on the questions above. Your plans should be written down using the agreed format for your setting, so they can be evaluated and reviewed. However, things happen spontaneously and so you will need to update your plans regularly in order to respond to children's individual interests and needs. Planning methods vary in different settings, but some examples are outlined in Figure 9.15 (below and on page 243).

Your assessment criteria:

Learning aim C2: Understand the importance of planning to support children's play and development

P7 Explain the role of planning in early years settings to support children's play and development.

? Reflect

Using the list on the left, revisit an observation of a child before you plan an activity for them. How could you enhance the information you have about the child before you plan for them?

Figure 9.15 Planning formats that you might come across in your setting

Type of planning format	Time range	Advantages	Disadvantages
Short term	An hour to a week	Reactive to children's needs Can make sure resources are available	It can be difficult to inform all staff of the plans Too much writing if plans change too often
Medium term	Half termly provision	Plans can develop in detail	Can lose track of children's stages of development Can lose track of children's interests
Long term	Yearly provision	Can incorporate annual events	Can lose track of children's stage of development Can lose track of children's interests Can become repetitive and out of date
Continuous	Every day provision	Provides variety in activities that are available all the time, e.g. sand and water play can include different toys to play with from one day to the next	Becomes redundant if not conscientiously completed and updated

Type of planning format	Time range	Advantages	Disadvantages
Spontaneous	Immediate/ ongoing	Completely reactive to child's interests and stage of development	All resources need to be available all the time Recording what has been done might be overlooked

Contents of plans

Whichever type of planning is used in your setting, the plans might contain the following information:

- date
- member of staff responsible
- activity
- resources
- which children will benefit
- group size
- links to the early years guidance
- space for evaluation.

Reviewing plans

Settings need to evaluate the effectiveness of the plans frequently, so that systems can be altered if necessary. As well as daily evaluation of individual plans, there should also be some overall evaluation of plans to make sure that certain factors are being covered. These include:

- The plans cover all children's needs, stages of development and interests over time.
- The plans are linked to the early years guidance of the country.
- The plans cover all areas of learning (in England, emphasis is placed on the prime areas of learning for the youngest children).
- There are adequate resources.
- There is a large enough variety of activities and group sizes.
- The plans are responsive to the children's ideas and stages of development.

Key term

Prime areas of learning: the three areas of learning that are 'particularly crucial for igniting children's curiosity and enthusiasm for learning...form relationships and thrive.' (EYFS 2012) In England they are PSED, CL and PD.

When you are making plans for the children for the first time, it's a good idea to ask a more experienced practitioner for advice and suggestions

Design

Using one of the observations you have made on children in your work for this unit, make some suggestions for activities that will promote the child's learning and development. If possible, try the activities with the child and reflect on how appropriate and successful your planning was.

Case study

Sumitra is a newly qualified practitioner working with two-year-old children in a pre-school. She has been named as the key person for three children in the group and has started to record observations of their learning and development. Sumitra has found it difficult to write about one of the children, as he has not settled. As she is a new practitioner, Sumitra's supervisor has asked to see her records.

1. Explain the key information that should be identified in Sumitra's observation records.
2. Suggest some of the ways that Sumitra's observation records of her three key children could be used.

Creating and reviewing plans to support children's play and development

Preparing activities for children

Having learned how to observe, record and assess children's play and development carefully and accurately, you are now ready to prepare activities for children using all the information you have gathered. You may not always get this right at first, but when you and your supervisor review and reflect on the plans, you will have the opportunity to make amendments.

Competent planning should always be flexible, so that you can make changes if the child wants to develop other aspects of their learning further. Remember to use the early years guidance when preparing your activities and to take on board the child's own views if they are old enough and willing to contribute to the process. You can also observe children's non-verbal communication about whether or not they are interested in an activity. Taking note of the child's voice in this way is often overlooked.

The activity plan in Figure 9.16 (below and on page 245) is based on the observation record of Ebony in Figure 9.11 on page 236. This plan provides several ideas for Ebony's development. If the plan is used well, the link between observing and planning becomes well established.

Your assessment criteria:

Learning aim D: Be able to create, implement and review activity plans for children

P8 Present appropriate activity plans for an observed child to support their play and development linked to the relevant curriculum.

P9 Review the effectiveness of the planning methods, plans and implemented activities in supporting the child's play and development.

M6 Analyse the extent to which the plans and implemented activities supported the child's play and development.

D3 Evaluate own practice in the planning, creation and implementation of activities in terms of how it supported the child's play and development.

Figure 9.16 An example of an activity plan

Child's name: Ebony Williams	Date: 25.07.12 (Observation dated 24.07.12)	Context: Ebony has shown an interest in animals and in reading books – she is able to predict sounds associated with the stories. She has also started to use the musical instruments.		
Rationale: Ebony has shown repeated interest in books and a new interest in making sounds with instruments. These two interests can be combined to develop Ebony's listening, attention and expression.				
Possible planned activities	Reading stories with repetitive refrains such as 'The Gingerbread Man'	Singing lots of nursery rhymes Encourage Ebony to listen to the rhymes	Provide musical instruments and emphasise the beat in more songs	Use music with a good beat to encourage Ebony to dance rhythmically
Resources required	Quiet corner, books	No resources required	Musical instruments	Dance music CD, CD player
Group size	Alone with Ebony or with a small group of children	Alone with Ebony or with a small group of children	Small or large group of children	Large group of children

Early years guidance links (Development Matters in the EYFS, England)	Pages 15 'Listens with interest to the noises adults make when they read stories.' Page 16 'Joins in with repeated refrains and anticipates key events and phrases in rhymes and stories.'	Page 15 'Shows interest in play with sounds, songs and rhymes.' Page 43 'Joins in singing favourite songs.'	Page 43 'Creates sounds by banging, shaking, tapping or blowing.'	Page 44 'Beginning to move rhythmically.'
Health and safety	None specifically	None specifically	No small parts or damaged instruments	Sufficient space
Evaluation/ observation				

Implementing plans

Once you have made your plans, you need to implement them promptly, otherwise they become redundant. However, this is sometimes not straightforward. Flexibility and good preparation are very important and, if your prepared plans do not engage the children, you will need to adapt them accordingly. Similarly, the needs and stages of development will differ between the children in any group, so you should be ready to differentiate the activity in order to meet the needs of all the children.

Reviewing and evaluating plans

Good planning formats will allow space for comments, so that you can keep a record of how the activities went for future reference. Plans can be reviewed both from the child's and the practitioner's point of view. The following questions will help you to evaluate your plans:

- Did the children enjoy themselves?
- Were the children engaged? Could I have engaged them more?
- Did the children learn what I intended them to learn?
- Did they learn anything extra at the same time?
- Did I prepare well enough?
- Did I choose the right/sufficient resources?
- Was the group size right?
- Did the activity suit the children's needs and interests?
- Did the activity support the children's play and development?

Design

Using the same format as the table in Figure 9.16, devise some other suitable activities for Ebony, perhaps exploring her interest in animals.

Key term

Differentiate: *adapt an activity so that it can meet the differing developmental needs of all the children in a group*

Research

With permission, complete and record an observation of a child using your own or the setting's format. Use the observation to plan an activity for the child to extend their learning. Complete the activity then review and evaluate the child's learning.

Assessment criteria

This table shows you what you must do to achieve a Pass, Merit or Distinction.

	Pass	Merit	Distinction
Learning aim A: Understand the importance of observation and assessment in work with children			
	3A.P1 Explain the importance of observing and assessing children in early years settings.	3A.M1 Analyse issues to be considered when observing and assessing children in early years settings.	
Learning aim B: Be able to present records of observations of children			
	3B.P2 Justify the selection of a set of observational methods to observe the development of a child in an early years setting, giving valid reasons for your choice.	3B.M2 Analyse the appropriateness of selected observational methods for assessing the play and development of a child in an early years setting.	3B.D1 Evaluate the validity of the selected observational methods used, making recommendations to address potential weaknesses.
	3B.P3 Present full and effective records to show that valid observation of a child's play and development has taken place.		

	Pass	Merit	Distinction

Learning aim C:

1 Be able to draw valid conclusions from observations of children

2 Understand the importance of planning to support children's play and development

Pass	Merit	Distinction
3C1.P4 Describe how observations of the child's stages of development and interests can be used to contribute to planning to meet play and development needs.	3C.M3 Analyse how observation and assessment have contributed to planning to meet a child's play and development needs.	3C.D2 Evaluate how observation, assessment and planning have contributed to the observed child's progress in relation to theories of development.
3C1.P5 Describe the observed behaviour making use of relevant theories of development.	3C.M4 Discuss the relevance of theories of development to what has been observed about a child's progress.	
3C1.P6 Select, giving valid reasons, different play activities and strategies which could enable the observed child to progress further.	3C.M5 Assess different play activities and strategies which could enable the observed child to progress further.	
3C2.P7 Explain the role of planning in early years settings to support children's play and development.		

Learning aim D: Be able to create, implement and review activity plans for children

Pass	Merit	Distinction
3D.P8 Present appropriate activity plans for an observed child to support their play and development linked to the relevant curriculum.	3D.M6 Analyse the extent to which the plans and implemented activities supported the child's play and development.	3D.D3 Evaluate own practice in the planning, creation and implementation of activities in terms of how it supported the child's play and development.
3D.P9 Review the effectiveness of the planning methods, plans and implemented activities in supporting the child's play and development.		

10 | Diversity, equality and inclusion in the early years

Learning aim A:
Understand the importance of valuing diversity and countering discrimination in early years practice

- Principles of equality and diversity
- Current anti-discriminatory legislation
- Barriers to implementing equality and challenging discriminatory practice

Learning aim B:
Understand inclusive practice in early years settings

- The benefits of inclusive practice
- Strategies for inclusive practice
- The role of adults in promoting inclusive practice

Learning aim C: Understand how children with additional needs may be supported in early years practice

▶ Regulatory frameworks to support children with additional needs

▶ Planning to meet children's individual needs

▶ Additional help and support

Principles of equality and diversity

Definitions

Diversity and equality

Diversity refers to the differences between people. One of the most obvious changes in the population of Britain over recent years is the greater number of inhabitants of different nationalities. Less obvious though is the fact that people within all groups display enormous diversity. Practitioners should not assume that all children are the same, as this is simply not true. What is important is to give all children the same opportunity to enjoy themselves, to make progress and to learn to recognise, respect and value their differences. By doing this, you are providing children with equality of opportunity. Figure 10.1 gives some definitions of diversity that you will need to understand as a practitioner.

Inclusion

In order to enable all children to enjoy learning and to achieve their potential, you will need to make sure that you meet the needs of all the children you care for. Inclusion involves adapting the environment and the activities to cater for all children's needs, whatever they are.

Key terms

Discrimination: *unequal treatment of a person or group based on prejudice*

Diversity: *differences between people*

Equality: *having the same opportunity to enjoy and achieve*

Inclusion: *ensuring all children can access and benefit from the provision*

Prejudice: *a pre-judgement of someone without making certain of the facts*

Stereotyping: *making assumptions about an individual because of certain characteristics*

Inter-group diversity Differences **between** different groups of people	Practitioners must recognise, respect and value the differences between people at all levels.	**Intra-group diversity** Differences **within** different groups of people

Figure 10.1: Definitions of diversity

All children are different, mentally as well as physically

 Discuss

Make a list of minority groups in your school or college community. Discuss in your group whether you have experienced or witnessed any stereotyping or prejudice within the community. Consider your placement setting and discuss whether you are aware of any overt or private stereotyping or prejudice.

Stereotyping

Stereotyping involves making incorrect assumptions that all people from a certain group will behave in the same way or believe in the same things. For example, many people think that black children are good at sports or that children in a wheelchair cannot be active. The danger of stereotyping is that it might lead to a practitioner being unable to recognise the individual needs and abilities of a child.

Children's learning needs will differ as much as their dietary needs

Prejudice

Prejudice in early years settings involves making assumptions about children who belong to a particular group, which can lead to treating them differently.

? | **Reflect**

Reflect on the local community you live in, or your college or school community. Think about how stereotyping can influence how one group of people think about another group. What equality issues are important in your own community?

Discrimination

As a result of stereotyping and prejudice, some children from minority groups or with different needs, might not receive equality of opportunity to take part and achieve their potential. This is discrimination, which is completely unacceptable in early years settings and is illegal.

Vulnerable groups

In theory, any group of people could face prejudice and discrimination. In practice, however, it is usually people from minority groups that are the most vulnerable. In early years settings, there are a number of groups of children who might suffer and Figure 10.2 gives some examples.

Key terms

Vulnerable: more likely to be harmed either mentally or physically

Special educational needs (SEN): physical, sensory, communication, behavioural or learning disability that causes a child to need additional help in order to access or achieve learning

Figure 10.2 Differences that might cause individuals to suffer from prejudice in an early years setting

Difference	How children might suffer from prejudice
Culture	Opinions about gypsy, Roma and traveller people, for example, could affect practitioners' attitudes towards them.
Gender	Boys and girls might not be given the same opportunities.
Age	Older and younger children may be treated differently without good reason.
Socio-economic	Poorer children might not be given the same opportunities as richer children, or assumptions might be made about their abilities.
Appearance	Dirty and poorly clothed children might receive less preferential treatment.
Religion	Children from minority religious groups may not feel welcome.
Special educational needs (SEN)	Practitioners might not cater for the extra learning needs of children with SEN.
Disability	Children with disabilities might not be given opportunities to take part in activities.
Race	Children from different races might be treated disrespectfully.

Do all children in your setting feel included in all types of play?

Reflect

Choose one or two of the categories in Figure 10.2. Reflect on how practitioners who have a prejudice regarding that group might result in children in that group suffering from discrimination. Give some examples for each of the categories you have chosen.

The negative effects of discrimination on children's life chances

Prejudice and discrimination in early years settings are extremely harmful to the children who experience them. The reasons for this are summarised in Figure 10.3.

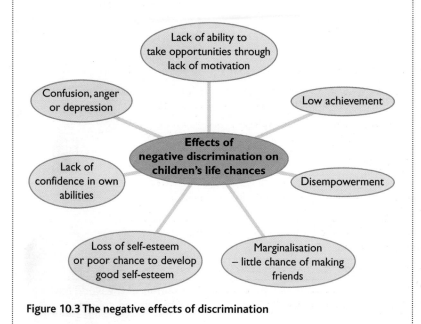

Figure 10.3 **The negative effects of discrimination**

Some children who wear different clothing from others might not feel part of the group

Case study

Old Oak nursery is preparing to celebrate different foods from the ethnic groups in the setting. All parents have been asked to contribute a savory and a sweet dish for a lunchtime feast for parents, staff and children. The majority of parents are happy to do so, and the children are excited about having their parents in to eat lunch with them.

A visitor to the setting from the local authority overheard two staff talking together saying how they weren't going to try any of the Indian food as it will be too spicy. They also commented that they wouldn't be eating any food from one parent because 'she is too dirty'.

1. Explain why these comments could be regarded as harmful in an early years setting.

2. Describe how the visitor should respond in this situation.

Discuss

Look at the statements below and discuss with your group the negative effects such attitudes might have on young children.

'Boys don't play with dolls.'

'Grow up – you're too big to cry now.'

'Look at that silly hat he's wearing.'

'He's smelly.'

'She always eats smelly food.'

Can you add any others from your own experiences?

Current anti-discriminatory legislation

Relevant legislation

The problems that people experience because of discrimination are so serious that **legislation** is now in place to prevent prejudice and discrimination from destroying children's life chances. All children's services have to comply with legislation and **codes of practice** to promote equality and inclusion.

There are several major pieces of legislation that promote inclusion and these are listed in Figure 10.4. Until 2010, there was a large range of equality and anti-discrimination laws in the UK. These were brought together and simplified in one act called the Equality Act 2010. The key principle of this law is that all people must be treated fairly and with equal respect.

Your assessment criteria:

Learning aim A: Understand the importance of valuing diversity and countering discrimination in early years practice

P1 Outline the role of legislation and regulatory frameworks to counter discrimination and ensure equality in early years practice.

Figure 10.4 Legislation introduced to protect people from discrimination

Legislation	What does it say?
United Nations Convention on the Rights of the Child 1989	An international agreement, to which nearly all countries of the world have signed up, describing the need for equality for all children and defining children's rights
Human Rights Act 1998	Informed much of the legislation about discrimination that followed in later acts
Every Child Matters 2003	Identified five positive outcomes for all children and what service providers must provide to ensure these outcomes are achieved; they are: Being Healthy, Staying Safe, Enjoying and Achieving, Making a Positive Contribution and Achieving Economic Wellbeing
Children Act 2004	Strengthened the child's legal rights and made it compulsory to involve children in decisions affecting them; made the ideas from Every Child Matters a legal requirement
Childcare Act 2006	Focused on reducing inequalities between children
Equality Act 2010	Brought together as many as ten or more previous acts to ensure that it is illegal to treat people unequally

How does legislation affect early years practitioners?

Figure 10.5 on page 255 summarises how the relevant legislation affects the work of practitioners in early years settings. All practitioners need to understand and respect the aims of a fair and just society to provide equal opportunities for all its members.

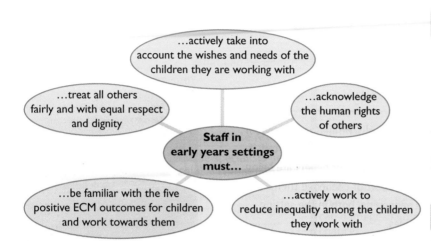

Figure 10.5 Legal responsibilities of staff in early years settings for inclusive practice

Code of practice: *guidance and standards for good practice*

Every Child Matters (ECM): *a government document produced in 2003 that outlines five positive outcomes for children*

Legislation: *the laws of the land*

 Design

Working in a small group, choose one of the acts from Figure 10.4 and research it on the internet. Make an illustrated poster and a handout summarising what your chosen act says. Display your poster for the other groups to share and learn from and give them a copy of your handout.

Case study

Little Fish is a small pre-school in a rural part of the UK, where there is a predominantly white population of children from farming backgrounds, some rich and some poor. The practitioners at Little Fish are also all white and have lived in the community all their lives.

Recently, several Romany children from three families have joined the pre-school. Their parents have come to the village to work with the summer fair.

The children do not speak very much and their demanding behaviour is taking much of the practitioners' time while they settle in. Some of the other parents and one member of staff have started to complain about the Romany children attending the setting.

1. Analyse some of the issues relating to stereotyping, prejudice and discrimination in this scenario.

2. Discuss how the manager of Little Fish pre-school should deal with this situation.

3. Reflect on why diversity should be valued in early years settings.

All children have the right to be respected

All people have the right to be respected

 Design

Using your notes from the Reflect activity on page 251, design a handout for fellow students in school or college to highlight the importance of addressing the equality needs you have identified.

The benefits of inclusive practice

Inclusive practice

In order to counteract inequality and promote a fair environment for all children, you must be committed to and demonstrate inclusive practice. This commitment comes from an inner belief that all children must have equal opportunities to make progress and reach their full potential.

It is important to remember that being inclusive does not mean treating all children in the same way, as individual children will have different needs. What it means is that you show all children equal respect and give them an equal chance to make progress, according to their individual needs.

Figure 10.7 describes some ways in which the setting and practitioners themselves can promote inclusion for all children.

Your assessment criteria:

Learning aim B: Understand inclusive practice in early years settings

P4 Explain the benefits of inclusive practice in early years settings for children and families.

P5 Examine different strategies an early years setting can use to demonstrate inclusive practice.

Key term

Inclusive practice: accepting all children and catering for their needs

Figure 10.7 Inclusive practice

How the setting can be inclusive	How you can be inclusive as a practitioner
Display a wide variety of images of different families and children.	Smile and welcome all families and children.
Ensure that all important information and messages are translated into relevant languages, if necessary.	Ask all families and children about their customs and lifestyle.
Contact parents in a variety of ways. Ask parents which method they would prefer: text, email, telephone, newsletter, etc.	Observe every child in your key person group as carefully as the others.
Have resources such as books and home corner tools or dressing up clothes that reflect a variety of cultures and special educational needs (SEN).	Learn a few important words and phrases in other relevant languages.
Provide some dual language labels for common words in other relevant languages.	Research information about people and cultures that you are not sure about.
Celebrate special days from all cultures represented in the setting.	Avoid stereotyping or prejudging people.
Provide opportunities for parents from different groups to share their culture with the children.	Challenge yourself and others if you suspect there is any discrimination.
Have effective SEN policies and procedures.	Reflect on your own thinking and be a good role model for children and other practitioners.

Benefits for children

Just as discriminatory behaviour can damage children's life chances, inclusive practice will have the opposite effect and will benefit children's life chances.

The principles of inclusive practice are designed to benefit children by:

- ensuring that all children feel equally valued

- developing children's confidence about their own identity

- ensuring that all children's individual needs are considered equally important and catered for

- giving all children a feeling of safety and belonging (see Maslow's hierarchy of needs in Unit 1: Child development, page 86)

- giving all children an equal opportunity to take part in activities

- giving all children an equal chance to learn and develop.

If we can do this for all young children, then later in life the children will take pride in themselves and contribute to society positively, achieve success in some way, and have high aspirations for themselves and for their own children.

Research

Investigate more about inclusive early years practice (for example, at: www.inclusive-solutions.com/earlyyears.asp or: https://www.pre-school.org.uk/practitioners/inclusion). Evaluate how your work setting or placement prepares the environment to promote equality and inclusion. Make a 'Good Inclusive Practice' guide for practitioners.

Inclusive practice will benefit children's life chances

Discuss

Working with a partner, look at the pictures of apples and cats. Make lists of how the apples and the cats are similar and dissimilar to each other. Now do the same for yourself and your partner. Discuss the process of noticing similarities and differences.

Reflect

Reflect on times when you have felt left out of a group. How did you feel? Have you ever excluded anyone from joining a group you have been part of?

Strategies for inclusive practice

Strategies for the setting

There must be a commitment in every early years setting to provide an inclusive environment and there must be strong policies and procedures in place to promote this. Settings can actively encourage inclusive practice by using some of the strategies described below.

Staff meetings

It is good practice to have inclusive practice as a fixed agenda item for staff meetings. This gives all staff the opportunity to discuss issues as they arise and to share best practice.

Staff discipline

Owners and managers must investigate, challenge and correct any sign of prejudice or discrimination that occur within the setting, whether they have witnessed it themselves or members of staff have reported it to them.

Resources

All children in the setting must feel equally welcome, so it is important to have a variety of resources reflecting other lifestyles and special educational needs. These resources can include books, role play equipment and dressing up clothes. Displaying images of people from different cultures and words in other languages welcomes people from other nationalities, particularly if their first language is not English.

It is important to have a range of resources for children that reflect their varied cultural and ethnic backgrounds

Your assessment criteria:

Learning aim B: Understand inclusive practice in early years settings

P5 Examine different strategies an early years setting can use to demonstrate inclusive practice.

M2 Analyse the extent to which different strategies contribute to effective inclusive practice in early years settings.

Key term

Strategies: *plans of action or policy designed to achieve an aim*

 ### Design

Find out about the cultural habits of some of the children in your setting. These need not be from another culture, as habits within cultures differ as well. Then design some A4 cards to be used to decorate the role-play corner when it is being used as a shop or a café.

Visitors

Parents of all children at the setting can be invited into the setting to talk to the children about their jobs, their culture, clothes, music or hobbies. This provides a rich opportunity for the staff and children to learn about different cultures and individual differences.

Allowing a flexible routine

Young children feel happier if there is a routine in their day. However, different children will need different amounts of time to complete activities. For example, introducing a rolling snack time instead of a fixed snack time will allow some children to become engrossed in something for longer or for hungry children to eat earlier. (For more on routines for learning and development, see Unit 3: Meeting children's physical development, physical care and health needs, pages 84–113.)

Providing flexible access for parents

Sometimes parents' work schedules involve unsociable hours, for example if they work in a supermarket or hospital. This might mean that they cannot make appointments or attend special events at the setting. Allowing parents to make appointments at their convenience will contribute to the general philosophy of inclusive practice in the setting. Similarly, providing information in a range of different formats (such as email or on a website) may also help parents stay in touch more easily.

Practitioners must provide extra input for children with English as an additional language

Case study

Melanie is a room supervisor at the Purple Rabbit pre-school, which operates from a community hall near the hospital in a large town. Many of the children who attend Purple Rabbit are from immigrant families from a range of nationalities, but most speak Malayalam or Polish, and many of the parents work at the hospital. Many of the children who arrive at the setting do not speak much English.

Imogen is a practitioner at the Purple Rabbit pre-school and she overhears Melanie saying, 'Well, I don't know why we have to accept all these children who don't speak English – how are we supposed to talk to them?'

1. Outline the reasons why this comment is unacceptable.

2. Explain what Imogen should do in this situation.

3. Analyse the importance of positive strategies in contributing to effective inclusive practice in early years settings.

Q | Research

Using the internet, find some traditional songs from the cultures of the children in your setting. Include songs for all nationalities of children. Learn them then try to sing them with some four-year-old children in the setting.

The role of adults in promoting inclusive practice

Sensitive adults

Even with the strongest equality policies and procedures in a setting, discriminatory attitudes from staff can be very damaging to children and their families. Practitioners need to be sensitive and respectful to every child's needs, values and ways of life, otherwise an inclusive philosophy cannot exist. There are many ways in which you can make sure that you are positively promoting inclusive practice.

Actively role model a delight in diversity

Some children will live in families where discriminatory comments are made and accepted. Early years practitioners need to actively celebrate the differences between different people, taking delight in diversity and emphasising how rich a culture we live in. This might mean deliberately introducing activities and resources to promote and help the children understand a positive attitude to diversity. This will enable all children to feel valued and respected.

Asking parents to provide photos from home will help you to learn more about the families' and children's lives

Sensitive and prompt responses

If you observe children regularly, you will get to know them well. Getting to know the parents is also important so that you can build up a picture of the child's home life and culture.

Your assessment criteria:

Learning aim B: Understand inclusive practice in early years settings

P6 Explain how adults in an early years setting can help children to value and respect others.

M3 Analyse the extent to which inclusive practice used by adults in early years settings could impact on outcomes for children.

D1 Evaluate the extent to which reflection on own attitudes and practice might contribute to the promotion of diversity, equality and inclusion in early years practice.

Design

In your group, make a collage of as many different types of faces as you can find from magazines and newspapers. Write a slogan to help convince people that prejudice and discrimination can damage children's life chances.

? Reflect

Privately reflect on your own feelings towards different groups of children. List any prejudices that you can detect in your attitudes or practice, and make a decision to try to eliminate them from your work with children.

Children's moods and non-verbal communication will also tell you a lot about the children. One of the best ways of promoting inclusive practice is to make sure that you seek, observe and record a child's interests, stages of development and feelings, so that you can respond to them quickly with appropriate plans, activities and resources. (For more on observing and planning, see Unit 9: Observation, assessment and planning for play and development, pages 222–247.)

Differentiating activities

All children need some new, fun activities to stimulate them, and children with learning difficulties, in particular, will need well-planned activities that cater for their individual needs. Experienced practitioners can see immediately if a child is finding something too hard or too easy and will be able to adapt the activity to suit all children's needs. This is called differentiation and is a skill that you will develop over time.

The environment will also need adapting for some children. For example, can a child in a wheelchair access the painting easels? Inclusive practice means making sure all children can access all resources and activities.

When working with a group of children, you must be alert to their differing needs and respond to them individually

Reflective practice

You will improve your practice if you develop the habit of reflecting on your daily interactions with children, asking yourself whether or not you have done the best for all children at all times. (For more on reflective practice, see Unit 11: Reflecting on own early years practice, pages 272–289.)

Key term

Differentiation: *making an activity easier or harder or adapting it in some other way to cater for individual children's needs*

A selection of different dressing up clothes can help children to respect other traditions

Reflect

Think about your last day in the setting. How did you try to find out about a child's likes and dislikes or about their background? How might you follow this up next time you are in the setting?

Regulatory frameworks to support children with additional needs

Regulations

Each country within the UK has its own legislation and codes of practice, which provide guidance on how to cater for children with special educational needs (SEN). As a practitioner, you need to understand the process that applies in the country you work in.

In the 1970s, Mary Warnock developed the first Code of Practice for children with SEN in England, and the same guidance is still in use. The first major act, the Special Educational Needs and Disability Act 2001, ensured that children with SEN would not be substantially disadvantaged. Currently, the government's green paper 'Support and aspiration: A new approach to special educational needs and disability' (July 2012) proposes major changes. All discrimination acts have been amalgamated into the Equality Act 2010, which makes all forms of discrimination illegal.

The Early Years Foundation Stage 2012 in England requires settings to have and to implement a policy to promote equality of opportunity for children in their care, 'including support for children with SEN or disabilities'.

Meeting individual needs

As with all children, you need to observe children with SEN carefully and discuss their needs with their parents in order to know how best to respond to them. Children with SEN sometimes also need input from other specialists. Sometimes practitioners can provide the support that a child needs, while at other times there will be a need for external support.

Observing and recording the development of children with SEN is crucial so that small steps for their development can be carefully planned

Your assessment criteria:

Learning aim C: Understand how children with additional needs may be supported in early years practice

P7 Outline the framework and requirements to provide support for children with additional needs in early years settings.

🔍 Research

1. *Study a copy of the relevant SEN Code of Practice for the country you live in. Look for definitions of SEN. Research and summarise the system in your country.*

2. *Investigate the government's green paper on special educational needs and disability (July 2012). Find out about the changes that it proposes.*

Different models of disability

There are two common views of disability that influence early years practice. The medical model is less popular now and the social model is more widely accepted. There is a move away from thinking that children must fit in with society and more towards the society enabling each child to achieve.

The medical model

In this model, a child's disability is considered to be a medical problem that can be solved in order to make the child better. This view puts a lot of emphasis on what the child cannot do and tries to fill the gaps.

The social model

The social model views disability as being caused by the people and the environment in which a child lives. It proposes that society is responsible for providing a suitable environment for the child to develop. This model concentrates on what the child can do in order to enable development.

How models of disability affect practice

The medical model in practice means that practitioners expect the child with a disability to fit into the setting, sometimes missing out on opportunities because they cannot take part. The social model in practice means that practitioners adapt the environment and activities so that all children can take part at their own level.

Your assessment criteria:

Learning aim C: Understand how children with additional needs may be supported in early years practice

P8   Describe the influence of models of disability on early years practice.

Practitioners must believe that all children are capable of learning and developing

Case study

Anna is three years old and has cerebral palsy. Anna cannot walk unaided but enjoys trying to do so. The nursery that Anna attends has a chair with a table and a support for Anna's back and neck for her use in the nursery. She has better use of her arms and hands and loves using play dough, which is very good for developing the strength in her fingers.

When the other children go outside to play, Anna is taken out in her chair but just sits and watches the other children. The manager has overhead some of the staff saying that they can't help Anna outside, as 'there is nothing we can do to make her legs better'.

1. Identify which model of disability is influencing the staff's attitude in this scenario.

2. Describe how the staff could improve their practice to meet Anna's needs outdoors.

? | Reflect

Think about your setting. How would it be suitable for a child with a visual impairment? How might you change the environment, and how would you assess the child's needs?

Planning to meet children's individual needs

Supporting children

All children need careful support to make sure they make progress. However, children with SEN will require extra support. Figure 10.8 below shows some of the ways that children with SEN can be supported.

Your assessment criteria:

Learning aim C: Understand how children with additional needs may be supported in early years practice

M4 Discuss ways in which children with additional needs can be supported in early years settings.

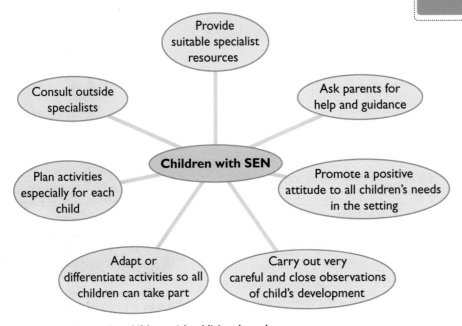

Figure 10.8 Supporting children with additional needs

Individualised planning

If you are observing children carefully and monitoring their progress regularly, you will become aware when a child is consistently showing signs of delay in any area of learning. It is your responsibility to speak with other members of staff and the special educational needs coordinator (SENCo) to seek advice.

Currently, once a delay is identified, practitioners should complete an individual education plan (IEP), together with the parents. A typical format is shown in Figure 10.9, although this will vary in different settings. The emphasis is on breaking tasks into very small steps, which the staff help the child to achieve using specific resources or language. Frequent reviews are held with the parents to monitor progress and to update the IEP as required.

Q | Research

In your placement, find out about the provision for children with SEN. Ask for permission to observe a child with SEN. Record what you have seen, assess the child's stage of development and plan some activities for them to focus on their stages of development and interests.

Figure 10.9 An example of an individual education plan (IEP)

Individual Education Plan No. 1						
Child's name Philippe Avenall		Child's DOB and age 30/01/10 – 3 years 6 months		IEP completed by: CPS and Mrs Avenall (Philippe's mother)		
Area of concern: Philippe's expressive language – he is achieving at the 24 month level						
Today's date	Observation	Target(s)	What resources?	Parents' comments		When to be reviewed
01/08/12	Philippe is just starting to put two words together when he speaks. He recently said 'Mummy gone' and 'Want banana'. He has started talking more when there is food on the table at snack and lunch times.	• To develop P's vocabulary • P will learn 5 new words to communicate his needs when eating. • P will learn 2 new two-word expressions to communicate his needs.	• Staff to introduce food nouns to Philippe, especially at snack time and lunchtime. • Staff to share books with foods in them with P. • Staff to repeat P's expressions and add extra words to model good language use.	I will try to maintain this practice at home, although in the evening P is tired and doesn't talk much at tea time.		1 month's time – 01/09/12

The government green paper on special educational needs and disability (see page 264) proposes the introduction of a single assessment process and a combined Education, Health and Care plan, which will focus on providing integrated support and improving outcomes for children and their families. (See also Unit 13, page 328.)

IEPs should by written by the child's key person and the parents together

Research

Ask your supervisor if you can see an IEP in your work setting or placement. Compare and contrast it to the one shown in Figure 10.9 and note the differences. Could either of them be improved?

The role of the special educational needs coordinator (SENCo)

This role requires an experienced practitioner who is interested in children with SEN. In most early years settings, there is one SENCo who will have received training in their role and how to develop provision for children with SEN in their setting. In larger settings, it is good practice to share the SENCo's workload between two or more staff. The SENCo does not have to be an expert in the individual needs of all the children with SEN, but they do have to be well organised and good at communicating with others. Figure 10.10 outlines some of the different aspects that are typically part of the SENCo's role.

Your assessment criteria:

Learning aim C: Understand how children with additional needs may be supported in early years practice

P9 Explain the role of the appointed special educational needs coordinator in an early years setting.

D2 Evaluate the role of adults in effective planning to support children with additional needs in early years settings.

Figure 10.10 The role of the SENCo in an early years setting

Case study

Aleisha is the key person for Oliver, a two-year-old boy who has just started at Acton Hill Day Nursery. Through observing and assessing Oliver as part of the Early Years Foundation Stage (EYFS) two-year-old progress check, Aleisha has noticed that his language development does not seem to be following the expected pattern. Aleisha discusses her findings with the setting's SENCo and the speech and language therapist.

1. Outline the role and responsibilities of the SENCo in working with Oliver and his parents.

2. Outline the role and responsibilities of the speech and language therapist in this situation.

3. Explain how an Individual Education Plan (IEP) could help to identify Oliver's particular needs.

Research

Arrange a meeting with the SENCo in your work setting or placement and ask them about their role. Write an account of their role and evaluate the importance of careful planning for children with SEN.

Reflect on your own interest in children with SEN. Do you think you could be a SENCo?

Additional help and support

Specialist support

One of the responsibilities of the SENCo is to signpost children and families to other specialists who can provide help and support. Figure 10.11 shows a few of the specialists you might work with to provide support for children with SEN.

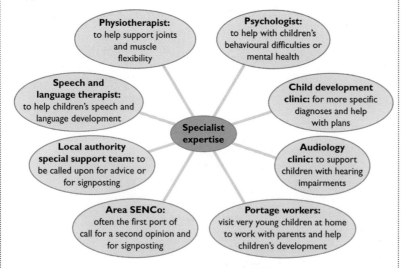

Figure 10.11 Specialist support for children with SEN

Physiotherapist: to help support joints and muscle flexibility

Psychologist: to help with children's behavioural difficulties or mental health

Speech and language therapist: to help children's speech and language development

Child development clinic: for more specific diagnoses and help with plans

Specialist expertise

Local authority special support team: to be called upon for advice or for signposting

Audiology clinic: to support children with hearing impairments

Area SENCo: often the first port of call for a second opinion and for signposting

Portage workers: visit very young children at home to work with parents and help children's development

Working with parents

It is very important for practitioners and SENCos to work closely with the child's parents to build up a complete picture of the child's development and individual needs.

Sometimes a parent might approach the key person in the setting to express a worry or concern about their child's development. On other occasions, the key person may have a concern that the parents do not agree with. Following up on this requires patience, confidence and determination in order to serve the child's best interests. Keeping careful records of observations will help to support decision making about extra help that might be required. You can only write an IEP for a child if the child's parent has given permission and parents should always be present when the IEP is written or reviewed.

Your assessment criteria:

Learning aim C: Understand how children with additional needs may be supported in early years practice

P9 Explain the role of the appointed special educational needs coordinator in an early years setting.

M4 Discuss ways in which children with additional needs can be supported in early years settings.

D2 Evaluate the role of adults in effective planning to support children with additional needs in early years settings.

Discuss

Choose one of the specialist job roles above and research what the job involves. Make an illustrated poster and handout so all class members can benefit from your research.

Talking to parents about their child's special educational needs requires sensitivity and good understanding of the child's identified needs

Assessment criteria

This table shows you what you must do to achieve a Pass, Merit or Distinction.

Pass	Merit	Distinction
Learning aim A: Understand the importance of valuing diversity and countering discrimination in early years practice		
3A.P1 Outline the role of legislation and regulatory frameworks to counter discrimination and ensure equality in early years practice.	3A.M1 Discuss the potential barriers to implementing equality in an early years setting.	
3A.P2 Explain why diversity should be valued in early years settings.		
3A.P3 Explain why discriminatory behaviour and attitudes should be challenged in early years settings.		
Learning aim B: Understand inclusive practice in early years settings		
3B.P4 Explain the benefits of inclusive practice in early years settings for children and families.	3B.M2 Analyse the extent to which different strategies contribute to effective inclusive practice in early years settings.	3B.D1 Evaluate the extent to which reflection on own attitudes and practice might contribute to the promotion of diversity, equality and inclusion in early years practice.
3B.P5 Examine different strategies an early years setting can use to demonstrate inclusive practice.	3B.M3 Analyse the extent to which inclusive practice used by adults in early years settings could impact on outcomes for children.	
3B.P6 Explain how adults in an early years setting can help children to value and respect others.		

Pass	Merit	Distinction
Learning aim C: Understand how children with additional needs may be supported in early years practice		
3C.P7 Outline the framework and requirements to provide support for children with additional needs in early years settings.	3C.M4 Discuss ways in which children with additional needs can be supported in early years settings.	3C.D2 Evaluate the role of adults in effective planning to support children with additional needs in early years settings.
3C.P8 Describe the influence of models of disability on early years practice.		
3C.P9 Explain the role of the appointed special educational needs coordinator in an early years setting.		

11 | Reflecting on own early years practice

Learning aim A:
Understand the purpose of reflective practice in relation to work with children

▶ What is reflective practice?

▶ Why is reflective practice important?

Learning aim B:
Be able to reflect on own early years practice with children aged birth up to 8 years in relation to promoting children's communication and language

▶ Reflecting on how you promote children's communication and language

▶ Gathering evidence of promoting communication and language

▶ The skill of self-evaluation

Learning aim C:
Understand how to develop own early years practice with children aged birth up to 8 years to promote children's communication and language through planning

▶ Planning for improvement

How does reflective practice happen?

Reflective practice should be part of your everyday activities. You will need to practise and develop the skill of thinking about what you are doing both 'in action' (as you are doing it) and 'on action' (after you have done it), as described in Figure 11.3.

Reflective practice

'in action' | 'on action'

This involves thinking 'as you go'. While you are engaged in a task, you are able to observe and think about how well, or not, you are performing and about how successful you are in relation to the child's learning and development.

- It is important to be **analytical** and **objective**.
- Does the evidence support the judgement?

This involves thinking 'after the event'. When you have completed a task, you are able to think back to a child's reactions, a colleague's comments and your own observations about how successful you were in relation to the child's learning and development.

Figure 11.3 Reflective practice 'in action' and 'on action'

Key terms

Analytical: able to examine something in detail to find out its meaning or features

Objective: based on the facts, not influenced by feelings or emotions

Reflect

Think about an activity that you have recently planned and implemented in your placement or work setting. Carry out this reflective exercise:

- *Describe what you did.*

- *How did you do it?*

- *How successful do you think you were?*

- *What did you learn from it?*

Has this exercise helped you identify any strengths or areas for development? Do you need more knowledge or information about a particular subject?

Case study

Aisha has been the leader of the toddler room for three years and is keen to improve her professional skills. She keeps herself updated by attending regular early years network meetings. She is also subscribed to popular professional journals and often joins online discussions.

Aisha has recently joined an online early years forum and has become interested in the topic of 'reflective practice'. She has asked other contributors the following questions:

- What exactly is 'reflective practice'?

- What difference will it make to the children and me?

- Does anyone have any ideas about how I can make it part of my daily practice?

How would you answer Aisha's questions if you were also taking part in the forum?

You will need to think about what you are doing both while you are doing it and after you have done it

Why is reflective practice important?

The importance of reflective practice

The quality of any setting is hugely dependent on the quality of its workforce. Practitioners who are actively and deeply committed to the learning, development and care experiences they provide for children are more likely to be reflective, and reflective practitioners are more likely to care about the experiences they provide for young children. This creates a virtuous spiral of quality improvement, as illustrated in Figure 11.4.

How can reflective practice contribute to work with children in early years settings?

Skilled and effective practitioners working in early years settings know that it is important to engage in reflective practice for the following reasons.

1. Effective early learning experiences can only happen when practitioners reflect on what they know about, for example:

    *   each unique child's needs and stages of development

    *   the appropriate next steps for that child

    *   the child's current interests and preoccupations

    *   the time, space and other resources (including human resources) they have available.

2. Personal and professional development happens when practitioners are self-aware, proactive and analytical. Developing the ability to recognise your strengths and the areas that need to be developed further will put you in the position of decision maker: choosing to make change happen rather than having it imposed on you.

3. Continuous quality improvement is dependent on reflection and self-evaluation. A willingness and ability to monitor, evaluate and revise practice is crucial in order to make changes. It follows that staff must welcome change in order to facilitate continuous improvement. The two processes (engaging in reflection/self-evaluation and embracing/welcoming change) go hand in hand with one another.

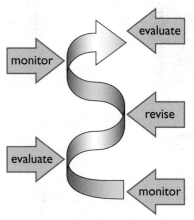

Figure 11.4 The virtuous spiral of quality improvement

Key terms

Facilitate: to make it easier for something to happen to

Preoccupation: something that completely takes over our mind and thoughts

Proactive: taking positive action to get something done

Virtuous spiral: the process of improving our care for children through reflective practice

4. Staff teams achieve shared understandings through professional dialogue and collaboration. The practitioners within a setting need to hold regular conversations to question and challenge professional perspectives, behaviours, attitudes and approaches. This will support the team to reach a consensus on what is best for young children and how they want to achieve it. Reflective practitioners will then be able to:

- critically question their own practice and that of their colleagues

- make informed judgements and decisions

- engage in constructive dialogue.

Reflective practice is also important because you are more likely to develop a deep and holistic understanding of your work through reflecting critically on everything you do. Figure 11.5 demonstrates the cycle of stages in reflective practices that bring out improved outcomes for children.

Key terms

Consensus: an agreement reached by the whole group

Constructive: helping to improve

Research

Next time you are on placement, ask your supervisor about the setting's approach to reflective practice.

- *Is it something the staff do consciously?*

- *Are the staff team encouraged to do this (either as individuals or the whole team)?*

- *Do they record their reflections?*

- *Can they give you any examples of how their reflections have changed or improved their practice?*

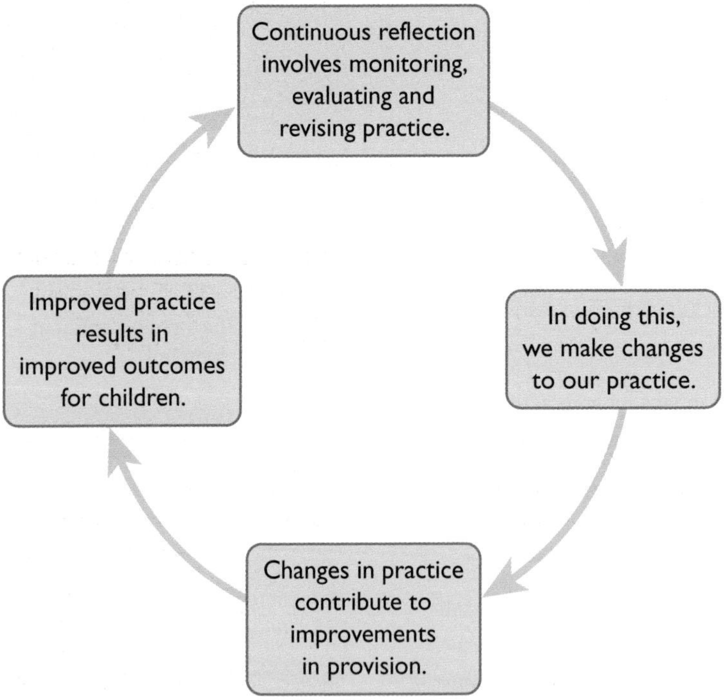

Figure 11.5 Reflective practice cycle for improving outcomes for children

Continuous reflection involves monitoring, evaluating and revising practice.

In doing this, we make changes to our practice.

Changes in practice contribute to improvements in provision.

Improved practice results in improved outcomes for children.

The impact of reflective practice in improving communication and language in children

You will remember from Unit 6 that language and communication are at the heart of children's learning and development, as they have strong links to both social and cognitive development. It is essential that you continuously monitor and evaluate your professional practices to ensure effective support for children in this 'prime area of learning' (EYFS, 2012).

Reflecting on how well you support children's communication and language involves:

1. **monitoring**

    - how you make assessments

    - the quality of your interactions

    - the range of activities and resources you provide

    - the quality of the environment

2. **revising and enhancing**

    - your knowledge base – about children, development and language acquisition

    - your observation, assessment and planning skills

    - the creation of communication-friendly environments

3. **evaluating against best practice.**

Your assessment criteria:

Learning aim A: Understand the purpose of reflective practice in relation to work with children

D1 Evaluate the impact of reflective practice in improving communication and language in children.

Reflecting on how you support children's communication and language will improve your professional practice

Case study

Bryony is on the senior management team at Highfields Nursery. She wants to introduce the staff to the idea of reflective practice and to set up regular sessions at staff meetings for this to happen. (Currently, staff meetings are more about business or organisational matters.) Bryony is planning to give a short presentation at the next meeting and is making herself some notes.

Describe the key points that Bryony must remember about:

- what reflective practice is

- why reflective practice is important

- how reflective practice can help to develop practice in early years settings.

? Reflect

Use the points made opposite to monitor the quality of what is currently happening in your setting to improve children's language and communication. Think about how, in your opinion, this practice could be revised and enhanced. What, on the evidence you have available, would your evaluation be measured against what you know of best practice?

Making the link from theory to professional development

Knowing about and understanding the different theories of language development and reflecting on how they influence practice can contribute to the continuous development of professional behaviours. Figure 11.7 gives some examples of how you can translate theory into practice. (For more information about the theories of language development, see Unit 1, pages 10–55, and Unit 6, pages 162–181.)

Figure 11.7 Putting theories about language and communication development into practice

Theorist	Theory	Influence on professional practice
Noam Chomsky	Nativist perspective	Having high expectations of babies and young children results in lots of encouragement for them to communicate and use language.
B.F. Skinner	Behaviourist theory (sometimes also known as Learning theory)	Reinforcing and rewarding the elements of children's language and communication that sound most like speech
Jerome Bruner	Interactionist theory	Consciously providing social, collaborative opportunities for children to engage with more skilled language users
Roger Brown	Mean length of utterances (MLU)	Having realistic expectations about the levels of language children are likely to use

Planning realistic 'next steps' when thinking about future developments |

Your assessment criteria:

Learning aim B: Be able to reflect on own early years practice with children aged birth up to 8 years in relation to promoting children's communication and language

P2 Select evidence about own practice with children aged birth up to 8 years to promote their communication and language.

M2 Compare own practice with current best practice in promoting children's communication and language development with children aged birth up to 8 years using evidence.

D2 Assess effectiveness of own practice, recommending areas for development.

Talking with your supervisor about professional practices will help you evaluate your own practice

Gathering information together

A useful and systematic way of gathering information together is to produce a learning journal (sometimes also known as a learning log or professional development diary). You can write this by hand on paper or produce and store it electronically.

What is important is that your learning journal will provide a focal point for your reflective thinking. A learning journal can demonstrate your increasing understanding of the professional perspectives, behaviours, attitudes and approaches you are developing. It provides an opportunity to communicate your thoughts about how and why you did what you did and what you now think about it.

The assessment for this unit requires you to 'collect, analyse and evaluate evidence about how you work with children to promote their communication and language'. Producing a learning journal (which you can build on as you move from placement to placement) is an ideal way of gathering evidence for this.

A learning journal is one way of gathering together evidence of how you work with children

🔍 Research

In your placement or work setting, ask your supervisor if you can observe one of the practitioners during an activity that has been planned to support children's language and communication. Explain that you need to observe how practitioners:

- *encourage babies or young children to use language*

- *reinforce and reward children's use of language*

- *support children to learn from more advanced language users*

- *demonstrate realistic expectations of children.*

When you have observed the activity, evaluate how effective the practitioner was, giving examples of the successful strategies you observed.

Case study

At The Bridge Nursery School, the staff team have decided to reflect on how well they support children to develop their communication and language skills. The questions they are asking themselves are:

- How do we know which children may need additional support with their communication and language skills?

- How often do staff/child interactions promote high-quality communication?

- Whereabouts in our setting does good communication happen and why?

- Which activities (or which times of the day) result in good communication?

1. Describe how the staff members could gather evidence and information for this reflective task.

2. Discuss some of the ways that the staff team could use this information to improve their practice in the setting.

Figure 11.10 Examples of influences on professional practice

Factor	Example of personal influence	Example of professional impact
Family values	'If I was naughty when I was little, I used to get a smack off my mum. It never did me any harm.'	'I know I can't smack children, but I don't know the best way to help them learn how to behave.'
Cultural norms and experiences	'When I was growing up, I was told it was rude to look directly at the adults who were talking to me, so when I was listening I used to glance down at the floor.'	'Now I find it difficult to fully look at someone talking to me, particularly if they are older than me or in a senior position. I've been told I need to maintain eye contact to show people I'm really listening to them.'
Community influences	'In my community, children are expected to be very respectful of adults and not answer back.'	'If children ignore me or answer back when I'm talking to them, I get really cross and I know I blame the parents for not teaching them proper manners.'
Education	'When I was at school, I found reading and writing really difficult.'	'I won't ever offer to read – even when the children ask me to read them a story.'

Case study

Nadine works in a private day nursery and is preparing for a meeting with her line manager. The nursery has been taking part in a local project called 'Talk Time' (looking at ways to support children's speech and language) and Nadine has been the lead practitioner. Her line manager is very keen to hear about this project and has asked Nadine to report on her involvement and the impact of the project on the setting.

1. Discuss some of the ways that Nadine could evaluate her own practice.

2. Describe some of the barriers she might experience in doing this.

3. Explain why she might find it difficult to be objective in providing a report for her manager.

? Reflect

Reflect on the influences that have made you the person you are now. Make a table like the one in Figure 11.10 and write in your own examples.

Constructive feedback from colleagues can support your self-evaluation and professional development

Reflecting on how you have become 'you', can be part of the self-evaluation process

Planning for improvement

Identifying areas for improvement

Successful monitoring and evaluation of your own performance will ensure that you can identify the areas of practice you want to develop. In the case of children's communication and language, you may identify:

- the quality of the interactions you have with children

- your playfulness when you engage with children

- your ability to provide play opportunities that support and enhance opportunities for language and communication

- a combination of elements from each of these areas.

You can then ask the questions shown in Figure 11.11 (below and on page 288).

Figure 11.11 Questions to help you plan for improvement

Where can I go to get help with this?
There are lots of ways of getting help.
• **Talk to people** – tutors, placement supervisor, other members of the staff team while you are on placement, other students. (All of these will have ideas about developing your practice.)
• **Read** – textbooks, professional journals, articles in magazines, course notes and handouts.
• **Attend training courses** – organised by the staff team at your placement, the local authority, private training providers or the local college.
• **Use the internet** – there is a wealth of online material, including online training courses, DVD clips, articles from journals and professional websites.

How do I make an action plan?
Action planning will help you to focus your ideas and decide what steps you need to take to achieve your goals. It involves SMART objective setting. Make sure the things you want to achieve (your objectives) are:

Specific:	'I will use the Every Child a Talker (ECaT) child monitoring tool...'
Measurable:	'...to assess six children.'
Achievable:	'I have the skills to do it.'
Realistic:	'I have the resources to do it '
Time bound:	'I will do this before the 31st January.'

Your learning criteria:

Learning aim C: Understand how to develop own early years practice with children aged birth up to 8 years to promote children's communication and language through planning

P4 Create appropriate plans to develop own practice with children aged birth up to 8 years to promote communication and language.

M3 Analyse the value of planning to develop own practice in promoting children's communication and language.

D3 Evaluate the contribution of continuous reflection in the development of own practice in promoting children's communication and language.

 Key term

Every Child a Talker (ECaT): a government-sponsored project to improve children's speech and language, which concluded in 2011

Figure 11.11 Questions to help you plan for improvement (*continued*)

The resulting SMART objective from this example would be: 'to use the ECaT monitoring tool to assess the language and communication skills of six key children before the 31st January'.

This is a SMART objective because it:

- clearly identifies the assessment tool being used (specific), how many children are to be assessed (measurable), and the timescale in which the assessments will happen (time bound)

- is both something that is possible to do (achievable) and likely to happen (realistic).

The objective would not be SMART if it simply said: 'to assess the children's language and communication skills'.

How do I know what my priorities should be?

Think about the tasks most likely to move you towards your goals. Which tasks will have the biggest impact on your practice and on the children?

How can I be sure that I am making progress?

If you have written SMART objectives on your action plan, you will be making progress. You can then check your progress by making sure you carry out what you planned in your SMART objective.

How can I be sure that my practice is changing?

To check that your practice is changing, go back to the reflective practice cycle (Figure 11.1 on page 274):

- **Monitor** what you are now doing now, taking note of what others say.

- **Evaluate** yourself against best practice, what you were doing before and the impact you are having.

- **Revise** your thinking and practice if there are changes you want to make.

? | **Reflect**

Think about how you could improve the quality of your interactions with young children. Write yourself some SMART objectives. Show them to your placement supervisor and ask for regular feedback on the progress you make over the next few weeks. At the same time make sure you critically evaluate your own performance so that you can discuss your progress.

Case study

Trevor has a Level 3 qualification in Children's Care, Learning and Development, which he completed four years ago. He now works in a Children's Centre. He has recently developed a particular interest in how children acquire language and communication and what he can do to support them. He wants to improve his knowledge and skills, and his manager has agreed that for the next three months she will support him with this. She has asked him to draw up an action plan.

1. Create an action plan, with SMART objectives, that will help Trevor to develop this aspect of his practice.

2. Describe how Trevor could use this plan to improve his own professional practice.

When you answer these questions, take into account the knowledge and skills that Trevor will have gained while studying for his initial qualification.

Assessment criteria

This table shows you what you must do to achieve a Pass, Merit or Distinction.

Pass	Merit	Distinction
Learning aim A: Understand the purpose of reflective practice in relation to work with children		
3A.P1 Explain the role of reflective practice in work with children in early years settings.	3A.M1 Assess how reflective practice contributes to work with children in early years settings.	3A.D1 Evaluate the impact of reflective practice in improving communication and language in children.
Learning aim B: Be able to reflect on own early years practice with children aged birth up to 8 years in relation to promoting children's communication and language		
3B.P2 Select evidence about own practice with children aged birth up to 8 years to promote their communication and language.	3B.M2 Compare own practice with current best practice in promoting children's communication and language development with children aged birth up to 8 years using evidence.	3B.D2 Assess effectiveness of own practice, recommending areas for development.
3B.P3 Explain personal factors that affect own practice in promoting children's communication and language.		
Learning aim C: Understand how to develop own early years practice with children aged birth up to 8 years to promote children's communication and language through planning		
3C.P4 Create appropriate plans to develop own practice with children aged birth up to 8 years to promote communication and language.	3C.M3 Analyse the value of planning to develop own practice in promoting children's communication and language.	3C.D3 Evaluate the contribution of continuous reflection in the development of own practice in promoting children's communication and language.

12 | Research skills

Learning aim C:
Be able to evaluate
the research project

▶ Reviewing your research
  project

▶ Evaluation and implications of
  your research

Planning your research project

The role of research

Research plays an extremely important role in early years practice. Practitioners can use research findings to inform their decisions about implementing new ideas, to change their practice or to meet individual children's needs. Carrying out research will enable you to investigate new approaches, assess the effectiveness of your work and make improvements to your practice.

Identifying a research focus

In thinking about your own research project, your first task is to identify a research focus. This will help you to concentrate on the main area you would like to investigate. For example, you might be interested in some aspect of play provision in your placement or work setting or you might want to investigate facilities for children with special educational needs.

Think about your own areas of interest and discuss your ideas with your tutor and placement supervisor. There may be a specific aspect of practice in your setting that would benefit from investigation and possible improvement, for example the way in which child observations are conducted. Observing practice and reading journal articles and research reports will help you to formulate a feasible topic for your research.

Objectives of the research proposal

To help you decide on your research objectives, you need to ask yourself the important questions shown in Figure 12.1 on page 293.

Research plays an extremely important role in early years practice

 Discuss

Start to think about your own research focus based on your own interests or aspects of the practice in your placement. Make a list of possible ideas and discuss these with your tutor and placement supervisor.

What do I hope to achieve from this research? (e.g. increasing knowledge, improving practice)

How achievable are these objectives in the time frame I am working with?

Research objectives

What **ethical issues** do I need to consider? (e.g. confidentiality, dealing with sensitive information)

How **feasible** is this research focus in relation to my current workplace or placement situation?

Figure 12.1 Questions to help you decide on your research objectives

Ethical issues in research

Any kind of research involving human beings is subject to a range of ethical issues. As a researcher, you will be investigating situations and using information that could be extremely sensitive and private. You will also be working with very vulnerable subjects who are often not in a position to defend themselves. It is very important that you fully understand the implications of:

- confidentiality in obtaining, storing and using information

- data protection legislation (the Data Protection Act (1998))

- authenticity of information and the use and misuse of statistics

- research policies and procedures

- children's rights, in accordance with the United Nations Convention on the Rights of the Child (1989) (see also Unit 8, page 218)

- the importance of informed consent

- dealing with sensitive subjects.

The Nuremberg Code is a set of principles for ethical research, which was established after the Second World War. These include 'informed consent, the absence of coercion, properly formulated scientific experimentation and beneficence towards experiment participants'.

Key terms

Authenticity: truthfulness, genuineness

Beneficence: the quality of being kind, helpful or generous

Coercion: forcing or threatening someone to do something against their will

Data Protection Act (1998): the UK law that protects the privacy of individuals, and ensures that information about them is kept securely and is processed fairly

Ethical issues: questions concerning what is moral or right

Feasible: capable of being done

Vulnerable: more likely to be harmed or exploited

Think about your own areas of interest and discuss your ideas with your tutor and placement supervisor

Research

Investigate the Nuremberg Code in relation to ethical research and examine the Data Protection Act (1998) regarding the use of confidential information in the research process.

Discuss the issue of informed consent with your tutor and placement supervisor. Who might you need to obtain consent from in order to carry out your research? How would you go about doing this and why is it important?

Research methods

Types of research

There are many different types of research and they can be carried out using a variety of research methods. Some of the different types of research are described in Figure 12.2.

Your assessment criteria:

Learning aim A: Be able to produce a research proposal related to work with young children

P4 Explain the suitability of the selected research methods for the research proposal, including related ethical issues.

Figure 12.2 Types of research

Type of research	Description	Example
Action research	This is initiated to solve a particular problem and to use the findings in a practical way.	Investigating why children are not using certain areas in the outdoor play area, with a view to improving the provision
Longitudinal research	This takes place over a long period of time in order to follow progress or development.	A child study that examines aspects of child development over the period of a year
Primary research	This is the research you actually carry out and involves you collecting your own data using primary research methods.	Questionnaires, interviews or observations (see pages 296–298)
Secondary research	This means studying material that has already been written on your chosen topic. It involves carrying out a literature review using books, journals and the internet.	Reviewing research reports and government documents in order to investigate the incidence of childhood obesity
Qualitative research	This focuses on thoughts and opinions rather than facts. Ideas and judgements are analysed rather than directly measured. Interviews are often used to obtain qualitative data.	An investigation into the quality of parent/child relationships
Quantitative research	This focuses on numbers and statistics, and produces quantitative data that can be measured and analysed.	An investigation into the number of children diagnosed with attention deficit hyperactivity disorder (ADHD)

Conducting a literature review:

When you are undertaking research, it is important to carry out a literature review. This provides background material for your study and valuable information on what is already known about the subject. You should begin your literature review early in your research work, as it will inform and shape your project and will help you decide on your choice of primary research methods.

You will need to use a variety of different sources for your literature review, for example books, government documents and reports, research articles and internet-based information.

Your assessment criteria:

Learning aim A: Be able to produce a research proposal related to work with young children

P2 Summarise reviewed research to inform the research proposal.

M1 Analyse how the literature review informed and shaped the research proposal and choice of research methods.

A good starting point is to make a list of the 'key words' in your study and begin your search for relevant documents and other source information. Try to be systematic and organised and make a list of useful sources as you come across them. Keep accurate records using an index system, as you will need all this information when you create your final reference list.

You will need to use a variety of different sources for your literature review

Case study

Khadija is a childcare student who is currently on placement at a nursery. She works with babies aged six months to one year. As part of her final college assessment, Khadija is planning to carry out a research project focusing on how observations of babies are carried out in the setting. She is preparing for a meeting with her placement supervisor to discuss the plans for her project.

1. Outline some of the questions that Khadija will need to ask her supervisor about carrying out research in the setting.

2. Explain why it is important for Khadija to carry out a literature review as part of her research.

🔍 **Research**

Practise some of the skills you will need when carrying out your literature review by doing the following exercises.

1. *Select four books from the library or learning resource centre. Make a note of the following information about each book: author, date of publication, title, name of publisher, place of publication*

2. *Use the internet to research the Foundation Years website (www.foundationyears.org.uk). Investigate the Child Development page and research some of the organisations listed there.*

3. *Write a brief report that analyses how your literature review helps inform your research proposal.*

Your own research might focus on a specific aspect of practice in early years

Primary research methods

There are many different primary research methods, all with specific features, advantages and disadvantages. The methods you choose will depend on your area of research, the objectives you want to achieve and the timescale you have available. Some key features of primary research methods are outlined in this section.

Questionnaires

You can use questionnaires to obtain facts (quantitative data) and opinions (qualitative data). Questionnaires are frequently used in quantitative marketing and social research, and they can be a valuable method of collecting a wide range of information from a large number of individuals.

To ensure that your questionnaire will be effective, you need to take care in writing the questions and constructing the questionnaire. Here are some useful pointers to help you when writing your questions:

- Only ask questions that are relevant and will give you the information you need.

- Avoid asking too many questions.

- Use simple language.

- Try to use mostly closed questions (for example, questions with yes/no answers, tick boxes or a rating scale).

- Including one or two open questions can provide more detailed information (for example, 'Describe in your own words, what do you think about…').

- Try to avoid ambiguous questions (questions that are unclear or open to more than one interpretation) such as 'Do you like travelling by bus and train?' (This is in effect two questions, which should be asked separately.)

If you are using a questionnaire as a research method, it is a good idea to test your questions with a friend or colleague. This is sometimes called a pilot study. You will also need to think about how you will distribute and collect your questionnaires (for example, by post, in person or using a collection box) and how much time this might take.

Learning aim A: Be able to produce a research proposal related to work with young children

P4 Explain the suitability of the selected research methods for the research proposal, including related ethical issues.

M1 Analyse how the literature review informed and shaped the research proposal and choice of research methods.

Key terms

Closed questions: questions that have a restricted range of answers, for example yes/no

Open questions: questions that allow respondents to express their views in the answer

Pilot study: a small-scale preliminary study conducted before the main research in order to check its feasibility

Research

Look at Figure 12.3 on page 297 and decide which questions are closed questions, and which are open questions.

Use these questions as a 'trial' pilot study to ask your own parents or other parents you know. Compare your responses with those of others in your group.

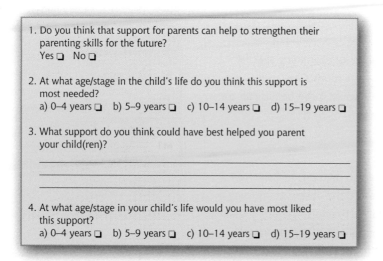

1. Do you think that support for parents can help to strengthen their parenting skills for the future?
   Yes ❑ No ❑

2. At what age/stage in the child's life do you think this support is most needed?
   a) 0–4 years ❑   b) 5–9 years ❑   c) 10–14 years ❑   d) 15–19 years ❑

3. What support do you think could have best helped you parent your child(ren)?
   _____
   _____
   _____

4. At what age/stage in your child's life would you have most liked this support?
   a) 0–4 years ❑   b) 5–9 years ❑   c) 10–14 years ❑   d) 15–19 years ❑

Figure 12.3 A questionnaire for a research project investigating support for parents

Interviews

Interviews enable face-to-face discussion and are often used to collect qualitative data. Some interviews can be conducted by telephone or email, but these tend to be less effective overall. You will need to decide whether you will:

- take notes (can be distracting)

- record the interview (accurate but time-consuming afterwards)

- rely on your memory (not always accurate)

- write in the answers as you go (can be misleading).

As with questionnaires, you will need to prepare either closed or open questions, or a mixture of both. Closed questions can limit the response from the interviewee, and open questions can result in almost endless responses that can be difficult for you to summarise and analyse.

If you decide to use interviews, make sure that you:

- have a clear purpose and an outline of the issues to be discussed

- prepare your questions in advance

- decide whether to record the interview by hand or digitally

- confirm the date, timing and location of the interview

- obtain all the relevant permissions and respect any promise of confidentiality.

? | Reflect

Consider the difference between these example questions. Which questions would provide the most effective and useful answers?

1. *Do you support children's emotional and physical wellbeing?*

2. *How do you support children's emotional and physical wellbeing?*

3. *Give one example of how you support children's physical wellbeing.*

4. *On a scale of 1 (lowest) to 4 (highest), how effectively do you think you support children's emotional wellbeing in your setting?*

Interviews enable face-to-face discussion and are often used to collect qualitative data

Case studies

Case studies are detailed investigations into the background of one person or a group of people. They can be useful for examining specific issues, such as the experience of being a teenage mum. Case studies can provide some very useful qualitative data. However, it can be difficult to generalise information from case study research.

Observations

Real life observation is widely used as a research method, particularly for studying children's behaviour. You can record the observations using a camera or digital recording device then analyse them using a rating scale or checklist. For example, you could rate your observations of parent/child attachment behaviour on a scale of 1 (lowest) to 4 (highest), as outlined in Figure 12.4. Alternatively, you could use a checklist to record the observations, as outlined in Figure 12.5.

Your assessment criteria:

Learning aim A: Be able to produce a research proposal related to work with young children

P4 Explain the suitability of the selected research methods for the research proposal, including related ethical issues.

M1 Analyse how the literature review informed and shaped the research proposal and choice of research methods.

Figure 12.4 Using a scale to rate observations

Attachment behaviour observed over a 10-minute period (Parent X)	1 (low)	2	3	4 (high)
Physical contact				X
Verbal communication	X			
Facial expression				X

Figure 12.5 Using a checklist to record observations

Attachment behaviour observed (Parent X)	Number of times observed in 10 minutes
Physical contact	IIII
Verbal communication	I
Facial expression	IIII

Observations can be useful for qualitative research, but they have some limitations for more quantitative work. Some of the problems include:

- It is very difficult to observe everything that you might want to study.
- The presence of an 'observer' can actually change the behaviour of those being observed (the Hawthorne effect).
- Observations can be interpreted subjectively and can therefore involve researcher bias.

Key terms

Hawthorne effect: a reaction in which individuals change their behaviour simply because they know they are being observed

Researcher bias: when a researcher's personal beliefs and values influence aspects of their research

Subjectively: making judgements based on individual feelings and opinions rather than the external facts

Scientific experiment

Scientific experiment as a research method is essentially a study of cause and effect. It sets out to prove that something is caused by or dependent on something else. For example, high levels of additives in fizzy drinks can cause changes in children's behaviour. In carrying out scientific experiments, the research subjects are generally divided into two groups: the experimental group and the control group. The experimental group will be exposed to the subject matter of the research, whereas the control group will not. For example, in an investigation into the effects of food additives on children's behaviour, half of the children will be given food additives and half will not (or they will be given a placebo instead). The behaviour of the children will then be compared over a period of time in order to determine if food additives changed the children's behaviour.

Scientific experiments involve the deliberate manipulation of one variable, while trying to keep all other variables constant. The variable that is changed is called the independent variable (IV). In this example, food additives will be the IV (or the 'cause'). The factor that is measured in the research is called the dependent variable (DV). In this example, the children's behaviour will be the DV (or the 'effect'). In other words, the research will set out to prove whether food additives cause a change in children's behaviour.

Scientific experiments study cause and effect, for example the impact of food additives on children's behaviour

Experimentation is regarded as one of the most scientific research methods, yet there are a number of problems associated with it, including:

- It is not always possible to control all the other variables that might affect the results of this kind of research (for example, personality, genetic predisposition, socio-economic influences, etc.).

- There are ethical issues involved in using human beings in experimental situations, particularly those involving the use of placebos.

Key terms

Control group: a group that does not receive a treatment, stimulus or intervention in an experiment

Dependent variable (DV): a factor that may change as a result of manipulating the independent variable in research (the outcome)

Experimental group: a group that receives a treatment, stimulus or intervention in an experiment

Independent variable (IV): a factor that can be manipulated by the researcher

Placebo: an inactive substance or false procedure, often administered to the control group in an experiment

Research subjects: the objects or individuals being studied in a research project

Variable: a factor that can change or be manipulated in research

Reflect

Start to think about the methods you might use to carry out your own research project.

What might be the advantages and disadvantages of different methods for your own study?

What other factors will you need to consider?

Discuss the possible methods with your supervisor or tutor.

Your research proposal

Creating a research proposal

A research proposal should present an outline of exactly how you intend to carry out your research project. Generally, it will include:

- a research question (or **hypothesis**)
- the objectives of your research (with reasons)
- your rationale (including the **validity** and **feasibility** of the proposal)
- the research methods you intend to use
- your target group and **sample selection**
- the timescale you are working within
- your action plan
- any modifications you have made (for example, as a result of your literature review).

The research question

Your research question should highlight the key focus of your research. This might be in the form of an actual question, for example:

'How can early years practitioners build and maintain attachment relationships with babies aged 0–1 year?'

Alternatively, it could be in the form of a hypothesis, for example:

'Sharing child observations with parents on a regular basis significantly improves parental involvement in their child's early learning.'

Application to practice

Your research project should not only be interesting for you to carry out, it should also have some direct application to working with young children. You need to consider the objectives and rationale (why you are doing this research and why you think it is important). You also need to consider how feasible the project will be in terms of factors such as:

- how your project relates to work with children and families
- what you hope to achieve
- the timescale involved
- how you intend to collect your **data**

🔑 Key terms

Data: *facts and information collected together for reference or analysis*

Feasibility: *how easily something can be done*

Hypothesis: *a tentative proposal that forms the basis of an investigation*

Sample selection: *the process of choosing subjects to be involved in a research project*

Validity: *the extent to which the research project measures what it sets out to measure*

Your research proposal should present an outline of exactly how you intend to carry out your research project

- your placement situation and/or your possible access to children and/or families

- ethical considerations such as confidentiality, obtaining relevant permissions and following research procedures.

Validity

You will also need to consider the validity of your research. This means making sure that your findings are a true representation of what you are claiming to measure. For example, if you are investigating people's opinions about the need for a new children's play park in a local community, it is likely that your findings will be different depending on who you interview. If you interview parents, then the results of your research could indicate an overwhelming need for a children's play park. However, the results might be very different if you interviewed elderly people instead. In both cases, the results could not be generalised as an opinion of the whole community.

When considering the validity of your research project, you need to think about your sample selection and some of the other factors that might influence the validity of your research, including the research methods you will use.

Discuss

Think about the focus of your own research and experiment with different research questions or hypotheses. Discuss the feasibility of your proposal with your tutor and placement supervisor.

When considering the validity of your research project, you need to think about your sample selection

Case study

A group of childcare students has been asked to consider the feasibility of these research questions:

- Can play therapy techniques positively improve the behaviour of challenging children?

- Can working in partnership with parents positively influence a child's behaviour in nursery?

  1. Discuss the possible variables that could influence the results in each case.

  2. Suggest how you could reword these research questions to make investigating them more feasible.

Design

Formulate a research proposal and discuss this with your tutor and/or placement supervisor.

Start to make a list of 'things to do'.

The research process

Research skills

A good researcher needs to be well organised. The research process requires skilful planning and efficient time management and you will need to monitor your project carefully. It is also important for researchers to be non-judgemental in order to avoid researcher bias. This can sometimes be challenging, particularly if your research involves people you know or if you have strong feelings about certain aspects of early years practice.

Carrying out your research

Your own research project will involve:

- reviewing a range of secondary sources (your literature review)

- carrying out your own primary research using your chosen methods (for example, questionnaires, interviews or case studies).

For example, you might choose to interview your placement supervisor and conduct a questionnaire with other students in your group. Your action plan should help you plan the time required to collect all your data and record your findings.

Recording your findings

Once you have carried out your primary research, you will need to record your findings and present your results. This will involve a number of different steps, including:

- collating your raw data

- summarising your data using percentages and statistical averages

- presenting your results.

Collating your data

This stage involves pulling together the findings from all your research methods, for example the results of your questionnaire, responses from interviews and analysis of observations. A useful way to collate the results from a questionnaire is to use a simple spreadsheet, as shown in Figure 12.6 on page 303. In this example, questions 1, 2 and 4 were multiple choice (with respondents choosing from answer options a, b, c or d) and questions 2 and 5 were simple Yes/No responses.

Your assessment criteria:

Learning aim B: Be able to carry out a small-scale research project related to work with young children

P6 Collect and record research findings relevant to the project objectives.

M2 Produce a coherent argument and relevant conclusions based on the research findings.

 Key terms

Collating: *the process of organising data into a form that you can analyse*

Raw data: *information collected from research that has not been processed or organised*

Researcher bias: *when a researcher's personal beliefs and values influence aspects of their research*

Respondents: *the people who participate in a research study*

Statistical average: *a value that is representative of all the values within a data set (often the mean value)*

Research

Using the data shown in Figure 12.6, summarise the following responses.

1. *What percentage of respondents answered 'Yes' to question 2?*

2. *What percentage of respondents chose answer b to question 4?*

3. *What percentage of respondents answered 'No' to question 5?*

4. *Write a brief report that produces a relevant conclusion from these findings.*

Figure 12.6 An example of collated data from a questionnaire

Respondent	Question 1	Question 2	Question 3	Question 4	Question 5
1	a	Yes	b	c	No
2	b	Yes	b	b	No
3	a	No	c	b	No
4	c	Yes	d	a	Yes

Summarising your data

This stage involves compiling your results using percentages and statistical averages. For example, the responses to question 1 from the four respondents in Figure 12.6 were:

a = 2   b = 1   c = 1

In summarising these results, we can say that:

50% of the respondents (2 out of the 4) chose answer a

25% of the respondents (1 out of the 4) chose answer b

25% of the respondents (1 out of the 4) chose answer c.

Analysing your findings

This stage involves presenting the findings from all your research methods and analysing the key points. Using a combination of different research methods is called triangulation and this is an effective way to increase the reliability of your results. You will need to compare similarities and differences, discuss your ideas and consider possibilities. For example, are the findings from your questionnaire similar to the responses from your interviews? When analysing your results, be critical and creative, ask questions and make suggestions. For example:

• Were there any surprises in your findings? (Discuss and comment on these.)

• Did the results match your expectations? (Why do you think this is?)

• What factors may have influenced your findings (for example, the sample selection or research methods used)?

• What do your results suggest?

 Design

Summarise the data from your own research methods.

Convert your questionnaire responses into percentages (where relevant) and summarise the results from the other research methods you used.

What are some of your key findings?

 Key term

Triangulation: using a combination of methods in a research study

Your own research project will involve using primary research methods, for example questionnaires

Presenting your findings

Presentation formats

The results of your research will be much easier to understand if you present them in a 'user-friendly' way. You can do this by creating graphs, charts and diagrams and using appropriate computer software. It is important to make sure that you present your results accurately and that you do not manipulate your results just to make your project look better! This would be regarded as unethical and would completely undermine the validity of your research. Some of the ways you can present your results are shown in Figure 12.7.

Your assessment criteria:

Learning aim B: Be able to carry out a small-scale research project related to work with young children

P6 Collect and record research findings relevant to the project objectives.

P7 Present research findings in a relevant format.

Pie chart: How children travel to school

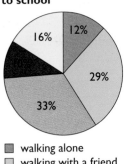

- ▨ walking alone
- ▨ walking with a friend
- ▨ walking with an adult
- ▮ by bus
- ▯ by car

Bar graph: Number of pets owned by boys and girls

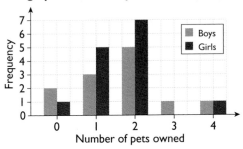

Simple chart or table: Children's favourite foods

Children's favourite foods	Girls	Boys
Pizza	45%	55%
Pasta	35%	20%
Fish fingers	15%	15%
Other	5%	10%

Figure 12.7 Three methods of presenting the results of research

Writing a research report

You will summarise your whole project in your research report, which should include the following sections:

1. **A title page:** this could state your research question or hypothesis, or you might decide on a different title for your work

2. **A list of contents:** showing the main chapters and page numbers

3. **An abstract (sometimes called a summary or précis):** a short summary of what you set out to do and what you achieved – you will most probably write this section last

 Discuss

Think about some of the ways you might present your own research findings. Talk to your tutor and discuss your ideas.

Investigate the computer software you might need to use.

4. **An introduction:** this section includes a statement of your research objectives and rationale

5. **Your literature review:** summarising your background reading and research into your chosen topic

6. **Research methodology:** an outline of your chosen research methods, including any ethical considerations

7. **Presentation and analysis of results:** this section includes a summary of your findings, with discussion and analysis

8. **Evaluation and conclusion:** a summary and reflection on the whole study, including recommendations and the implications of your research for work with young children

9. **List of references:** using a system approved by your tutor

10. **Appendices:** where used, these should be relevant, numbered and referred to in your work. You could include a copy of your questionnaire or interview questions as an appendix.

 Design

Write down the section headings for your own research report and discuss them with your tutor.

Make a rough draft of your contents page and think about the appendices you might want to include in your research report.

Your research report will include a number of different sections

Case study

Mari has been conducting a research study into the type of support available to parents of children in primary school. She has used a questionnaire as one of her research methods and is now thinking about how she could present her findings. The responses to one of her questions are summarised in the table below.

Question: Which type of support do you think could best help the parents of children aged 5–8 years old?	
Options	**Number of responses (out of a total of 100)**
Websites	25
Leaflets	10
Home visits from a teacher	5
Group work with other parents	1
Telephone advice from a parent support adviser	15
Teacher support in school	24
Extended family	5
Parent support advisers in school	12
Other	3

1. Describe and illustrate two different ways in which Mari could present the results from this question.

2. Evaluate the advantages and disadvantages of each of your chosen presentation methods.

Reviewing your research project

Evaluating your research

One of the first steps in evaluating your research is to return to your original objectives and research question. Did you achieve what you set out to do? What did you discover?

Your evaluation should discuss your findings in the context of current or previous research that has been conducted. How do the findings from your research compare with other studies that you have read about? Were there any major similarities or differences? Your evaluation should also attempt to summarise your work – this will involve reviewing both your aims and your findings. You should not introduce any new material into your evaluation, but reflect on what you have done.

Reviewing your research methods

An important part of evaluating any research project is to reflect on the research methods used. This should include an assessment of both the strengths and weaknesses of your methodology, in addition to an evaluation of improvements you could have made. Some examples are shown in Figure 12.8 (below and on page 307).

Your assessment criteria:

Learning aim C: Be able to evaluate the research project

P8 Describe how the research findings relate to the original research question.

Your evaluation should summarise the findings from your research

Figure 12.8 Strengths and weaknesses of research methods

Interview method	Advantages/strengths	Disadvantages/weaknesses	Possible improvements
Questionnaire	Covers a wide range of information Can reach a wide audience	Difficult to construct precise questions Distribution and collection problems Time-consuming Low response rate People don't always answer questions honestly	Give a specific date for return. Provide a collection box in a central area. Make sure questions are simple and unambiguous to avoid researcher bias.
Interview	Can obtain more in-depth information More personal Responses are immediate	Arranging suitable times and venues Recording responses accurately Can be subject to researcher bias (prompting the interviewee or 'putting words into their mouth')	Plan ahead. Prepare a set list of questions and stay on track. Send the questions to the interviewee in advance. Use a digital device to record the interview.

Interview method	Advantages/strengths	Disadvantages/weaknesses	Possible improvements
Case study	Provides very detailed information around a specific topic or issue Very personal approach	Can sometimes collect far too much information Ensuring confidentiality for participants Time-consuming Difficult to replicate or generalise results	Provide specific questions for the participants. Make sure the same criteria are used for all case study subjects (controlling variables).
Observation	Captures 'real life' situations Very useful for obtaining qualitative data	Very difficult to observe everything you might want to study The presence of an 'observer' can change the behaviour of those being observed (the Hawthorne effect) Observations can be interpreted subjectively (researcher bias)	Use more than one observer to try to standardise findings. Conduct observations over a period of time.
Scientific experiment	Provides accurate information for quantitative study; can be replicated; results can be analysed using statistical tests; limits researcher bias	Difficult to control all the relevant variables Can be considered unethical with human subjects	Ensure that participants are fully informed and ethical issues are addressed

Case study

Sally has recently carried out a research project to investigate the support available for the parents of children with attention deficit hyperactivity disorder (ADHD). The aims of her research were:

- to examine the services that are currently available in the Nether-Downs area to support parents of children with ADHD

- to investigate how parents currently access these services

- to consider the improvements that could be made in supporting parents to access these services in the future.

Sally used family case studies and interviews with parents for her research methods and is now evaluating her findings.

1. Give examples of some of the questions that Sally should address in evaluating the aims of her research proposal.

2. Outline some of the issues that Sally should consider when summarising and evaluating her findings.

Your assessment criteria:

Learning aim C: Be able to evaluate the research project

M3 Review the chosen research methods in relation to the results obtained, any sources of bias or error and ethical considerations.

Your own research may involve using family case studies

? | **Reflect**

Review your research methods and reflect on how effective they were.

Make notes on anything you would change for a future research project.

Evaluation and implications of your research

Making improvements

Having reviewed your research methods, you can now consider how your research could have been improved. It can be useful at this stage to ask yourself the following questions:

1. Did you achieve what you set out to do (in relation to your research objectives)?

    • If not, why not?

    • Were your objectives perhaps too vague or overambitious?

    • What could you have changed in order to achieve your objectives?

2. What problems did you encounter?

    • These could relate to your research methods, research sample, or to collating or analysing your data.

    • How could these problems have been overcome?

3. What were the limitations of your study?

    • These could relate to your research sample, research methods or time constraints.

4. How valid and reliable were your results?

    • Did you use triangulation?

    • Did you address any specific variables?

    • Did you acknowledge any variables you could not control?

5. How did you address any issues relating to researcher bias?

    • These could include personal knowledge of the research topic or making subjective judgements.

6. How did you address any ethical considerations?

    • These might include confidentiality, dealing with sensitive information and obtaining relevant permissions.

Implementing your research

The final stage in evaluating your project involves making recommendations based on your research findings. This will include making suggestions about how your findings might be used in a practical way when working with young children.

Review the findings from your research with your tutor

The recommendations from your research findings could be relevant for:

- your own professional practice

- early years practitioners in general

- specific procedures or ways of working

- local service provision for children and families

- local or national policy-making in early years.

For example, did the findings from your research indicate the need for better ways of working, new methods of carrying out routine tasks or more staff training in a particular area? You might also consider the wider implications of your research, for example changes to local early years services or national policies. Your recommendations should also include suggestions for extending your research, or possible areas for further study, which might improve and extend the research outcomes.

Recommendations

A recent study into the role of the key person working with babies aged 0–1 year made the following recommendations:

- Specific time should be planned into every day for each key person to provide undivided attention to the babies in their care (nurture time).

- Simple games such as 'Peek-a-boo' and 'This little piggy' should be a regular part of the interaction between babies and their key person.

- Music, rhyme and singing should feature prominently every day.

- All aspects of personal care (such as feeding, nappy changing, comforting) should be carried out by the key person wherever possible.

- There should be more staff training provided on the role of the key person, the importance of attachment and interactive play with babies.

- There should be a system of peer observation among staff to monitor the quality of interactions between babies and their key person.

- The role of the key person should be integrated into the policy of the setting and shared with parents and carers.

(Source: 'Tuning into Children', Centre for Excellence in Outcomes in Children's and Young People's Services, 2011)

These recommendations address issues relating to individual professional practice, staff teamwork and training, and the setting's policies and procedures.

Key term

Peer observation: *a process in which one practitioner observes the professional practice of another and provides supportive, constructive feedback*

Reflect

Consider the recommendations from your own research. What are the implications for:

- *your own professional practice?*

- *early years practitioners?*

- *service provision for children and families?*

- *local or national early years policies?*

Write a brief report to evaluate the extent to which the findings from your research could be implemented.

The recommendations from your research might include the need for staff training

Assessment criteria

This table shows you what you must do to achieve a Pass, Merit or Distinction.

Pass	Merit	Distinction
Learning aim A: Be able to produce a research proposal related to work with young children		
3A.P1 Explain the role of selected research relating to work with young children in early years settings.	3A.M1 Analyse how the literature review informed and shaped the research proposal and choice of research methods.	3A.D1 Discuss research objectives in terms of feasibility and application to practice.
3A.P2 Summarise reviewed research to inform the research proposal.		
3A.P3 Describe the objectives of the selected research proposal, giving reasons.		
3A.P4 Explain the suitability of the selected research methods for the research proposal, including related ethical issues.		
3A.P5 Create a realistic research proposal.		
Learning aim B: Be able to carry out a small-scale research project related to work with young children		
3B.P6 Collect and record research findings relevant to the project objectives.	3B.M2 Produce a coherent argument and relevant conclusions based on the research findings.	
3B.P7 Present research findings in a relevant format.		

Pass	Merit	Distinction
Learning aim C: Be able to evaluate the research project		
3C.P8 Describe how the research findings relate to the original research question.	3C.M3 Review the chosen research methods in relation to the results obtained, any sources of bias or error and ethical considerations.	3C.D2 Evaluate the extent to which the findings from the research undertaken can be implemented.
3C.P9 Explain the possible implications of the research findings for current practice.	3C.M4 Recommend possible improvements to the research, referring to any relevant implications and ethical issues.	

13 | Health, education and social services for children and their families

Learning aim C:
Understand the role
of multi-agency work
for children and their
families

▶ The provision of multi-agency
support

Types of services and benefits for children and their families

The right to services

Every local authority (district or council) in the UK has a responsibility to provide health, education and social services that meet the needs of children and families. Statutory service providers, such as the National Health Service (NHS), are required by law to support the rights of children and families to access and receive services.

Article 4 of the United Nations Convention on the Rights of the Child (UNCRC) states that governments have a responsibility to ensure that minimum standards in social services, health and education systems are set and maintained. The UNCRC is also discussed in Chapter 8, page 218.

Types of services

Health, education and social services in the UK are provided by the government, but also by a range of voluntary, independent and private service providers, for example private day nurseries, voluntary pre-schools and organisations like the NSPCC. Statutory service provision from the government offers a range of support for children and families, including those covered in the sections below.

Integrated child and family services

Integrated services were first introduced as a result of the Children Act (2004) as a way of improving service provision in response to the Every Child Matters government initiative. They offer joined-up health, education and social care services to children and their families. Examples of integrated child and family services include:

- Sure Start Children's Centres: providing childcare, parenting support, health and family services for vulnerable young children and their families

The National Health Service is required by law to support the rights of children and families to access services

- extended schools: offering out of hours activities for children, adult learning and recreational activities

- multi-agency disability teams: providing assessment and treatment for children with physical disabilities or learning difficulties.

Education services

Statutory education services in the UK are provided free for all children from the ages of 4 to 19 years. The services generally include:

- nursery, primary and secondary schools

- further education and sixth form colleges

- special educational services and support

- educational psychology services.

Most three- and four-year-old children also qualify for free pre-school education (up to 15 hours a week) in registered pre-schools, day nurseries or with accredited childminders.

Social services

Statutory social services are provided to support children and families, offer information and advice and assess specific needs. For example:

- social workers: providing support for vulnerable children and families, adoption and fostering services and safeguarding services for children 'at risk'

- family support workers: providing help with parenting skills and childcare services

- specific support for children with special needs: providing mobility aids and other resources.

Social workers provide support for children considered 'at risk'

Health services

A wide range of statutory health services is provided for children and their families. These include both hospital and community-based health care and supportive services. For example:

- GP services: providing health care in the community

- hospital provision: including paediatric, obstetric and midwifery services

- health visitors: providing developmental assessments and routine surveillance

- school health services

- dental services

- speech and language therapy.

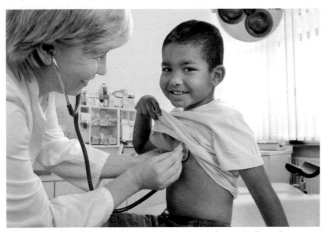

Statutory health services include both hospital and community-based health services

Financial benefits

Many families in the UK are also entitled to a number of financial benefits, including:

- maternity pay or allowance

- statutory paternity pay

- child benefit

- child tax credit

- disability living allowance (for a child who has care needs or mobility problems)

- free prescription medicines (for children under 16 years).

Access to services

Why families need access to services

There are many different reasons why a family might need to access health, education or social services in their local area. For example:

- **health services:** for childhood illness (such as acute infections or chronic conditions like asthma), routine medical check-ups, immunisations or therapeutic services (such as speech and language therapy)

- **education services:** for children with special educational needs, educational psychology support for children with emotional or behavioural difficulties

- **social services:** in situations of family breakdown, support for parental stress or depression, parenting support and adoption and fostering services.

Information for families

Families can find out information about services in their local area from a variety of different sources, including:

- professionals: for example, health visitors, family support workers, teachers, early years workers, GP

- local centres: for example, Sure Start Children's Centres, day nurseries, schools, child health clinics, local libraries

- voluntary organisations: for example, Citizens Advice Bureau, Action for Children, Children's Society

- the internet: local authority websites and information services such as:

  – Family Information Services (England) (www.direct.gov.uk)

  – Family Information Service (Wales) (http://wales.gov.uk)

  – Scottish Family Information Service (Scotland) (www.scottishfamilies.gov.uk)

  – Family Support (Northern Ireland) (www.familysupportni.gov.uk).

The provision of information needs to consider the communication needs of families, for example where English is not their first language, or the particular needs of individuals with sensory impairment. Many forms of information for families are provided in a variety of community languages, in addition to large print and Braille formats.

Key terms

Acute: with a sudden onset but of short duration

Chronic: persisting over a long period of time

Research

Investigate the Family Information Services relevant to your home country in the UK.

Make a list of some of the information provided for parents about:

- *finding and choosing childcare*

- *schools, learning and development*

- *adoption, fostering and children in care.*

Supporting children and families

Being a parent is a very difficult job, and most parents have no training for the role! Health, education and social services help parents by providing much-needed support for children and their families. The provision of information supports families in selecting and choosing the services they need. Access to services helps to strengthen parents' confidence in providing the best care for themselves and their children. Support from the different services helps to improve the health, welfare and long-term outcomes for children and their families. Some examples of the types of support available and the impact on outcomes for families and children are shown in Figure 13.1.

Your assessment criteria:

Learning aim A: Understand the provision of health, education and social services for children and their families

M1 Assess how services and benefits support children and families, with examples.

D1 Evaluate the extent to which services and benefits could impact on outcomes for children.

Figure 13.1 Support services for children and families

Service	Examples of support provided	Impact on outcomes
Health care services (in pregnancy)	Antenatal care, advice and guidance (e.g. the effects of diet, smoking, alcohol and medicines) GP, hospital and midwifery services Routine screening tests Preparation for childbirth Parenting classes Preparing for the baby	Healthier pregnancy Early detection of potential problems More confident mothers Less complicated childbirth Healthier babies
Education services (child with special needs)	Assessment of child's individual needs Access to home visits Specialist groups, centres and services Educational support Specialist equipment and/or resources (e.g. vision, hearing or mobility aids)	Maximising children's potential; Enabling achievement Empowering parents Assisting teachers
Social services (family breakdown)	Social work or family support services Parenting support groups Help with childcare Temporary foster care Referral to specialist services (e.g. therapy, counselling) Advice about financial benefits and other practical resources	Helps to minimise distress and disruption Encourages parents to support their children Helps to maintain stability Can prevent more serious problems (e.g. emotional and/or behavioural difficulties, chronic depression or abuse)

Case study

Yvonne is 20 years old and is a single parent to Josh, who is one year old. Yvonne suffered from postnatal depression after Josh was born and struggled to care for him on her own. Yvonne's health visitor encouraged her to see her GP, who provided some treatment for her postnatal depression and referred her to the Young Mums group at the local Children's Centre. Yvonne now attends the group every week and has found out about other services and some of the financial benefits she can claim. She has also made some new friends, whom she often meets in the local park, where the children can enjoy playing together. Yvonne is now planning to take Josh to a local pre-school group and is thinking about a enrolling in a part-time training programme.

1. Describe how the services that Yvonne accessed provided support for both her and Josh.

2. Discuss the possible long-term implications of these services on the future outcomes for both Yvonne and Josh.

Research

In your placement or workplace, ask your supervisor about the information provided for families about different kinds of services in the local area. Is any information provided in languages other than English?

Keep a record of different information sources for future reference.

Support from the different services helps to improve the health, welfare and long-term outcomes for children and their families

Case study

Genine and Kevin have three children: Wayne aged seven years, Emma aged five years and Ryan aged three years. The family live in a fourth floor flat on a council estate. Kevin is unemployed and Genine is currently six months pregnant.

Wayne attends the local primary school and has recently been diagnosed with Attention Deficit Hyperactivity Disorder (ADHD). Ryan attends the local nursery school every morning, and is currently being assessed because of some speech and language difficulties.

1. Outline the different kinds of support that this family may need over the next few months.

2. Describe the different services and professionals that may be involved in providing support for this family.

Types of early years settings

Settings providing early years education

The range and availability of early years settings can sometimes be confusing. Early years provision can be private, voluntary or maintained (managed by the local authority). In all four countries of the UK, three- and four-year-old children are entitled to free early years education (up to 15 hours a week) in registered settings. In addition, some areas in England are also offering free early years provision for vulnerable two-year-olds.

Although there are many variations across the UK, some of the key features of the different early years settings providing early years education are summarised in Figure 13.2.

Your assessment criteria:

Learning aim B: Understand the context in which early years education is provided

P3 Explain the differences between settings which provide for children's early years education.

Figure 13.2 Types of early years settings

Type of provision	Management	Age range	Cost	Hours
Children's centres	Maintained (Sure Start areas)	0–4 years	Free (for eligible families only)	Full day care
Pre-schools and playgroups	Voluntary or private	2–5 years	Hourly rates	Sessional care
Nursery schools and classes	Maintained (local authority)	3–5 years	Free	Regular school hours
Reception classes/Early Years Foundation Stage units in primary schools	Maintained (local authority)	4–5 years	Free	Regular school hours
Independent schools	Private	2–5 years	Termly fees	Regular school hours
Crèches (workplace and independent)	Private	0–4 years	Hourly rates	Sessional care
Day nurseries (independent and business chains)	Private	0–5 years (some with facilities for older children)	Fees payable	Extended day care
Registered childminders (home-based care)	Private	0–8 years	Hourly rates	Flexible

Differences in provision

When choosing the place that is right for their child, parents need to evaluate the advantages and disadvantages of different settings and consider factors such as:

- type of service provided (individual, home-based, group care)

Your assessment criteria:

Learning aim B: Understand the context in which early years education is provided

M2 Compare the advantages and disadvantages to children and families of different types of early years education.

- organisation of the service (grouping of children, age ranges, room layout)

- suitability and convenience (location, opening hours, flexibility)

- cost implications

- range of services provided (such as parenting support, family health services, advice groups)

- range of activities provided (such as specialist music or art, outdoor activities)

- facilities for children with special needs (such as specialist staff, equipment and other resources).

Some parents of pre-school children may consider that individualised care is more beneficial for young children and will choose home-based care with a childminder. Some parents may prefer the stimulation of group-based care and the range of additional services offered in a Children's Centre. Alternatively, the extended opening hours at a private day nursery might be advantageous for some working parents, while the range of activities and facilities for children with special needs could suit the requirements of other parents.

There is a wide variety of early years provision in the UK

🔍 Research

Find out more about the benefits of early years education, for example at www.education.gov.uk or www.early-education.org.uk, or from articles in Early Years Educator Magazine (www.earlyyearseducator.co.uk) or Nursery World Magazine (www.nurseryworld.co.uk).

Investigate some of the early years settings in your own area.

Create a table of the provision in your local area, organised by the type of provision.

Case study

Hannah and Matt Josey have two children, Martha aged three years and Tom aged ten months. Hannah is planning to go back to work as a receptionist at the doctor's surgery, from 8am to 3pm every day. Matt works as a car mechanic at a local garage, from 7.30am to 5pm every day. He drives the family car to work and Hannah is planning to take the bus.

Martha has been attending a local private day nursery every morning from 9am to 12am.

1. Describe the factors that Hannah and Matt will need to consider in making arrangements for the care of their children once Hannah goes back to work.

2. Outline the advantages and disadvantages of the different types of provision available for the care of Hannah and Matt's children.

Parents need to consider how different types of early years provision meet their individual needs

The structure and inspection of early education services in the UK

The structure of early years education

All settings on the Early Years Register that provide early years education, including childminders and group-based care, must be registered with the relevant regulatory organisation and offer the accredited early years curriculum. The structure of the education system and the compulsory school age are different in the four home countries of the UK, as outlined in Figure 13.3.

Your assessment criteria:

Learning aim B: Understand the context in which early years education is provided

P4 Explain how early years education is inspected in the home country.

Figure 13.3 Education in the four countries of the UK

Country	Regulatory organisation	Early years curriculum	Compulsory school age	School curriculum (excludes private schools)
England	Office for Standards in Education (Ofsted)	Statutory Framework for the Early Years Foundation Stage (0–5 years)	The term following the 5th birthday (or September following the 4th birthday at parent's request)	National Curriculum (5–16 years)
Scotland	Education Scotland (Her Majesty's Inspectors)	Early Years Framework (Pre-Birth to Three: Positive Outcomes for Scotland's Children and Families)	The term following the 5th birthday	Curriculum for Excellence (3–18 years)
Wales	Estyn (Her Majesty's Inspectorate for Education and Training in Wales)	Foundation Phase in the Framework for Children's Learning (3–7 years)	The term following the 5th birthday	National Curriculum for Wales (starting from Key Stage 2) (7–16 years)
Northern Ireland	Education and Training Inspectorate (ETI)	The Northern Ireland Curriculum: Foundation Stage (0–4 years)	The term following the 4th birthday	The Northern Ireland Curriculum (4–16 years)

The role of early years inspectorates

The inspection of early years education is carried out on a regular basis in all settings that provide early education for children. This includes early years and childcare settings, Children's Centres, accredited childminders and maintained schools. Although there are some differences in the inspection systems between the four home countries of the UK, some of the overriding principles are the same. The main purpose of inspection in an early years setting is to judge the quality and standards for the welfare, learning and development of the children. To reach an overall judgement, inspectors will ask themselves, 'What is it like for a child here?'

 Key term

Early Years Register: a record of all childcare providers caring for children from birth to aged five

The inspection process

Inspectors usually visit the setting unannounced and spend time observing staff and children and speaking with parents and carers. During an inspection, inspectors collect first-hand evidence based on the practice they observe and what they learn from the people using the service. They use this evidence and other information to make their professional judgements, which are published in inspection reports. These reports are publicly available (usually on the inspectorate's website) and must be shown to parents, if requested.

The inspection report

The format of inspection reports varies between the four home countries of the UK, but in general, the report will summarise:

1. the overall effectiveness of the early years provision

2. the steps that need to be taken to improve provision further.

The regulatory organisation collates and publishes statistics, and uses them to monitor improvements in service provision. Inspection reports enable parents to make informed decisions when choosing an early years setting. Information from inspections is also used to create action plans to develop the provision and improve quality in the setting.

The overall effectiveness of registered early years providers inspected by Ofsted from January to March 2012 is shown in Figure 13.4. The summary of actions required to improve provision in settings inspected by Ofsted during the same period is shown in Figure 13.5.

Figure 13.4 Overall effectiveness of early years registered providers inspected between 1 January 2012 and 31 March 2012, by provider type (provisional)

Provider type	Outstanding	Good	Satisfactory	Inadequate
Childminder (3208)	8	63	27	3
Childcare on non-domestic premises (1643)	17	62	18	3
All provision (4866)	11	62	24	3

Legend: ☐ Outstanding ■ Good ☐ Satisfactory ■ Inadequate

Note: Percentages are rounded and do not always add exactly to 100.

Source: Ofsted Official Statistics Release for the period 1 September 2008 to 31 March 2012

Research

Investigate the education structure and early years curriculum in your own country.

Reflect on the differences between starting school at five years old and at four years old. What do you think the advantages and disadvantages are of each?

Investigate the compulsory school age in some other European countries. How do these compare with the UK?

Inspectors will spend their time observing staff and children and speaking with parents and carers

Discuss

Look at the overall effectiveness of early years providers in Figure 13.4. What type of provision had the highest number of settings rated 'outstanding'?

Figure 13.5 Actions at early years registered inspections between 1 January 2012 and 31 March 2012, by the statutory requirements of the Early Years Register (provisional)

	Total number of inspections	Number with actions	Percentage with actions
Any action	4,866	1,123	23
Learning and development requirements			
Early learning goals	4,866	14	0
Educational programmes	4,866	11	0
Assessment arrangements	4,866	3	0
Welfare requirements			
Safeguarding and welfare	4,866	548	11
Promoting good health	4,866	122	3
Behaviour management	4,866	12	0
Suitability of adults	4,866	71	1
Qualifications, training, knowledge and skills	4,866	43	1
Staffing arrangements	4,866	13	0
Premises, environment and equipment	4,866	273	6
Organisation	4,866	104	2
Documentation	4,866	388	8

(Source: Ofsted Official Statistics Release for the period 1 September 2008 to 31 March 2012)

Inspection of early years education

There are some differences in the process of inspection for early years education in the four home countries of the UK, as outlined below:

England

Ofsted inspections are carried out on all newly registered settings and at least every 3 to 4 years after that. The inspection includes judgements in the following categories:

- the overall effectiveness of the early years provision

- the effectiveness of leadership and management of the early years provision

- the quality of the provision in the Early Years Foundation Stage

- outcomes for children in the Early Years Foundation Stage.

Each category is graded as follows:

1 (outstanding)   2 (good)   3 (satisfactory)   4 (inadequate)

Your assessment criteria:

Learning aim B: Understand the context in which early years education is provided

P4 Explain how early years education is inspected in the home country.

 Discuss

Look at the 'Percentage with actions' column in Figure 13.5. Which category required the highest percentage of actions (improvements required in the setting)? Which other categories required actions?

The inspection report will also include information on:

- the quality of the provision for children and how this helps them to develop

- how well the setting is led and managed

- what improvements have been made since the last inspection

- what still needs to be done to improve the quality of the provision.

Scotland

Education Scotland inspects and reports on the quality of education in voluntary and private pre-school centres, nursery schools and family centres and nursery classes within schools. Her Majesty's Inspectors carry out inspections in those pre-school centres that are funded to provide pre-school education for children aged three to five years.

Education Scotland designs inspection procedures in line with 10 underlying principles to ensure that inspections are independent, responsive, fair and open. The principles are:

1. Independence, impartiality and accountability

2. Having all learners or users at the heart of inspection and review

3. Equality and diversity

4. Transparency and mutual respect

5. Observing practice and experiences directly: focusing on outcomes and impact

6. Building on self-evaluation

7. Partnership working with the users of our services and other providers/scrutiny bodies

8. Improvement and capacity building

9. Proportionality, responsiveness and assessment of risk

10. Best value

Wales

Her Majesty's Inspectorate for Education and Training in Wales (Estyn) provides advice to the Welsh Assembly Government on:

- the quality and standards of the nursery education provided

- how far the setting meets the needs of the range of children in the setting

The inspection report includes information on the quality of the provision for children

- the quality of leadership and management of the setting

- the contribution that the setting makes to children's wellbeing

- the spiritual, moral, social and cultural development of the children.

Northern Ireland

The Education and Training Inspectorate (ETI) evaluates the quality of provision across the range of activities in the setting. The inspection includes a report on the quality of:

- the children's development and learning

- the pre-school programme

- pastoral care and child protection

- teaching

- leadership and management.

Q | Research

Investigate the website of the inspectorate for your own country. Select a recent inspection report from a setting and examine the content and grading.

Write an email to the manager of the setting, outlining the improvements that have been suggested in the inspection report.

The inspection process will involve assessing the quality of relationships with parents and carers

Case study

Read the following extract from an inspection report:

'Children are cared for within four rooms and have access to a secure outdoor play area. The nursery is open Monday to Friday, from 7am to 6.30pm, throughout the year. The nursery supports children who speak English as an additional language. Staff know the children's needs and backgrounds, and they organise interesting activities to help them learn about diversity.

The environment is bright and welcoming, with a very spacious and well-equipped outdoor area. There are some good-quality play materials to support children's enjoyment and learning.

Overall, the setting runs efficiently, but the organisation of lunchtime results in some children waiting too long for their food.

Staff form positive and friendly relationships with parents and carers. They keep them informed about the children's day and they are beginning to introduce systems to involve parents more in children's learning.

Most of the staff are well trained and demonstrate secure knowledge of the Early Years Foundation Stage framework, but there are some inconsistencies in practice. Learning journals include observations of children's development, but the next steps in their learning are not consistently identified.

Children behave well in the setting because the staff set appropriate boundaries and help children to learn the difference between right and wrong.'

1. As a parent, what might you identify as the strengths of this setting?

2. As the manager of this setting, what might you include in your action plan as areas for improvement?

The provision of multi-agency support

Multi-agency working

Multi-agency working refers to different agencies, services or teams of professionals working alongside parents to provide services that meet the needs of the children and families. Some of the professionals involved and the range of support provided are outlined in Figure 13.6.

Figure 13.6 Agencies providing support for children and families

Agency	Some of the professionals involved	Support provided
Health services	General Practitioners (GPs) Health visitors Midwives Speech and language therapists Hospital and health care staff	Support and advice about health care, medication or treatment, child development, language and communication
Social services	Social workers Family support workers	Helping families to access local services Support with children's welfare or concerns about safeguarding
Education services	Teachers Teaching assistants SENCos Parent support advisers (PSAs)	Support with children's educational progress Help and advice for children with special educational needs
Psychology services (child and adolescent mental health services: CAMHS)	Educational psychologists Therapists	Support with mental health issues Emotional and behavioural support Help for children with learning difficulties

Meeting the needs of children and families

Multi-agency working fulfils a very important role in the early identification of children's needs. This includes not only the statutory recognition of children who are 'in need', but also the needs of children who are at risk of significant harm and children with special educational needs.

Children in need

Children are defined as 'in need' if their health and development will be significantly impaired without the provision of services. It is important for their specific needs to be recognised and for multi-agency services to work together to provide support.

The **Common Assessment Framework (CAF)** was introduced in England in 2005 as a standardised framework for assessing the needs of children and their families. It is an important tool for multi-agency working and supports practitioners to make a **holistic** assessment of children's additional needs, identify any support required and work more effectively together.

🔑 Key terms

Common Assessment Framework (CAF): *a standardised process for assessing the needs of children and families and identifying the support required from different professionals*

Holistic: *emphasising the importance of the whole child*

Case study

Tony is six years old. His father is currently in prison for drug-related offences and his mother, who has recently given birth to a baby girl, is being treated for depression. Tony is currently living with his mother and maternal grandmother, and he attends a local primary school.

Before his father went to prison, Tony was always an outgoing boy, who enjoyed football and social play with his friends. However, in school recently, he refuses to participate in any group activities and is aggressive towards other children. Tony often arrives late for school, he is frequently dirty and sometimes he does not attend at all.

1. Outline the key professionals who may be involved in supporting and providing services for Tony and his family.

2. Discuss how multi-agency working would contribute to meeting the needs of Tony and his family and improving outcomes for them.

🔍 Research

Investigate the Common Assessment Framework at: www.education .gov.uk/childrenandyoungpeople/ strategy/integratedworking/caf. Examine the CAF form. List the different elements that are considered when assessing the strengths and needs of children and their families.

Children are defined as 'in need' if their health and development will be significantly impaired without the provision of services

Children at risk of significant harm

Some children need support because they are suffering, or likely to suffer, significant harm, for example abuse or neglect. Multi-agency working is extremely important in this situation and justifies compulsory intervention in family life in the best interests of children. The statutory guidance in the government document Working Together to Safeguard Children (2010) clearly outlines the importance of multi-agency working to support children and families (see also Unit 8, pages 206–221).

Children with special educational needs

Children with special educational needs may need multi-agency support for a range of factors, including physical or sensory impairment, emotional or behavioural problems, difficulties with speech and language, or the need for specialised equipment or resources. The government green paper on special educational needs and disability (July 2012) places greater emphasis on a multi-agency approach. It proposes a single assessment process and a combined 'education, health and care plan', which would focus on providing integrated support and improving outcomes for children and their families. (See also Unit 10, page 264.)

🔍 Research

Investigate the government green paper on special educational needs and disability 'Support and aspiration: A new approach to special educational needs and disability'.

Write a brief report to evaluate some of the recommendations relating to multi-agency working and improving outcomes for children.

Assessment criteria

This table shows you what you must do to achieve a Pass, Merit or Distinction.

Pass	Merit	Distinction
Learning aim A: Understand the provision of health, education and social services for children and their families		
3A.P1 Explain the services and benefits children and families have a right to access, to include: • health • education • social services. 3A.P2 Explain why families may need to access named services.	3A.M1 Assess how services and benefits support children and families, with examples.	3A.D1 Evaluate the extent to which services and benefits could impact on outcomes for children.
Learning aim B: Understand the context in which early years education is provided		
3B.P3 Explain the differences between settings which provide for children's early years education. 3B.P4 Explain how early years education is inspected in the home country.	3B.M2 Compare the advantages and disadvantages to children and families of different types of early years education.	
Learning aim C: Understand the role of multi-agency work for children and their families		
3C.P5 Explain the role of a multi-agency approach in work with children and families.	3C.M3 Discuss how multi-agency working contributes to meeting the needs of children and families, with examples.	3C.D2 Evaluate the extent to which multi-agency working might impact on outcomes for children.

14 | Food and mealtimes in the early years

Learning aim A1:
Understand how
to provide food
for children to
encourage health and
development

- ▶ Nutrition for health and
  development

- ▶ Meeting children's individual
  dietary needs

Learning aim A2:
Understand the
role of the adult in
encouraging children
to develop healthy
eating habits

- ▶ Children's attitudes towards
  food

- ▶ Developing healthy eating
  habits in early years settings

Learning aim B:
Understand the
role of the adult in
preparing and serving
food safely

▶ Food hygiene and safety

Nutrition for health and development

Nutrition for health and development

A healthy, balanced diet is essential for children's growth and development. Research has shown that unhealthy diets in childhood can lead to long-term health problems in later life, and that healthy eating habits need to start from an early age. The food children eat provides essential nutrients for healthy development, including macronutrients such as protein for muscle development and micronutrients such as calcium for strong bones. Nutritional deficiencies can also affect children's development, behaviour, concentration and emotional wellbeing.

Right from the start, a healthy diet during pregnancy is extremely important for foetal growth and development. Folic acid (Vitamin B9) is particularly important during the pre-conception period and early pregnancy in helping to prevent neural tube defects, including spina bifida. Studies have also shown that iodine deficiency during pregnancy and childhood can cause permanent brain damage.

A healthy diet during pregnancy is extremely important for foetal growth and development

During infancy and early childhood, healthy brain development is dependent on an adequate intake of macronutrients such as protein, carbohydrate and fats.

A steady supply of glucose is crucial for children's brain development, most importantly, the glucose that is released slowly from the breakdown of complex carbohydrates, such as pasta.

A deficiency in micronutrients (vitamins and minerals) such as vitamin B12, zinc and iron, have been associated with poor cognitive functioning. A 2010 study from the University of Maryland, USA found that infants with iron deficiency anaemia had:

- lower cognitive scores

- lower motor development

- altered social and emotional development.

Other studies have shown that dietary omega-3 (polyunsaturated fat, which is found in certain foods such as seeds, beans and oily fish) can result in improved cognitive ability, memory, attention and concentration in children.

(This topic is also covered in Unit 3, pages 88–90.)

Healthy eating

Children need to eat a variety of food from the four main groups.

Figure 14.1 Examples of foods from the four main food groups

Fruit and vegetables	Meat, fish, eggs, beans and other non-dairy sources of protein

Bread, rice, potatoes, pasta and other starchy foods	Milk and dairy products

All these foods contain nutrients that are essential for good health. A healthy diet contains a balance of these important nutrients, which all perform a different function in the body. Figure 3.2 on pages 88–89 of Unit 3 provides a summary of the main nutrients, why they are important and what foods they are found in.

Key terms

Iron deficiency anaemia: *a shortage of oxygen-carrying red blood cells due to lack of iron in the diet*

Macronutrients: *nutrients that the body needs in large quantities, such as carbohydrates, fats, and proteins*

Micronutrients: *nutrients that the body needs in small quantities, such as vitamins and minerals*

Neural tube defects: *defects of the brain and spinal cord*

Nutrients: *substances providing nourishment for growth and development*

Pre-conception period: *the time during which a couple are trying to conceive a baby*

Dietary guidance

The Children's Food Trust guide *Eat Better, Start Better: Voluntary Food and Drink Guidelines for Early Years Settings in England - A Practical Guide* (2012) provides the dietary recommendations for children aged one to five years, as shown in Figure 14.2.

Figure 14.2 Dietary recommendations for children aged 1–5 years

Food groups	Examples of food included	Main nutrients provided	Recommended servings
Starchy foods	Bread, potatoes and sweet potatoes, starchy root vegetables, pasta, noodles, rice, other grains, breakfast cereals	Carbohydrate, fibre, B vitamins, iron	Four portions each day Provide a portion as part of each meal (breakfast, lunch and tea) and provide as part of at least one snack each day
Fruit and vegetables	Fresh, frozen, canned, dried and juiced fruit and vegetables, and pulses	Carotenes (a form of vitamin A), vitamin C, zinc, iron, fibre	Five portions each day Provide a portion as part of each main meal (breakfast, lunch and tea) and with some snacks
Meat, fish, eggs, beans and non-dairy sources of protein	Meat, poultry, fish, shellfish, eggs, meat alternatives, pulses, nuts*	Protein, iron, zinc, omega 3 fatty acids, vitamins A and D	Two portions each day Provide a portion as part of lunch and tea (Two to three portions for vegetarian children)
Milk and dairy foods	Milk, cheese, yoghurt, fromage frais, custard, puddings made from milk	Protein, calcium, and vitamin A	Three portions each day provided as part of meals, snacks and drinks

*Be allergy aware – information about food allergies and developing an allergy plan is available from www.allergyuk.org

Source: Children's Food Trust, *Eat Better, Start Better: Voluntary Food and Drink Guidelines for Early Years Settings in England – A Practical Guide*, 2012, p. 15

Diet-related illness

The food that children eat affects their health and development in both the long and short term.

Children who eat food that contains more calories than they use in energy can easily become obese. Obesity can cause problems in the short term, as it is more difficult for obese children to be active. It can also cause more long-term problems, as overweight children are more likely to develop conditions such as diabetes, heart disease and high blood pressure later in life.

In 2010, the Advisory Panel on Food and Nutrition in Early Years found that over a fifth of children were either overweight or obese by the time they reached their final year in the Early Years Foundation Stage.

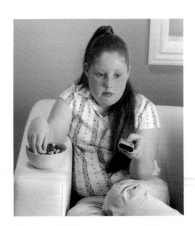

Obese children are more likely to develop conditions such as diabetes

Diet and dental health

Too much sugar in the diet can be very harmful to children's teeth. Bacteria in the mouth react with the sugar to form acid, which attacks the tooth enamel and causes decay. Natural sugar is present in many foods, such as fruit, but foods with added sugar such as fizzy drinks and biscuits are the most harmful to children's teeth. These foods should be strictly limited and replaced with healthier alternatives such as fresh fruit, breadsticks and unsweetened juice. The use of artificial sweeteners is prohibited in any foods for infants and young children (aged birth to three years).

Natural sugar is present in many foods, such as fruit

Portion size

The Children's Food Trust guide *Eat Better, Start Better* (2012) provides excellent advice about good food choices and typical portion sizes for children aged one to five years. Figure 14.3 shows some examples from the guidance.

Research

Investigate the Children's Food Trust guide Eat Better, Start Better *at www.childrensfoodtrust.org.uk.*

Examine the recommended portion sizes for children of different ages and design a chart to display in your setting.

Key terms

Diabetes: a condition characterised by a high blood sugar level as a result of the body not producing enough insulin

Obesity: the condition of having excessive body fat; weighing more than 20% (males) or 25% (females) more than the ideal weight

Figure 14.3 Extract from the Children's Food Trust *Eat Better, Start Better* guidelines on serving fruit and vegetables to children

Good choices of food to serve	Typical portion sizes as served*
Vegetables: includes vegetables served with meals and within dishes, such as carrots, green beans, broccoli, cauliflower, cabbage, courgettes, peppers, leeks, onions, okra, swede, pak choi and sweetcorn.	1–2 tablespoons cooked vegetables (40 g) Small bowl vegetable soup (150 g)
Salad vegetables: includes lettuce, other leaves, watercress, celery, cucumber, tomato, raw carrot, raw pepper, radish and beetroot.	4–6 raw vegetable sticks (40 g)
Pulses: includes beans (such as kidney beans, haricot beans, butter beans, pinto beans, broad beans), chickpeas, red and green lentils, split peas, processed peas and baked beans.	½ –1 tablespoons pulses (40 g)

*Portion sizes are typical example portion sizes for children aged one to five years, and are not suitable for children under one year old.

Source: Children's Food Trust, *Eat Better, Start Better: Voluntary Food and Drink Guidelines for Early Years Settings in England – A Practical Guide*, 2012, p. 19

Weaning

Healthy eating habits develop from a very early age, so introducing babies to a range of healthy food during the weaning process can help to establish a solid foundation for the future. During the process of weaning, a baby should be offered a wide variety of foods, as this helps the baby to experience different foods and encourages their sense of taste.

The Department of Health currently recommends that babies should not be introduced to solid food until the age of six months. Before this time, a baby's digestive system is still developing, and introducing solids too early can increase the risk of infections and allergies.

The guidance also recommends avoiding certain foods during the weaning process, for example:

- raw eggs, including mayonnaise (to minimise the risk of salmonella)

- shellfish (to minimise the risk of food poisoning)

- salt (which can be damaging to the baby's kidneys)

- sugar (to help prevent tooth decay)

- honey (can produce toxins leading to the condition infant botulism)

- whole nuts (in addition to allergy concerns, nuts should never be given to children under the age of five because of the risk of choking)

- low-fat foods (fat is an important source of calories and some vitamins for babies).

Key terms

Infant botulism: a rare but serious illness that can result in paralysis

Salmonella: a bacterium that causes diarrhoea and food poisoning

Toxins: poisonous substances

Research

Investigate a variety of weaning foods for babies at www.nhs.uk.

Design

Create an illustrated guide for parents showing some ideas of different foods to try when babies first start the weaning process.

Babies should not be introduced to solid food until the age of six months

Case study

Gemma is five years old and attends the local primary school. She has breakfast at home every day and takes a packed lunch with her to school. Her childminder picks her up from school at 3pm each day and she has a snack at the childminder's home before her mum picks her up at about 5pm. All the food that Gemma ate yesterday is listed below.

- Breakfast: small bowl of rice pops cereal with milk; small glass of fresh orange juice

- Snack at school: two breadsticks; small carton of milk

- Packed lunch: cheese sandwich on white bread with sunflower spread; packet of plain, salted crisps; small fromage frais; chocolate biscuit; small carton of unsweetened juice

- Snack at the childminder's: toasted sandwich on white bread with cheese, tomato and butter; banana; small glass of milk

- Tea at home: wholewheat pasta with tomato sauce and cheese; strawberry yoghurt; chocolate milkshake

- Supper: two plain digestive biscuits; small glass of milk

1. Use the current guidance on nutrition to analyse Gemma's food intake and list all the nutrients that she ate yesterday.

2. Discuss examples of Gemma's healthy eating and some of the ways that Gemma's diet yesterday could have been improved.

Meeting children's individual dietary needs

Working with parents

It is extremely important to work closely with parents and carers in order to ensure that children's food and drink meets their individual dietary needs. As a practitioner, you need to communicate effectively with parents in order to respect their wishes, and make sure that any information about dietary restrictions is recorded in the setting. This information needs to be easily accessible to all staff in the setting, including volunteers and students. Simple mistakes with children's dietary requirements can result in serious and sometimes tragic consequences.

Some of the information that may need to be recorded includes:

- parental choice or lifestyle (e.g. vegan or vegetarian)
- religion or cultural differences
- food intolerance or allergies
- specific illnesses or medical conditions that require a special diet.

Information about children's dietary restrictions should be clearly recorded in the setting

Religion and culture

Some religions and cultures have strict guidance about what kinds of food should be eaten and even about how animals used for food should be killed. Some of these dietary restrictions are summarised in Figure 14.4.

Your assessment criteria:

Learning aim A1: Understand how to provide food for children to encourage health and development

P2 Explain how to work with parents in early years settings to meet children's individual dietary needs.

🔍 Research

Investigate how the individual dietary needs of children are communicated and recorded in your placement or work setting.

Make a note of where this information is kept and which staff have access to it.

Some religions and cultures have strict guidelines about what kinds of food should be eaten

🔑 Key terms

Halal: Islamic dietary laws that regulate the preparation of food

Kosher: Jewish dietary laws

Lactose: a sugar present in milk

Figure 14.4 The dietary requirements of different religions

Religion	Dietary restrictions	Periods of fasting?
Buddhist	Many are vegetarian. Some may eat fish. Some may be vegan.	Yes
Hindu	Most are vegetarian. Some may be vegan. Dairy is generally acceptable. Those who eat meat, poultry, and fish will exclude beef.	Yes
Jewish	Pork and pork products are excluded. Kosher beef, lamb, poultry and fish (with fins and scales) are eaten. Shellfish is not eaten. Meat and dairy are never eaten at the same meal. The Jewish diet also excludes gelatin, fats, emulsifiers, stabilisers and additives from an animal origin that is not kosher.	Yes
Muslim	Pork and pork products are excluded. Halal beef, lamb, poultry and fish are eaten. Dairy products are eaten by most. The Muslim diet also excludes gelatin, fats, emulsifiers, stabilisers and additives from an animal origin that is not halal.	Yes
Sikh	Many are vegetarian. Those who eat meat, poultry and fish will exclude beef and possibly pork.	No
Rastafarian	Pork and pork products are excluded. Many will be vegetarian. Some may be vegan.	Yes

Vegetarian and vegan

Some parents choose to be vegetarians or vegans and may want their children to follow similar eating patterns. Vegetarians do not eat any meat or fish and vegans do not eat any animal products, including eggs and cows' milk. Soya and other sources of plant protein are therefore very important. If children follow a vegetarian or vegan diet, then special care will need to be taken to make sure all the essential nutrients are included in their diet.

Food intolerance

A food intolerance is not the same as a food allergy. Children with a food intolerance may have difficulties digesting certain substances, such as lactose, which can lead to digestive symptoms such as diarrhoea. You should communicate with parents about the ingredients in different foods and always check food labels carefully. Some specialist food products are available for children with food intolerance, for example soya milk for children with cows' milk intolerance.

 Design

Plan a healthy, balanced meal, including drinks, for the following children:

1. *A school lunch box for Jamie, aged five years, whose parents want him to be vegetarian*

2. *Dinner for Parveen, aged three years, who is a Muslim*

3. *Breakfast for Ana, aged 18 months, whose parents are Jewish*

List all the nutrients you have included and give reasons for your choices.

Food allergies

A food allergy is when the body's immune system reacts abnormally to specific foods. Some common symptoms include an itchy sensation inside the mouth and an itchy red skin rash (urticaria). In children, the foods that most commonly cause an allergic reaction are:

• milk

• eggs

• peanuts

• fish and shellfish.

It is vitally important to communicate with parents about any specific food allergies their children may have, as some allergic reactions are severe and can be life-threatening.

Children with special needs

Children with complex needs may have additional dietary requirements (such as having their food prepared to a particular texture to enable them to eat). They may need support to eat (such as specially designed cutlery or seating) and may need staff to feed them if they are unable to feed themselves.

Children with complex needs may need help if they are unable to feed themselves

Children's attitudes towards food

Influences on children's attitudes to food

Children's food preferences develop between the ages of one and five. It is therefore very important to encourage children to develop healthy eating habits and to experience a wide variety of foods during this time.

There are several factors that can influence children's attitudes towards food and many of these are linked to their family situation. Some parents use food, particularly sweets, as a reward or a treat, which can lead to children developing a link between food and their behaviour. Similarly, in some families, providing food is associated with giving love and affection. In contrast, some parents use food in a more controlling way, for example insisting that children eat all of the food on their plate before they can leave the table or go out and play.

The Advisory Panel on Food and Nutrition recommends that food should not be used as either a reward or punishment. It also suggests that children who are made to eat everything on their plate learn to dislike those foods and this may lead to food aversions in adulthood.

Food refusal

As children develop more independence, they can become fussy about what they eat, which can lead to food refusal (not eating their food). Evidence shows that fussy eating affects about 10 to 20 per cent of children under five. Although food refusal is considered to be a normal developmental stage in young children, it can be a very worrying and frustrating time for parents. Some of the reasons that children refuse their food include:

- They are starting to practise their independence and saying 'no'.

- Food may not be the most important thing on their mind, for example they would rather be playing.

- Their appetite will vary depending on how active they have been during the day.

- They may enjoy the attention from their parents when they refuse food.

Children rarely become ill because of food refusal. All children are individuals and are developing their own likes and dislikes. They may like a particular food one week, but will refuse to eat it the next. Sweets and snacks should not be given to children between meals. Parents should be encouraged to be patient during this phase and should continue to offer attractive, nutritious meals at regular mealtimes.

Your assessment criteria:

Learning aim A2: Understand the role of the adult in encouraging children to develop healthy eating habits

P3 Explain how children's attitudes to food are influenced.

? | Reflect

Reflect on your own experiences with food as a child.

Was food ever used as a reward or a treat in your family?

What kind of memories do you have of family mealtimes?

Compare your experiences with a colleague in your group or placement.

Food should not be used as either a reward or a punishment

Working with parents

It is very important for early years practitioners to work in partnership with parents to encourage children's positive attitudes towards food and to support the development of healthy eating habits. This will involve factors such as:

- being sensitive to family situations that influence food choices (for example, culture, religion or lifestyle preferences)

- providing information about healthy eating (for example, menus, recipes and leaflets)

- having a healthy eating policy in the setting (including healthy snacks and lunch boxes)

- involving parents with food in the setting (for example, cooking or baking sessions or healthy eating workshops)

- working with other professionals (for example, health visitors or dieticians).

Your assessment criteria:

Learning aim A1: Understand how to provide food for children to encourage health and development

M2 Discuss the role of partnership working with parents in relation to children's attitudes to food.

Research

Research some healthy eating recipes to cook with children by searching for '5 a day recipes' on the NHS website (www.nhs.uk).

Ask if you can try some of them out with children in your placement or work setting.

Early years settings should provide a variety of healthy food for children

Case study

Olga is a childminder who cares for three children in her own home. She provides the children with breakfast, lunch and an afternoon snack every day. One of the children, Sammy, aged two years, is a very fussy eater, frequently refusing the food he is offered and spitting out food he says he doesn't like. Olga is struggling to encourage Sammy to eat and is planning to meet with his mother to discuss this.

1. Discuss some of the reasons why Sammy may have developed his fussy eating habits.

2. Explain why it is important for Olga to work in partnership with Sammy's parents in order to support Sammy in developing healthy eating habits.

Family meals can be a special time for enjoying good food and each other's company

Developing healthy eating habits in early years settings

The role of the adult

In 2010, the Advisory Panel on Food and Nutrition in Early Years published the report *Laying the Table*, which outlines food and nutritional guidance for early years settings in England. In addition, the Children's Food Trust launched *Eat Better, Start Better: Voluntary Food and Drink Guidelines for Early Years Settings in England* in January 2012. These reports both highlight the importance of the role of early years practitioners in supporting healthier eating habits for young children. Some of the ways you can do this as a practitioner include:

- organising snacks and mealtimes

- encouraging the enjoyment of food, offering interest and variety

- developing independence through self-serving and making choices

- supporting socialisation by eating together and developing table manners

- involving children in food preparation by cooking, baking and growing their own food.

Snacks and mealtimes

The Statutory Framework for the Early Years Foundation Stage currently requires that where children are provided with meals, snacks and drinks, these must be healthy, balanced and nutritious. The Children's Food Trust *Eat Better, Start Better* guidance (2012) includes a menu planning checklist, and an example from this is shown in Figure 14.5.

Your assessment criteria:

Learning aim A1: Understand how to provide food for children to encourage health and development

Learning aim A2: Understand the role of the adult in encouraging children to develop healthy eating habits

P4 Explain the role of adults in developing children's healthy eating habits.

D1 Evaluate the extent to which an early years setting contributes to children's health and development through the provision of food.

Figure 14.5 Menu planning checklist (breakfast)

1.1	Provide a portion of starchy food as part of breakfast each day.
1.2	Provide at least three different varieties of starchy food across breakfasts each week.
1.3	Provide a variety of wholegrain and white starchy foods each week. It is good practice to provide wholegrain varieties at least once a week at breakfast.
1.4	Choose breakfast cereals with low or medium sugar content. Avoid cereals high in sugar such as sugar-coated or chocolate-flavoured cereals.
1.5	Provide a portion of fruit and/or vegetables as part of breakfast each day.
1.6	If fruit juice is provided as part of breakfast, this should be unsweetened and diluted half juice, half water.
1.7	Ensure children have access to fresh drinking water.

Source: Children's Food Trust, *Eat Better, Start Better: Voluntary Food and Drink Guidelines for Early Years Settings in England – A Practical Guide*, 2012, p. 61

Encourage enjoyment

Research has shown that enthusiastic modelling by adults is effective in encouraging children to try new foods and participate more eagerly in mealtimes. You should eat with the children where possible and talk enthusiastically about the appearance and taste of the food. Seat fussy eaters with willing eaters and, if children are resistant to trying new foods, negotiate smaller and smaller tastes, allowing children to refuse once they have tried something. Using food in activities and learning experiences can add to children's interest and enjoyment, for example through songs, stories and craft activities.

Encourage children to try new foods

Encourage independence and socialisation

Practitioners can help children develop independence at snack and mealtimes by including them in planning menus, supporting decision making and encouraging children to serve themselves. This will require careful planning and the appropriate provision of resources, for example using child-sized utensils and containers. Some settings provide drinks and snacks on a continuous basis (sometimes called 'rolling' snack time), to enable children to help themselves whenever they want to. Although this can help to support children's independence, it needs to be balanced with the advantages of sitting together to enjoy a snack as a social occasion, when children can be encouraged to communicate, share food and practise using table manners. (See also Unit 3: Meeting children's physical development, physical care and health needs, page 105.)

Involving children

Evidence from the Children's Food Trust has shown that children are more likely to develop healthy eating habits if they are involved in activities such as cooking, baking and growing their own food. Cooking with children is both an enjoyable activity in its own right and an effective way of encouraging all children to try to eat a wide range of foods. Even young children can enjoy simple activities such as chopping soft fruit and vegetables like bananas and cucumbers. Older children will enjoy mixing, combining and assembling ingredients and baking simple pizzas, scones and muffins. Before you carry out food activities with children, it is best practice for you to complete a basic food safety and hygiene certificate – most settings will have arrangements for you to do this.

Some settings are able to involve children in growing their own food in a garden or allotment, and this can be a wonderful way to enhance children's enjoyment of food and healthy eating. If there is limited growing space, you can grow many vegetables and herbs on windowsills and in pots or bags. Most children will take great pleasure in planting vegetables, tending seedlings and nurturing plants before harvesting their crop and enjoying the end results in a stir fry, soup or sandwich.

Special occasions

It is important to give children the opportunity to celebrate special occasions, and food and drink are often used to mark these events. Some settings now encourage parents to bring in healthier food or non-food items such as stickers instead of cakes or sweets for birthdays and other celebrations. Providing information for parents will help everyone to understand the setting's policy and approach to special occasions.

Improving professional practice

The Children's Food Trust guide *Eat Better, Start Better* (2012) includes a Code of Practice Checklist for settings. This checklist is designed as a tool for settings to assess their practice and make improvements to the provision of food and drinks for children. The seven areas of the Code of Practice are:

- developing a food policy
- communication with children and families
- menu planning and food provision
- the food and drink guidelines
- special dietary needs and diverse diets

Your assessment criteria:

Learning aim A1: Understand how to provide food for children to encourage health and development

Learning aim A2: Understand the role of the adult in encouraging children to develop healthy eating habits

P4 Explain the role of adults in developing children's healthy eating habits.

D1 Evaluate the extent to which an early years setting contributes to children's health and development through the provision of food.

D2 Recommend improvements to an early years setting's contribution to children's healthy eating habits.

Cooking with children provides many different learning opportunities

- eating environments and social aspects of meals

- training (in food safety and hygiene, and basic nutrition).

An extract from the checklist is shown in Figure 14.6.

 Design

Learning about food can enhance children's interest in healthy eating. List some of the ways that food could be integrated into the seven areas of learning and development of the Early Years Foundation Stage (EYFS):

- *Personal, social and emotional development*

- *Physical development*

- *Literacy*

- *Mathematics*

- *Communication and language*

- *Understanding the world*

- *Expressive arts and design*

Figure 14.6 Extract from the Children's Food Trust *Eat Better, Start Better* Code of Practice Checklist

Recommendation		Do I/we meet this recommendation?			Actions to take
1.	Developing a food policy	Yes	Planning to	No	
1.1	I/We have a food policy in place which covers all aspects of my/our approach to food and healthy eating, and which is actively used and shared.				
1.2	I/We consulted with staff and families to develop the policy, and they are familiar with what it includes.				
1.3	I/We share and discuss my/our food policy with families when their children start attending my/our setting and it is clearly displayed.				
1.4	I/We review my/our food policy regularly (at least once a year) to monitor its progress and evaluate its impact.				
1.5	I/We use food to support other aspects of children's learning, and use food in activities with the children.				

Source: Children's Food Trust, *Eat Better, Start Better: Voluntary Food and Drink Guidelines for Early Years Settings in England – A Practical Guide*, 2012, p. 59

Involving children in growing their own food can be a wonderful way to enhance their enjoyment of food and healthy eating

Research

Investigate the Children's Food Trust Eat Better, Start Better Code of Practice Checklist, available at www.childrensfoodtrust.org.uk. Use the checklist to evaluate the food and drinks policies at your placement or work setting, and make a list of suggestions for improvements that could be made.

Food hygiene and safety

Safe food practice

The Food Standards Agency (FSA) operates in all four countries of the UK and outlines the regulations about the safe storage and preparation of food.

The food hygiene requirements in the Statutory Framework for the Early Years Foundation Stage state that 'managers/leaders must be confident that those responsible for preparing and handling food are competent to do so. In group provision, all staff involved in preparing and handling food must receive training in food hygiene.'

Everyone involved in preparing food for young children, or helping them to eat, needs to understand the importance of food safety and hygiene and be aware of the requirements of the Food Safety Act (1990).

The importance of personal hygiene

Good hygiene practice is very important when preparing food for children. Infection can easily spread if strict personal hygiene procedures are not followed. You should always do the following.

- Wash your hands before touching food, after using the toilet and after handling raw meat or anything dirty.
- Wear an apron and keep long hair tied back.
- Cover any cuts with waterproof plasters.
- Avoid coughing or sneezing over food.

Children should also be taught good hygiene habits from an early age. Encourage them to develop routine hand washing habits before meals or snacks, after using the toilet and following any messy or outdoor play.

Food preparation and storage

Safe food preparation and storage are essential for children's health and wellbeing. Food can become infected with harmful bacteria, which multiply rapidly and produce toxins. These toxins can cause food poisoning and other dangerous illnesses.

One of the most common causes of food poisoning is from salmonella bacteria found in raw chicken and eggs. It is very important that frozen chicken is thoroughly defrosted before cooking it, and that chicken and eggs are cooked thoroughly in order to kill these harmful bacteria.

Your assessment criteria:

Learning aim B: Understand the role of the adult in preparing and serving food safely

P5 Explain responsibilities and practices for working safely in an early years setting when preparing and serving food to children.

🔍 **Research**

Investigate the FSA regulations in your own home country about safe storage and preparation of food.

Discuss some of the practical examples you have observed in your placement and compare your experiences with others in your group.

Good hygiene practice is very important when preparing food for children

🔍 **Research**

Make a list of the ways in which the practitioners in your setting encourage young children to develop good hygiene habits.

✎ **Key term**

Bacteria: single-celled organisms, some of which are harmful to the human body

Bacteria can also spread through the process of cross-contamination. This is when bacteria from raw contaminated food spread to other food, for example if the juices from a joint of beef in the fridge drip onto some cooked ham on the shelf below. Bacteria can also contaminate food by using the same utensils for different foods, for example using the same knife to cut up raw chicken and then to make sandwiches.

Some key points about the safe storage and preparation of food are outlined in Figure 14.7.

Key term

Cross-contamination: the transfer of harmful bacteria from one source to another

Figure 14.7 Storing and preparing food safely

Storage	Preparation
Always keep food covered: wrap food with plastic film or foil once opened.	Use separate utensils and chopping boards for raw meat and cooked foods.
Store cooked food above raw food in the fridge.	Wash knives and utensils thoroughly after cutting raw meat.
	Wash your hands thoroughly between handling raw and cooked foods.
Keep food in the fridge at a temperature between 0 and 5°C.	Wash fruit and vegetables before using them for snacks or meals.
	Clean and disinfect all food preparation surfaces regularly and always use clean utensils.
	Empty kitchen rubbish bins regularly.
Always check 'use by' dates on food products.	Always cook food thoroughly and avoid reheating food.
	Defrost food thoroughly and never refreeze food once it has been thawed.

Serving food safely

It is vitally important to be aware of any food allergies or intolerances affecting children in early years settings. When choosing and preparing foods for children, you need to check the ingredients thoroughly in order to prevent serious illness and sometimes even death. Information about children's food allergies and intolerances should be clearly and prominently displayed and communicated to all staff.

Always store cooked food above raw food in the fridge

Case study

Cynthia Bowman is an Ofsted inspector who is about to visit the home of a registered childminder who cares for two children, aged six months and three years.

1. Write a checklist of all the food hygiene and safety measures that Cynthia will be looking for in the kitchen or other areas where food is prepared and stored in the childminder's home.

Assessment criteria

This table shows you what you must do to achieve a Pass, Merit or Distinction.

Pass	Merit	Distinction
Learning aim A1: Understand how to provide food for children to encourage health and development		
Learning aim A2: Understand the role of the adult in encouraging children to develop healthy eating habits		
3A1.P1 Explain the impact of diet on children's health and development.	3A1.M1 Analyse a child's diet in relation to current expert guidance.	3A.D1 Evaluate the extent to which an early years setting contributes to children's health and development through the provision of food.
3A1.P2 Explain how to work with parents in early years settings to meet children's individual dietary needs.	3A1.M2 Discuss the role of partnership working with parents in relation to children's attitudes to food.	3A.D2 Recommend improvements to an early years setting's contribution to children's healthy eating habits.
3A2.P3 Explain how children's attitudes to food are influenced.		
3A2.P4 Explain the role of adults in developing children's healthy eating habits.		
Learning aim B: Understand the role of the adult in preparing and serving food safely		
3B.P5 Explain responsibilities and practices for working safely in an early years setting when preparing and serving food to children.		

Index

Acknowledgements

The publishers gratefully acknowledge the permission granted to reproduce the copyright material in this book. While every effort has been made to trace and contact copyright holders, where this has not been possible the publishers will be pleased to make the necessary arrangements at the first opportunity.

Pages 334, 335, 343–344 and 345–346 contain excerpts from the *Voluntary Food and Drink Guidelines for Early Years Settings in England – A Practical Guide*, available from the Children's Food Trust, www.childrensfoodtrust.org.uk. Through ensuring a balanced diet in their early years and at school, together with better family cooking skills, lifestyle and food education, the Trust exists to help protect every child's right to eat better – and so, to do better.

The publisher would like to thank the following for permission to reproduce pictures in these pages (t = top, b = bottom, c = centre, l = left, r = right, m = most):

pp 10–11 Tetra Images/SuperStock, p 12 michaeljung/Shutterstock, p 13 Sebastian Kaulitzki/Shutterstock, p 15l Teresa Kasprzycka/Shutterstock, p 15r Dgrilla/Shutterstock, p 16 S.Borisov/Shutterstock, p 17 courtesy of Anna Ranson (http://www.theimaginationtree.com), p 18 Anita Patterson Peppers/Shutterstock, p 19r SnapshotPhotos/Shutterstock, p 20t S.Borisov/Shutterstock, p 20ct greenland/Shutterstock, p 20c Antoine Juliette/Oredia/Oredia Eurl/SuperStock, p 20cb Marlon Lopez/Shutterstock, p 20b Tyler Olson/Shutterstock, p 21 fStop/SuperStock, p 22 Asia Images Group/Getty, p 23 Rossario/Shutterstock, p 24t Elena Yakusheva/Shutterstock, p 24c Christy Thompson/Shutterstock, p 24b EML/Shutterstock, p 25 Emese/Shutterstock, p 26 Corbis/SuperStock, p 27 Flirt/SuperStock, p 28t mayak/Shutterstock, p 28c Ingrid Balabanova/Shutterstock, p 28b Sergey Nivens/Shutterstock, p 29 Cultura Limited/SuperStock, p 31 Ocean/Corbis, p 33t Laura Dwight/Corbis, p 33b Adam Przezak/Shutterstock, p 35t Losevsky Photo and Video/Shutterstock, p 35b Marcie Cheatham/iStockphoto, p 37b Timofeyev Alexander/Shutterstock, p 37t Lucian Coman/Shutterstock, p 41 Monkey Business Images/Shutterstock, p 42 michaeljung/Shutterstock, p 43 Monkey Business Images/Shutterstock, p 44 Fancy Collection/SuperStock, p 45t Fancy Collection/SuperStock, p 45b JS Photo/Alamy, p 47 Denis Kuvaev/Shutterstock, p 48 Nadasazh/Shutterstock, p 51 Capifrutta/Shutterstock, p 52 Zurijeta/Shutterstock, p 53 Ersler Dmitry/Shutterstock, pp 56–57 oliveromg/Shutterstock, p 59 Blend Images/SuperStock, p 60 Gladskikh Tatiana/Shutterstock, p 61 gunnargren/Shutterstock, p 63 courtesy of Anna Ranson (www.theimaginationtree.com), p 64 courtesy of Catherine Denman, pre-schoolplay.blogspot.co.uk. Used with permission. p 65t mu_che/Shutterstock, p 65b OJO Images/SuperStock, p 66t kickers/iStockphoto, p 66ct brebca/iStockphoto, p 66cb bikerider london/Shutterstock, p 66b Anita Patterson Peppers/Shutterstock, p 67t Nicholas Sutcliffe/Shutterstock, p 67ct Moodboard_Images/iStockphoto, p 67cb macka/Shutterstock, p 67b Radharani/Shutterstock, p 68 Image Source/SuperStock, p 71 Olesia Bilkei/Shutterstock, p 75 Image provided courtesy of Tiziana Ciccone of reggiokids.blogspot.com, p 77 David L. Moore - ED/Alamy, p 79 AISPIX by Image Source/Shutterstock, p 80 Pressmaster/Shutterstock, pp 84–85 Iakov Filimonov/Shutterstock, p 87 Tatiana Morozova/Shutterstock, p 88t victoriaKh/Shutterstock, p 88c Yauhen Buzuk/Shutterstock, p 88b Svetlana Lukienko/Shutterstock, p 89t Lilyana Vynogradova/Shutterstock, p 89ct Gayvoronskaya_Yana/Shutterstock, p 89c Africa Studio, p 89cb Payless Images/Shutterstock, p 89b Pamela Uyttendaele, p 90l Department of Health, p 90r bikeriderlondon/Shutterstock, p 91 thislife pictures/Alamy, p 92 imageegami/Shutterstock, p 93 Elena Shashkina/Shutterstock, p 94 Golden Pixels LLC/Shutterstock, p 95 Elena Schweitzer/Shutterstock, p 96 urbancow/iStockphoto, p 97 Velychko/Shutterstock, p 98 MJTH/Shutterstock, p 99 Samuel Borges Photography/Shutterstock, p 100t Oleksiy Khmyz/Shutterstock, p 100b Fotosearch/SuperStock, p 101 Lian Deng/Shutterstock, p 102 Igor Sokolov (breeze)/Shutterstock, p 103 Golden Pixels LLC/Shutterstock, p 104 Adrov Andriy/Shutterstock, p 105l Caro/Alamy, p 105r Stokmen/Shutterstock, p 106 Gary Ombler/Getty, p 107 NatUlrich/Shutterstock, p 109t Shchipkova Elena/Shutterstock, p 109b INSADCO Photography/Alamy, p 110l Beneda Miroslav/Shutterstock, p 110r GUILLAUME/BSIP/SuperStock, p 111 MAY/BSIP/SuperStock, pp 114–115 Kzenon/Shutterstock, p 116 tattywelshie/iStockphoto, p 119 Seth Joel/Shutterstock, p 121 Blamb/Shutterstock, p 122 JESSICA RINALDI/Reuters/Corbis, p 123 hartphotography/Shutterstock, p 125 Kitch Bain/Shutterstock, p 126 imageegami/Shutterstock,